Scotland's Golf Courses

The Author

Robert Price has held research and teaching appointments in universities in Scotland, Canada and the United States. Most of his professional life has been spent as Reader in Physical Geography at the University of Glasgow. His research in the fields of glacial geomorphology and Quaternary environments has resulted in the publication of three books and numerous papers in scientific journals. He was awarded the degree of Doctor of Science for his contributions to the study of glacial environments, past and present.

The first edition of this book was the product of his research interest in the origins of Scottish landscapes and their use as sites for golf courses. Over the past 15 years, Dr Price has undertaken research and consultancy projects on many aspects of Scotland's golf industry. He has acted as a consultant to companies establishing and operating new golf facilities and has produced reports on the management and marketing of Scotland's golf facilities.

Dr Price is a keen golfer, and while visiting all of Scotland's golf courses for research purposes, he has taken the opportunity to play many of them.

SCOTLAND'S GOLF COURSES

Robert Price

THE MERCAT PRESS

EDINBURGH

First edition published in 1989 by Aberdeen University Press
This second edition published in 2002 by Mercat Press Ltd
10 Coates Crescent, Edinburgh EH3 7AL
www.mercatpress.com

ISBN: 1 84183 030 5

Printed in Spain by Santamaria

✿ Contents

❧ Tables

✿ Figures

Appendix

✸ Photographs

✹ Preface

Hearing a man who has only recently discovered the game of golf holding forth on the beauty of what I should have thought to be a comparatively ordinary course, I fell to marvelling at the extraordinary variety of experience offered by this singular game and the extraordinary reluctance of the average player to take advantage of it.

Every other game is played on the same kind of pitch the world over. One football field is like another; one cricket pitch like the next, except that in one case the background may be the village chestnuts and in another the gasometers.

Yet not only is every golfing pitch different from all others, but it consists of 18 little pitches within itself. Thus an almost inexhaustible supply of golfing problems presents itself.

How strange, therefore, that men of imagination in other walks of life so lack that quality as golfers that they will cheerfully play month by month, year by year, decade by decade, over the same 18 holes.

Ten to one, too, that they play with the same people every Sunday at the same hour, make the same remarks on the first tee, and what is more, play a four ball. Human ingenuity could scarcely devise golf in a duller form.

from *The Best of Henry Longhurst*, ed. MW Wilson & K Bowden
(Collins, 1979), pp. 174-5.

The above quotation is a very apt justification for writing a book which attempts to explain why 'every golfing pitch is different from all others'. The first edition of this book (1989) was the product of combining my professional scientific interest in the origins of Scottish landscapes (Price 1983) with my lifelong participation in the game of golf as an enthusiastic but very mediocre amateur golfer.

The publication of *Scotland's Golf Courses* in 1989, at a time when a new golf boom was underway in Britain, opened up a number of opportunities for me to undertake further research and consultancy work related to the development of new golf businesses providing mainly 'pay and play' golf facilities. While the providers and managers of golf courses in Scotland had traditionally been members clubs (mutual trading organisations) or local authorities (municipal courses), the second golf boom in Scotland has been led by commercial companies (Price 1998).

During the past decade, one hundred new golf courses have been opened in Scotland, i.e. a 25% increase in the level of supply. An analysis of these new courses and their operation is incorporated in this new edition.

SCOTLAND'S GOLF COURSES

Because of my involvement as a golf consultant to many new golf projects in Scotland, my perception of how the service industry which provides and operates Scotland's golf courses is structured, has changed radically and therefore there have been numerous alterations and additions to the text of the first edition. To many people the terms 'golf club' and 'golf course' are synonymous. 'Golf club' has two meanings, a kind of stick used in playing golf and an association of persons united by a common interest (i.e. playing golf). Because so many of the early golf facilities were created by an association of persons (club) interested in playing golf, the term golf club is often applied to any facility created for that purpose, i.e. the golf course and golf club have, by common usage, become synonymous. However, in this book the term 'golf club' refers only to the association of persons which operates or manages a golf facility. A golf facility consists of one or more golf courses at one location, operated/managed by one organisation. The golf courses of Scotland are either operated by members clubs (72%), by Unitary Authorities including Links Management Trusts (13%) or by commercial companies (15%).

In some parts of the world the term 'golf links' is applied to any golf course regardless of its landscape characteristics. In Scotland, many of the older golf courses are located on 'The Links' which is '...a tract of low-lying seaside land often held in common and used since the Middle Ages for sports, including archery, bowls and golf.' (Davies 1993). This land is usually underlain by gravel and covered by wind-blown sand in the form of sand plains, hummocks and dune ridges. 'Links' is an old Scots word, '*lynkis*', meaning ridges and hummocks or open rough ground. In its original usage it was not restricted to coastal locations (e.g. Bruntsfield Links in the centre of Edinburgh). On the west coast of Scotland the Gaelic term '*machair*' is used to refer to similar wind-built sand surfaces.

There is no official list of Scotland's golf courses and research by the writer shows that those lists which do exist are incomplete. The list of golf courses in the Appendix of this book refers to all the golf courses known to exist or to be under construction in March, 2001. There are several new golf projects at the planning stage and assuming that most of these come to fruition, then Scotland will have some 550 golf courses within a few years. However, this book is concerned with the 538 courses currently in existence. While every effort has been made to ensure that the facts, contained both in the appendix and the text, are correct, there will inevitably be some errors in such a large quantity of data assembled from a wide variety of sources. In order to assemble and present the data systematically, Scotland has been divided into four regions (A, B, C and D—see appendix), based on combinations of the new administrative single unitary authorities established in 1998. Each golf course has been assigned a regional number which is used in the text, on maps and in the appendix.

❦ Acknowledgements

Since writing the first edition of this book I have become increasingly involved with research and consultancy work in the golf industry. The past decade has seen the emergence of new commercial golf facilities in Scotland as well as the increased 'commercialisation' of members clubs. Club secretaries, facility managers, course designers and constructors have contributed to my golf education.

One of the major rewards of working in the golf industry is the opportunity to travel, not only throughout Scotland but around the world, and to play a variety of golf courses. 'I fell to marvelling at the extraordinary variety of experiences offered by this singular game' (Henry Longhurst, 1979). To those golfers with whom I shared these experiences, I offer my sincere thanks.

My wife Mary has been responsible for the production of the text for this book and has been a constant companion and assistant on my golf travels. Most of the photographs, except where otherwise acknowledged, were taken by the author. I am particularly indebted to Mike Williamson and Angus McNicol for providing photographs. Mike Shand produced the maps and diagrams.

❧ One
The History of the Game of Golf

Although this book is primarily concerned with golf courses, it is necessary to provide some historical background about the origins and evolution of the game, the equipment and golfing societies (clubs). Scotland can rightly claim to be the home of modern golf in that it was here, between 1740 and 1900, that all the major developments in the game, its equipment and administration, took place. It was also from Scotland that the rules, players and course designers spread throughout the world. Many of the game's traditions started on the classic links courses of Scotland. The pre-eminence of the Royal and Ancient Golf Club of St Andrews as rule-maker and administrator of the game and the 'export' of golf course designers, greenkeepers and players to all corners of the globe demonstrate the importance of Scotland to the game of golf.

Many books have been written about the history of golf. This author will confine himself to a brief discussion of four phases in the development of the game:

1. Pre-1735: historical references to the game of golf and connections between Scotland and the Low Countries.

2. 1735–1849: early Scottish Golfing Societies (clubs) and golfing equipment.

3. 1850–99: the expansion of golf in Scotland, the organisation of the game and the development of balls and clubs.

4. 1900–2002: the 'modern' era.

The reader requiring more detailed information on the history of the game of golf is referred to the Bibliography, in particular those books marked *.

GOLF IN SCOTLAND BEFORE 1735

If golf is defined as a game involving the driving of a ball with a club over a long distance into either a hole in the ground or against a small post, tree or door, then close links with *colf*, played in the Low Countries between the fourteenth and eighteenth centuries and the game of *gouff* (or '*gollfe*' or '*golf*'), played in Scotland between the fifteenth and eighteenth centuries, can be established. Van Hengel (1985), has made a detailed study of manuscripts and paintings (450 paintings between 1500 and 1700) in the Low Countries, which not only provide information about the game of *colf* but which clearly establish close trade and political connections between the Low Countries and the east coast of Scotland between 1485 and the mid-seventeenth century. Large quantities of *colf* balls were exported from Holland and Zeeland to Scotland and in the mid-seventeenth century Scottish wooden clubs were exported to and used in Holland. Van Hengel (1985, p. 11) states, 'There is absolutely no doubt that *colf* was an early form of golf.'

The first documentary evidence of 'colf' in the Low Countries is dated at around 1360, while the first documentary evidence which refers to golf in Scotland is an Act of Parliament of 1457 which forbids the playing of 'Gouff'. There are various references to Scottish golf being played in the churchyards and streets during the sixteenth century and that game may well have been similar to *colf*. Throughout the period 1550–1650, there are records of the game being played mainly on the links land along the east coast of Scotland, and also at Perth, Forfar and Glasgow (Fig. 1.1 and Table 1.1). Many of these early records are only passing references to golfers and the earliest description of the Scottish game of golf is to be found in a Latin Grammar for Aberdeen schools produced in 1632. This work refers to bunkers, iron clubs, holes and sand for teeing up (D. Hamilton, 1985).

In his book, *Golf—Scotland's Game*, David Hamilton (1998) establishes that prior to 1600 Scottish golf had at least two forms. The 'long game' was played by the wealthy minority on the links with expensive balls and clubs. The common people played the 'short game' in town streets and churchyards using rough sticks and cheap balls. The short game was similar to the game of *colf* played in the Low Countries. Both *colf* and the Scottish short game faded out in the mid-seventeenth century, but the long game of golf continued to prosper in Scotland, particularly in the east on common links land.

It seems highly likely that during the sixteenth and seventeenth centuries the Scottish game of golf moved out of the streets and churchyards either to common ground known as 'greens' or on to the coastal links land. By 1650, the links at Gullane, Leith, St Andrews, Carnoustie, Montrose, Aberdeen, Banff and Dornoch were golfing grounds, and the seeds of modern golf had been sown in the sands which would remain such a strong feature of the Scottish golfing landscape. Little is known about the way in which the game of golf was actually played in the sixteenth and seventeenth centuries. Not until 1721 is there an eye-witness account of the game being played. This is contained in a poem published by James Arbuckle, a Glasgow University student. Hamilton (1985) states: 'That the poem should contain a section on the game of golf suggests that the game was then a familiar feature of Glasgow life. Arbuckle describes a game between fairly skilful players, and the poem shows that the match was played on the "Glasgow Green".' Glasgow Green was a relatively small area on the north bank of the Clyde, to the west of the only bridge over the river. It was a gravel terrace where a summer crop of grass was grown and sold by auction. The game described by Arbuckle took place in winter. Summer golf was almost impossible throughout Scotland in the sixteenth and seventeenth centuries because the links and commons upon which it was played yielded an important grass crop during the summer. It is likely that the courses upon which golf was played at this time were natural landscapes consisting of links land or river terraces.

2

TABLE 1.1

List of Early References to Golf, Golfers and Golf Equipment in Scotland

1457 James II (Parl. 14, cap. 64). Act of Parliament discouraging football and 'Gouff'.

1503 King James IV bought clubs from a bow-maker in Perth (D. Hamilton, 1982).

1538 Golfers at play in Aberdeen, Aberdeen Burgh Records, 1538 MS, Vol XVI.

1552 St Andrews Charter: the document reserves to the Provost and Town Council and townspeople the right of using the links for 'golfe, futeball, shuting and all games...'

1554 Reference to a dispute between 'the cordiners [cobblers] of the Cannongate and the cordiners and gouff ball makers of North Leith'. The inference is that cobblers were stitching leather balls, but we do not know what they were filled with (*The Chronicle of the Royal Burgess Golfing Society*).

1565 Golf included in a list of unlawful games in Aberdeen.

1567 Mary, Queen of Scots, was charged with playing golf and pall mall at Seaton House, East Lothian, a few days after the murder of her husband. (*Inventories of Mary Queen of Scots*, Preface, p. lxx, 1863).

1589 Glasgow Kirk Session ruled that there be 'no golf in the High at the Blackfriars Yard, Sunday or weekday'. (James Colville, *The Glasgow Golf Club*, 1907, p.1).

1616 Records of golf being played at Dornoch (D. Hamilton, 1982).

1627 James Pitt recorded as clubmaker of St Andrews.

1628 *Memoirs of the Marquis of Montrose*, Mark Napier, Edinburgh, T.G. Stevenson, 1856, gives account of golfing expenses at St Andrews, Leith and Montrose.

1636 David Wedderburn's *The Vocabula, a description of the game of golf*, Aberdeen. (D. Hamilton, 1982).

1637 Banff—a record that a boy was hanged for stealing, among other things, two golf balls.

1641 Record of golf at Cullen.

1650 Record of golf at Carnoustie.

1650 Gullane: the weavers of Dirleton played the weavers of Aberlady on Old Handsel Monday (A. Baird, 1982).

1651 Non-documented claim that golf was played at Forfar.

1721 Description of the game of golf by a Glasgow University student, James Arbuckle (D. Hamilton, 1985).

The land was well-drained and, at least outside the summer months, had close-cropped turf. Such courses may have consisted of only a few holes and the locations of these may have been changed from time to time.

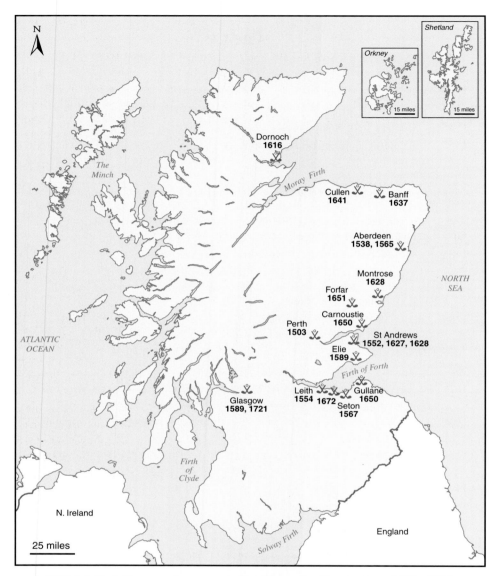

N

The Minch

Orkney

Shetland

15 miles

15 miles

Dornoch
1616

Moray Firth

Cullen
1641

Banff
1637

Aberdeen
1538, 1565

NORTH SEA

Montrose
1628

Forfar
1651

Carnoustie
1650

Perth
1503

St Andrews
1552, 1627, 1628

Elie
1589

ATLANTIC OCEAN

Firth of Forth

Leith
1554 1672

Gullane
1650

Seton
1567

Glasgow
1589, 1721

Firth of Clyde

N. Ireland

25 miles

Solway Firth

England

FIG 1.1 *Early literary references to golf, golfers and golf equipment, 1503–1721*

There can be little doubt that golf was well established in Scotland by the middle of the seventeenth century. All the available records suggest that, apart from at Glasgow and Perth, the game was mainly played on the east coast links. It was played by all classes of society. According to Archie Baird, Gullane's golf historian (Baird, 1985, p. 7), 'As far back as 1650, the weavers of Dirleton played the weavers of Aberlady annually on Old Handsel Monday'. However, the wooden clubs and the 'feathery' ball used in the seventeenth century were relatively expensive, and it is likely that these could be more easily afforded by merchants and the aristocracy. Whether the poorest golfers played with the same expensive equipment is not known. There is no doubt that the next stage in the development of the game of golf in Scotland, the formation of Golfing Societies or Clubs, was very much in the hands of wealthy merchants, landowners, professional men and academics.

EARLY SCOTTISH GOLFING SOCIETIES (CLUBS) 1735–1849

The arranging of matches, wagers and dining facilities eventually led to the formation of Golfing Societies or Clubs. The earliest days of these organisations are shrouded in mystery. Two Edinburgh Golfing Societies—the Royal Burgess and the Honourable Company of Edinburgh Golfers—both began in the early decades of the eighteenth century. It is believed that the Royal Burgess Golfing Society was founded in 1735, but the earliest documents in the club's possession go back no further than 1773. However, it is clear from the Minutes that golf was being played by members of the Society for some considerable time before that date. The Society played golf at Bruntsfield links, then moved to Musselburgh and then to Barnton in 1895.

In the early eighteenth century golf was played on Leith links. It was following a request to the Magistrates and Council of Edinburgh from a group of Leith golfers, described as 'gentlemen of honour, skilful in the ancient and healthful exercise of the golf', that a silver club to be played for annually, that the first rules of golf were drawn up. The 13 rules of the Gentlemen Golfers of Leith (later to become the Honourable Company of Edinburgh Golfers) laid down for the inaugural competition for the silver club were as follows:

Articles and Laws in Playing at Golf 1744:

1. You must tee your ball within a club's length of the hole.

2. Your tee must be upon the ground.

3. You are not to change the ball which you strike off the tee.

4. You are not to remove stones, bones or any break club for the sake of playing your ball, except upon the fair green, and that only within a club's length of your ball.

5. If your ball comes among watter, or any wattery filth, you are at liberty to take out your ball and bringing it behind the hazard and teeing it, you may play it with any club and allow your adversary a stroke for so getting out your ball.

6. If your balls be found anywhere touching one another you are to lift the first ball till you play the last.

7. At holling you are to play your ball honestly for the hole, and not to play upon your adversary's ball, not lying in your way to the hole.

8. If you should lose your ball, by its being taken up, or any other way you are to go back to the spot where you struck last and drop another ball and allow your adversary a stroke for the misfortune.

9. No man at holling his ball is to be allowed to mark his way to the hole with his club or any thing else.

10. If a ball be stopp'd by any person, horse, dog or any thing else, the ball so stopp'd must be played where it lyes.

11. If you draw your club in order to strike and proceed so far in the stroke as to be bringing down your club; if then your club shall break in any way, it is to be accounted a stroke.

12. He whose ball lyes farthest from the hole is obliged to play first.

13. Neither trench, ditch or dyke made for the preservation of the links, nor the Scholars' Holes or the soldiers' lines shall be accounted a hazard but the ball is to be taken out teed and play'd with any iron club.

John Rattray. Capt

Although the game of golf had been played for hundreds of years on an informal basis, the rules laid down by the Gentlemen Golfers of Leith in 1744 mark the beginnings of the formalisation of the game—membership fees, clubhouses, club secretaries and committees were soon to follow.

In 1754, ten years after the formation of the Honourable Company of Edinburgh Golfers, twenty-two gentlemen met in St Andrews and each contributed five shillings for a silver club to be competed for annually. The St Andrews Golfing Society was formed in 1766 (Behrend and Lewis, 1998) and they adopted the rules devised by the Leith Golfers. The St Andrews Society played over a links course of 11 holes out and the same number back. The course was very narrow and lay between dense banks of whin. In 1764 it was decided to make the first four holes into two, and since the same fairways and greens were used going out and back, the round was thus reduced to 18 holes which then became the standard round.

Seven other Golfing Societies were established in Scotland before the end of the eighteenth century: Bruntsfield Links, 1761; Musselburgh, 1774; Aberdeen, 1780; Crail, 1786; Glasgow, 1787; Port Errol (Cruden Bay), 1791; Burntisland, 1798. Members of these ten golfing societies were expected to wear the appropriate uniform while playing the game, participate in wagers and attend dinners after a game. For the social activities the 'Golf House' at Bruntsfield, which was a tavern owned by a club maker, one Thomas Comb, and the 'Golf House' at Leith, constructed by the Gentlemen Golfers at a cost of £760 in 1767, were the forerunners of modern clubhouses.

Between 1800 and 1849 a further thirteen golf clubs were established:

    1810   Montrose (Royal Albert)
    1815   Kingsbarns, Leith Thistle
    1817   Tayport (Scotscraig), St Andrews Thistle
    1820   Innerleven
    1832   North Berwick
    1841   Peterhead
    1842   Carnoustie, Royal Perth
    1843   St Andrews Mechanics
    1845   Barry Panmure
    1847   Leven

Thus, during the first 114 years of 'organised' golf in Scotland only 23 Golfing Societies or Clubs had been formed. Little is known of the early history of many of these clubs because of the absence of written records. This may reflect the fact that masonic traditions of secrecy dominated the early golfing societies. Only when non-masons had joined the Golfing Societies in such numbers that the character of the clubs changed, were formal records kept. It would appear that golf in Scotland was at a fairly low ebb at the beginning of the nineteenth century. The 23 clubs in existence by 1850 probably had a total membership of less than 500, although there is little doubt that informal golf was still played by non-members on the links land.

Apart from the courses at Bruntsfield (Edinburgh), Glasgow Green and the North Inch at Perth, all of the other Scottish courses were coastal links. Although there were 23 clubs in existence by 1849, this does not mean that there were 23 courses. At least three clubs were playing on the St Andrews links by 1843: St Andrews Golfing Society, St Andrews Thistle and the St Andrews Mechanics. Similarly, more than one club played on both the Leith and Musselburgh courses. The links land was ideally suited to the game of golf. Well-drained and closely cropped turf (grazed by sheep and rabbits) permitted the game to be played throughout the year. Play was curtailed in the summer months on the 'inland' courses of Bruntsfield, Perth and Glasgow because of the summer grass crop.

Each of the golf clubs had their own rules, but most of them closely followed the 13 rules drawn up in 1744 by the Honourable Company and subsequently adopted by the

St Andrews Society. By 1830 the Honourable Company was in temporary decline and in 1834 the St Andrews Golfing Society became the Royal and Ancient Golf Club of St Andrews, and so began its pre-eminence not only in Scottish golf, but on a global basis.

The earliest document relating to golf in St Andrews is a charter of 1552 which reserves to the Provost and Town Council and Townspeople the right of using the links for '...golfe, futeball, shuting and all games, as well as casting divots, gathering turfs [to roof their houses], and for the pasturing of their livestock'. No formal golf course existed in the sixteenth and seventeenth centuries. Even at the time of foundation of the Society of St Andrews Golfers in 1766, the course was a sterile wasteland of heather and whin with narrow fairways of short grass. There were many hazards and only crude 'greens' with rough, often deep 'holes'. Not until 1806 were greenkeepers employed at St Andrews. The matches, often accompanied by much betting, were decided by the number of holes won. Most matches were 'foursomes' in which members of each side played alternate strokes. Not until 1759 was stroke or medal play used to decide the winner of the silver club at St Andrews. It would appear that, in the mid-eighteenth century, St Andrews had already become the *Alma Mater* of the Golf. The original minute book of the Society of St Andrews Golfers (later to become the Royal and Ancient) states as much:

> The noblemen and gentlemen above named being Admirers of the Anticient (sic) and healthful Exercise of the Golf, and at the same time, having the Interest and Prosperity of the Ancient City of St Andrews at heart, being the Alma Mater of the Golf, did in 1754 Contribute for a silver club ...having a St Andrew engraved on the head thereof to be played for on the Links of St Andrews upon the 14th Day of May of said year, and yearly in time coming.

It is indeed remarkable that by this declaration these 22 men had laid the foundations for the establishment of St Andrews as the world's headquarters of golf administration, although they were not the original members of a newly formed golfing society (Behrend and Lewis, 1998, p. 10). The challenge match for the Silver Club was first played on 14 May 1754 and was won by William Landale who was a St Andrews merchant. Although he became Captain of the Golf, there was no Society of St Andrews Golfers to captain. Such a Society did develop in later years and is referred to in Minute Book 2, May 1766, which states that the members:

> Did this day agree to meet once every fortnight by eleven of the clock at the Golf House and to play a round on the links (in terms of the Regulations for the Silver Club), to dine together at Bailie Glass's and to pay each a shilling for his dinner the absent as well as the present.

In the latter half of the eighteenth century golf was a relatively expensive game to play. The clubs and balls used were costly and only the wealthy were members of the Golfing Societies. The 'feathery' ball was made of leather and filled with a 'top-hat full' of boiled goose or chicken feathers. The leather cover was soaked in alum water before being filled with feathers, so that when it dried it shrank but the feather stuffing expanded, hence producing a hard ball. These balls cost between two shillings and sixpence and four shillings each. About 1800, the feathery ball had a standard size of about 1¼ inches in diameter and weighed between 26 and 30 drams.

Because the 'feathery' ball was easily damaged by iron clubs, irons were only used in ruts or bunkers. It is very likely that the first makers of wooden clubs were bowmakers. The first record of the purchase of golf clubs is dated 1502 when James IV of Scotland purchased clubs from a bowmaker in Perth. The first Royal warrant holder was William Mayne (1603), Bower Burgess of Edinburgh, who was appointed Clubmaker to James I of England and VI of Scotland. Clubmakers were associated with the early golfing centres at Bruntsfield, Leith and Musselburgh (see Henderson and Stirk, 1985). The heads of the early wooden clubs were long, narrow and shallow and the face was concave. The shafts were ash or hazel and the heads were made of beech, apple, pear or thorn. The early clubs had no grips but sheepskin was used as a grip from about 1800.

Early irons were made by blacksmiths and were heavy and cumbersome. Throughout the 'feathery' era only two irons were used—the sand iron with a large concave face and the rut iron which had a very small head. There were no 'sets' of clubs, the individual player ordering his clubs to suit his particular preference and no two clubs were the same.

Although the St Andrews Golfing Society became the Royal and Ancient Golf Club in 1834, both the town of St Andrews and the links went through hard times during the 1840s. J. K. Robertson (1974, p. 48) states: 'The town was in debt to the tune of £10,000... a vast sum then for a small community that was dwindling every year. The University had sunk to a handful of students, there had even been talk of moving it to Perth. By 1848 the links, the townspeoples' heritage, had been illegally sold to the neighbouring landowner, Mr George Cheape, of Strathtyrum. Cholera, the black plague, had hit the town'. However, two things happened between 1845 and 1850 which were to transform both the fortunes of St Andrews and other golfing centres and the future of the game of golf—the arrival of the railway and the making of a new golf ball. In 1845 it was proposed to route a railway line through the links at the Burn Hole. The Royal and Ancient was successful in having the line re-routed alongside the links, and the line was opened in 1851. The railway era was to have a marked effect on the growth of the game of golf in Scotland throughout the second half of the nineteenth century.

There is some debate as to who was the first person to make and use a golf ball made of gutta percha (see Henderson and Stirk, 1985). It is believed that in 1843 a Dr Paterson, of St Andrews University, received a large black marble idol of Vishnu from Singapore which was wrapped in gutta percha. His son Robert made a golf ball from this malleable material and used it on the Old Course in the early hours of an April morning in 1845. Subsequently Robert's brother made a batch of these balls and sent them to London in 1846 under the name of 'Paterson's Composite Golf Balls'. Allan Robertson, the St Andrews ball maker, was not interested in the new ball because he was afraid it would ruin his trade in 'feathery' balls, but his assistant Tom Morris decided to open his own shop to make and sell the cheaper and more durable golf ball. There are other claims for the making of the first gutta percha ball, but wherever it originated it transformed the game of golf. Because of its cheapness (one shilling each) it opened up the game to artisans and peasantry. Between them, the railway and the gutta ball brought a new prosperity to St Andrews and allowed the game to expand, both in terms of numbers of players and numbers of clubs and golf courses, throughout Scotland and the rest of the United Kingdom.

EXPANDING GOLFING HORIZONS 1850-99

Between 1850 and the end of the century the number of golf clubs in Scotland increased from 18 to 211. There were two distinct facets to this expansion. Between 1850 and 1880 only 24 new clubs were formed, but between 1880 and 1900 nearly 169 new clubs were established. This was a period of industrial growth in Scotland which was accompanied by a rapid increase in the urbanisation of the population. For example, the City of Glasgow doubled its population between 1851 and 1901 (329,000 to 761,000) while the region of West Central Scotland increased its population from 900,000 to 1,900,000 over the same period. This rapid population increase, associated with industrial prosperity, provided a new, relatively well-off, middle class who were reasonably mobile as a result of the expanding railway network. It is therefore not surprising that leisure activities, such as golf, also underwent considerable growth. The factors affecting the number of golf courses and their location in Scotland will be discussed in more detail in Chapter 2.

By 1880 the dominance of links courses in Scottish golf was coming to an end, and by 1900 about half the courses were on inland sites with many of them in suburban locations around the main population centres of Glasgow and Edinburgh.

The *Golfers Handbook* of 1881 lists 49 clubs in Scotland with a total membership of over 3,800, but there are some notable gaps in the membership data. It is likely that there were over 5,000 golf club members in Scotland by 1881, by which date the Royal and Ancient had a membership of 750. It is probable that by the end of the century there were some 20,000 golf club members in Scotland and many others who played the game without joining a golf club.

Throughout the second half of the nineteenth century the clubs and balls changed very little. Long-headed wooden clubs were carried loosely by the player or caddy. The first canvas golf club container was not used until 1890. The gutta percha ball, made in moulds, was replaced by the gutty, which was a composite ball, in the 1880s. Both of these types of ball cost about one shilling while, throughout the period, wooden clubs cost between four and five shillings and iron clubs about three shillings and sixpence. During the latter part of the nineteenth century the condition of golf courses was steadily improved. By the beginning of the 1880s teeing areas were being separated from the greens, 4¼ inch diameter hole-cutters were being used and grass cutting and weeding being undertaken. The significance of the use of grass-cutting machinery will be discussed in Chapter 2.

The Royal and Ancient built its first clubhouse in 1854 and organised a foursomes championship in 1857. In 1860 the first Open Championship was held at Prestwick and in 1865 Tom Morris was appointed as the Royal and Ancient's first professional. In 1873 the Open Championship was played at St Andrews. This was the era of widespread recognition of the game of golf. Players, professionals and equipment-makers were responsible for taking the game to England, to Europe and to North America. Although Scots had taken the game to London in the early seventeenth century, the first club, Blackheath, was not founded until 1766 and other clubs were not established until the 1860s (Westward Ho! 1864, London Scottish 1865, Royal Liverpool 1869). The first club in Europe was at Pau in France (1866) and Scots immigrants carried the game to Canada (Montreal 1873, Quebec 1874, Toronto 1876). There are records of golf clubs and balls being exported from Leith to Charleston, South Carolina in 1743, and the South Carolina Golf Club was founded in 1786 and the Savannah Golf Club in 1795. The new era of golf in the United States is associated with the foundation of the St Andrews Club in Yonkers in 1888 and Shinnecock Hills Golf Club in 1891. It was the early successful Scottish golfers who travelled to instruct others how to play the game and to advise on how to lay out a course. Tom Morris travelled from St Andrews to Westward Ho! to lay out their course in 1864. Large numbers of Scots crossed the Atlantic and became golf professionals and course designers. It is said of Tom Bendelow, who designed over 600 courses in the American Mid-West, that his only qualification to be a golf course designer was his Scottish accent. The most famous Scottish-born golf course designer to work in the United States was D.J. Ross of Dornoch, who learned club making at Forgan's Shop in St Andrews and was taught his golf by 'Old' Tom Morris. In 1893 he returned to Dornoch as greenkeeper and professional and then emigrated to Boston in 1898. He was involved in designing over 500 courses in the USA and Canada, including Pinehurst.

Within Scotland there was certainly variety in the types of golf clubs which emerged during the big expansion between 1880 and 1900. By the very nature of Victorian society there was inevitably a social stratification within the private clubs. Many clubs became predominately male preserves (e.g. the Royal and Ancient). The first ladies' golf competition was held in Musselburgh in 1810 and the first ladies' golf club was established in St Andrews in 1867. That club had 500 members by 1886. The ladies often played on separate short courses. In Scotland, however, unlike England and the United States, the concept of the common links land was retained and persons not belonging to any golf club could play a game on the links. It is remarkable that any resident of St Andrews had the right of playing on the Old Course, free of charge, until 1946, and even visitors did not have to pay a fee until 1913. Similar circumstances prevailed on other links at Carnoustie, Montrose, Aberdeen, Gullane and North Berwick. This tradition was strengthened in the large cities such as Edinburgh, Dundee and Glasgow where municipal golf courses provided facilities for non-club members. It is therefore not surprising that the game of golf in Scotland has been enjoyed by all classes of society for the past two hundred years.

At the end of the nineteenth century golf was an established part of Scottish life and landscape. The Championships gave it publicity among the non-playing public. The Royal and Ancient was becoming the centre of administration for the game—it issued the Rules of Golf to all clubs in 1888 and was given the sole control of the Rules of Golf Committee in 1897. Golf was already playing an important part in the newly emerging tourist industry of Scotland, but no-one could have guessed what a significant role was yet to be played by the 'Home of Golf' as the new century began (Ph. 1.1, 1.2).

THE LAST ONE HUNDRED YEARS

About 40% of Scotland's present golf courses were in existence by 1900. A further 130 were opened by 1930, mainly in suburban locations in central Scotland but also in tourist areas in the south-west and north-east of the country. A further 51 courses were opened between 1930 and 1980. During the last twenty years a hundred and seventeen new courses have been built in Scotland and this second golf boom is comparable with the boom which took place during the last two decades of the nineteenth century. The underlying pattern of the distribution of Scotland's 538 golf courses had been clearly established by 1930. The reasons behind this distribution pattern will be discussed in Chapter 2.

Two important technical developments which took place during the first 30 years of the twentieth century had important impacts on the game of golf both in Scotland and throughout the world. In 1902 a rubber-cored ball—the Haskell—was made in America by the Goodrich Tyre and Rubber Company of Akron, Ohio. By the mechanical winding of elastic thread or tape, a core was formed which was then covered by gutta percha. This ball went further when hit properly, and even if miss-hit it still performed better than the previous balls. The widespread adoption of this ball did much to stimulate the growth and spread of the game of golf.

Various experiments had been made with steel-shafted golf clubs prior to the First World War. The USGA ruled that they could be used in their competitions in 1924 but they were not approved by the Royal and Ancient until 1930.

By 1930, therefore, Scotland contained 342 golf courses and Scottish players had access to both good quality mass-produced golf balls and clubs. For the next 30 years golf in Scotland was largely an amateur participatory sport played by a wide cross-section

Ph. 1.1 *Golf Club House (1854) and Grand Hotel (1895) at St Andrews, with Tom Morris on the tee c.1896 (courtesy of G.W.W. Special Collection, University of Aberdeen).*

Ph. 1.2 *Golf on St Andrews Links: 'Holing out' c.1890 (courtesy G.W.W. Special Collection, University of Aberdeen).*

of society. Although professional golfers were based in many local clubs, the National and even Open Championships received only minimal media coverage. When the Open Championship was held in St Andrews in 1900 there were 81 entrants. When it was played at Carnoustie in 1931 there were 215 entrants, but when it returned to St Andrews in 1960 there were 410 entrants and it was won by Kel Nagle of Australia. By 1948 there were 1,413 entrants for the Open at St Andrews. By the end of the millennium, the Open Championship attracted 2,300 entrants and the total prize money was £1.7 million. These few statistics are a measure not only of the development of the professional game on a global scale but also of the popularity of the game at all levels. Whether measured by the earning capacity of the top professional golfers (on-course earnings of £2 million per year plus several millions in off-course earnings) or by the size of the UK golf equipment and clothing market (£350 million) or by the fact that there were 600 new golf courses and 800,000 additional golfers in the UK during the past decade, the past twenty years have seen a transformation in the status of the game of golf.

In what ways have these remarkable changes affected the golfing scene in Scotland? Both the number of golfers and the number of golf courses have increased in Scotland during the past two decades so that what has been described as Scotland's second golf boom has occurred. Many Scottish golf courses have been upgraded as their owners' revenue has been boosted by increased membership fees and visitors' green fees. However, for many thousands of Scottish golfers, particularly in rural areas, playing the game of golf is still relatively cheap. Major golfing centres such as St Andrews, Gleneagles, Turnberry, Troon, Loch Lomond and Royal Dornoch participate in the global golf tourism market. There has also been a significant increase in the number of commercial golf facilities in Scotland (Price, 1998). The Scottish nation owes a great debt to the pioneers of the game of golf. Their recognition of the golfing potential of both the links and inland landscapes of Scotland has not only produced a fine selection of golf courses for the Scots people, but has also laid the basis for a very significant international tourist market. The economic significance of this resource—the golf courses of Scotland—is as yet appreciated only to a limited extent.

A series of reports has been published on the provision and usage of Scotland's golf courses. In 1987 the Scottish Tourist Board commissioned a 'Study of Golf Facilities in Scotland' from Arthur Young, Management Consultants. In 1989 the first edition of this book was published which was the first comprehensive description and analysis of Scotland's golf courses, and in the same year the Royal and Ancient Golf Club of St Andrews' Development Panel published 'The Demand for Golf'. In 1991 the Scottish Sports Council commissioned Cobham Research Consultants to produce a 'Study of Golf in Scotland' which was the first systematic study of the demand for, provision of and use of golf facilities in Scotland.

In November 1997, the Henley Centre produced a report, 'EMAP Golf Futures' which was described as a 'definitive study of future trends in the British Golf Market'.

The report analysed the present state of the British golf industry and examined the potential changes which may occur within the industry over the next decade. The Scottish segment of the industry is included as a part of the British golf industry. Because this writer believes that the Scottish golf industry and golf markets are quite different when compared with the rest of Britain, he produced two research reports: 'The Golf Industry in Scotland—Current Status and Future Prospects' in 1998, and 'The Management and Marketing of Scotland's Golf Facilities' in 2000. Any attempt to analyse golfing activity in Scotland is severely constrained by the lack of accurate statistics. There is no accurate national data on who plays golf where, when and how often, and detailed data on golf tourism is very limited. There is an urgent need for a National Golf Database if sound strategic decisions are to be made with regard to the best utilisation of the existing golf facilities and for future developments. A start has been made by the Scottish Enterprise 'Golf Tourism Review' (1998), co-ordinated by MW Associates, and the Highland and Islands Enterprise/Highland Golf Development Group, 'Highland Golf Development Strategy' (1999). In July 2000 the Scottish Executive announced a 'New Strategy for Scottish Golf Tourism' and appointed a National Golf Tourism Development Manager. A Golf Tourism Monitoring Survey was undertaken in 2001.

Major developments in golf took place in Scotland at the end of the nineteenth century which laid the foundations for the very high level of golf facility provision which the country now enjoys. As the twenty-first century begins there are equally dramatic changes taking place in both the means of provision and management of Scotland's golf courses. The remainder of this book is concerned with the description and explanation of the landscapes of these golf courses and their management.

ꙮ Two
The Location of Golf Courses— Where and Why

Scotland's 538 golf courses occupy approximately 50,000 acres of land. At present day prices these courses, clubhouses and related facilities probably represent a capital investment in excess of £500 million. However, many of these courses were created for a few hundred pounds and even today it is possible to develop a basic nine-hole course in a rural area for about £200,000. The cost of ground purchase and subsequent development into a championship course with associated high quality facilities in an urban or suburban area may be several million pounds. Scottish golfers, along with the many thousands of golfers who visit Scotland each year, owe a great debt to the pioneers of the modern game in Scotland who established so many golf courses between 1880 and 1920 when land and labour were relatively cheap.

This chapter attempts to explain the distribution patterns of Scotland's golf courses over the past 250 years. The present distribution (Fig. 2.1) reflects a variety of controls which affect the provision of golfing facilities. Many of the traditional, long-established golfing areas have been supplemented by the creation of large numbers of courses in response to a demand from the residents of urban areas in the Central Belt—about half of Scotland's golf courses are to be found in the urbanised central belt stretching from the Ayrshire coast to Dundee. About one-third of Scotland's golf courses are of nine holes and two-thirds of 18 holes.

The rural areas of the south of Scotland contain a fairly even spread of courses. In the north-east, courses are mainly situated along the coast and in the Spey and Dee Valleys. The north-west Highlands has very few courses.

Scotland's golf courses have been created and are managed by three types of organisation. The first golf boom (1880–1910) was the result of groups of golfers forming members clubs which laid out golf courses and maintained them primarily for the use of their members. This type of mutual, non-profit making organisation still operates 388 golf courses (356 facilities), i.e. 71% of golf courses and 74% of facilities. Municipal authorities and Links Management Trusts operate 13% of the courses (12% of the facilities) and commercial companies operate 15% of the courses (14% of the facilities). While members clubs still dominate the provision of golf courses in Scotland, the commercial sector has significantly increased. During the last decade 72% of the new courses in Scotland have been developed by commercial companies.

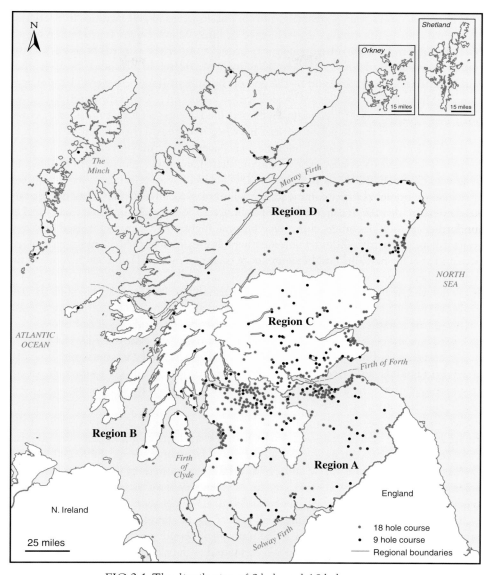

FIG 2.1 *The distribution of 9-hole and 18-hole courses.*
Region A: South and South-east Scotland
Region B: West-central Scotland
Region C: East-central Scotland
Region D: The North

SCOTLAND'S GOLF COURSES

There has always been a great tradition of public access to golf facilities in Scotland. Municipal courses (including those managed by Links Management Trusts) often began on common land which subsequently was brought under the control of town, city or county councils. By 1909 there were 32 municipal courses in Scotland; by 1940 that number had increased to 50 and by the end of the millennium there were 71 municipal courses. Many of these courses are located within cities and towns (Edinburgh, Glasgow, Dundee, Aberdeen) and have traditionally provided cheap golf for city residents. However, in recent years municipal authorities have begun to regard these facilities as sources of revenue rather than financial liabilities, and average weekday green fees have risen sharply. The average weekday green fee at municipal and links management facilities in 1980 was £2, but in 2001 it was £16.

The development of new commercial 'pay and play' facilities over the last decade has resulted in an increase in the number of public access courses. At the same time, most of the former 'private' members clubs have become increasingly commercialised and welcome the use of their facilities by non-members. It is estimated (Price 1998) that 43% of Scotland's members clubs now generate more than one-third of their total revenue from non-members.

When the first edition of this book was published in 1989, I was able to state (p. 20):

> On only half a dozen of the Scottish courses does a round of golf cost over £18, while on some 100 courses the cost per round is between £7 and £14 and there are still over 200 courses where a round of golf costs between £3 and £6. It is still possible to find the occasional unsophisticated nine-hole course where the deposit of a one pound note (or coin) in an honesty box entitles you to play the course.

In 2000 there were 21 courses (4%) where the weekday visitors green fee was over £50 (Table 2.1), 156 courses (29%) with a fee of between £20 and £49, 290 courses (54%) with a fee of between £10 and £19 and 70 courses (many of nine holes) with a fee of less than £10. Since 1990 weekday visitors green fees have increased by 150% while average annual membership fees have doubled to £300 per year.

In comparison with other countries (Table 2.2), Scotland has a very high level of provision of golf courses. Not only is the number of people per golf course low, but the cost of playing golf is relatively low when compared with other parts of Britain and with the rest of the world.

The remainder of this chapter is concerned with the description and explanation of how, when and where Scotland's golf courses came into existence. Collecting information about the chronology of golf course development is not an easy task. The one date which most golf club secretaries can readily provide is the date of foundation of their club. However, that date does not necessarily coincide with the opening of the course they presently play over. Some clubs (e.g. Glasgow Golf Club and the Honourable Company

TABLE 2.1

The number of 9-hole and 18-hole courses and the percentage of courses in each green fee category in each region

REGION	No. 9-hole courses	No. 18-hole courses	Total no. courses	Cost per weekday round (see Note 1) % in each category					
				A	B	C	D	E	F
A	36	81	117	12	54	20	9	1	3
B	45	129	174	19	41	28	6	1	5
C	34	91	125	7	55	24	6	1	6
D	42	80	122	12	67	12	5	2	2
Total	157	381	538	av. 13	av. 54	av. 21	av. 7	av. 1	av. 4

Note 1

Cost per round, 2000 prices

Category **A**: less than £10
Category **B**: £10–£19
Category **C**: £20–£29
Category **D**: £30–£39
Category **E**: £40–£49
Category **F**: over £50

TABLE 2.2

Population per Golf Course in Various Countries

Scotland	10,000
Ireland	13,000
U.S.A.	17,000
Wales	18,000
Sweden	22,000
England	26,000
Japan	50,000
France	112,000
Germany	142,000
Spain	210,000

of Edinburgh Golfers) have played over several different courses throughout their long history. Conversely, several clubs play over the same course, while other clubs have never had a course of their own. However, in the majority of cases the foundation date of a golf club coincides with the opening date (plus or minus a couple of years) of its own course. Therefore, since the date of foundation of a club is the most readily available information, unless other information suggests that a particular course pre-dates the foundation of the club, most of the analyses which follow are based on the published date of club formation. If more than one club has regularly used a particular course then the date of the foundation of the oldest club has been used.

It has been possible to determine the date of opening of 510 out of the 538 golf courses in Scotland. Table 2.3 summarises this information for each decade from 1730 to 2000. Although it has been established in Chapter 1 that golf was played in at least 15 locations in Scotland (Fig. 1.1) in the sixteenth and seventeenth centuries, little is known about the character of the courses used or about the organisation of the game. It is only after the formation of the Golfing Societies and golf clubs in the mid-eighteenth century that information about Scotland's golf courses becomes available.

THE OLD LINKS COURSES (FIG. 2.2) 1730–1849

Although golf was almost certainly continuously played from the seventeenth century on the various links sites shown on Figure 1.1, formal records of golf clubs using specific courses indicate only three golf courses in existence in Scotland by 1754—Bruntsfield Links in the centre of Edinburgh (1735), Leith Links (1744), and St Andrews (1754). A further seven clubs had come into existence by 1800: the Thorn Tree Club at Musselburgh (1774), the Society of Aberdeen Golfers (1780), Crail (1786), Glasgow (1787), Port Errol, Cruden Bay (1791), Dunbar (1794) and Burntisland (1797). A total of ten courses were in existence by the end of the eighteenth century. Eight of these occupied coastal links land and therefore continued the Scottish golfing traditions of the sixteenth and seventeenth centuries, while two courses were found in the very centre of expanding cities on common land used for a variety of purposes.

During the first half of the nineteenth century, the coastal links tradition was maintained with clubs/courses being established at Montrose (1810), Tayport, Scotscraig (1817), Leven (1820), North Berwick (1832), Peterhead (1841), Carnoustie (1842) and Perth (1842). The use of the North Insch at Perth by the Royal Perth Golf Club continued a tradition of golf being played on the gravel terraces beside the Tay which goes back to the sixteenth century.

EARLY EXPANSION 1850–79

This period saw the beginning of the expansion of golf throughout Scotland. A further 24 courses were opened between 1850 and 1879 (Fig. 2.3). The railway reached St

TABLE 2.3

Number of New Golf Courses Opened in Each Decade (1730–1999)
and the Population per Golf Course in Scotland.

Date	Total	Cumulative total	Decade %	Cumulative %	Population per Course (1000s)	% of courses opened in each period
1730–39	4	4	0.8	0.8		
1740–49	1	5	0.2	1.0		
1750–59	–	5	0.0	1.0		
1760–69	1	6	0.2	1.2		
1770–79	2	8	0.4	1.6		
1780–89	3	11	0.6	2.2		*1730–1879*
1790–99	–	11	0.0	2.2		8%
1800–09	–	11	0.0	2.2	145	
1810–19	1	12	0.2	2.4		
1820–29	1	13	0.2	2.6		
1830–39	1	14	0.2	2.8		
1840–49	4	18	0.8	3.6		
1850–59	8	26	1.6	5.2	111	
1860–69	4	30	0.8	6.0		
1870–79	12	42	2.4	8.4		
1880–89	42	84	8.2	16.6	41	*1880–1919*
1890–99	127	211	25.0	41.6		51%
1900–09	73	284	14.3	56.9	15	
1910–19	16	300	3.1	59.0		
1920–29	42	342	8.2	67.2	14	
1930–39	16	358	3.1	70.3		
1940–49	4	362	0.8	71.1		*1920–1979*
1950–59	10	372	2.0	73.1	13	18%
1960–69	9	381	1.8	74.9		
1970–79	12	393	2.4	77.3		
1980–89	24	417	4.7	82.0	12	*1980–1999*
1990–99	79	496	15.5	97.5	10	20%
(2000–2001) 14		510	2.7	100		*2000–2001* 3%

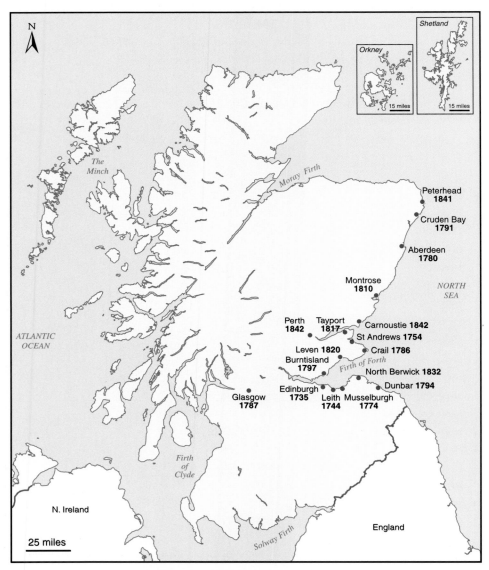

FIG. 2.2 *The location of golf courses, 1730–1849.*

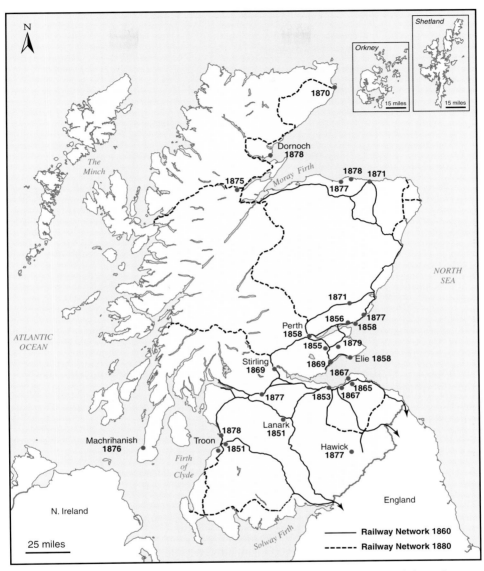

FIG. 2.3 *The location of golf courses opened between 1850 and 1879 and the railway network in existence in 1860 and 1880.*

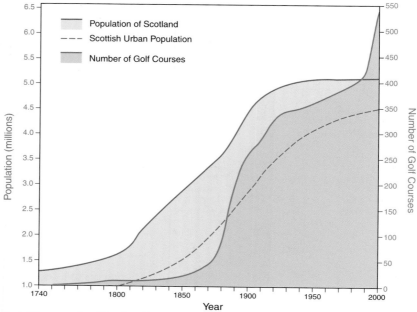

FIG. 2.4 *The growth of Scotland's population and the growth in the number of golf courses.*

Andrews in 1851, the Royal and Ancient clubhouse was built in 1854 and the first Open Championship was held in 1860. The population of Scotland also increased at a steady rate: in 1800 it was 1.6 million; in 1850, 2.9 million; and in 1880, 3.4 million (Fig. 2.4). After 1850, the growth in urban population was a significant contributor (50–60 per cent) to the total population with the population of Edinburgh increasing by 30 per cent, and that of Glasgow by nearly 60 per cent between 1850 and 1880. This was also the railway era in Scotland. By 1860 the rail links between Glasgow and Edinburgh, Glasgow and Carlisle, Edinburgh and North Berwick, Edinburgh and Carlisle, Glasgow/Edinburgh and Stirling, Perth, Dundee, Aberdeen, Fraserburgh, Elgin and Inverness had been completed. By 1880 the network had been extended to Oban in the west and Wick and Thurso in the north-east. The opening up of Scotland by the provision of a rail network coincided with a marked change in attitude to the Highlands. The area became fashionable as a place to take a holiday or buy property. Such attitudes stemmed from the decision by Queen Victoria to buy the Balmoral Estates in 1852 and to undertake numerous regal tours in Scotland. The period 1860–80 saw the foundations of the modern Scottish tourist industry being laid. The provision of golf courses in rural areas was no longer to depend only on local demand, as there would be a desire by visitors to play golf as part of a holiday. The relentless impact of the Industrial Revolution was beginning to produce a relatively wealthy upper- middle class who were mobile and had sufficient

24

free time to engage in sporting activities. The main impact of visiting golfers was yet to come but the signs of its beginnings can be seen in the spread of golf courses up to 1879.

Of the 26 courses opened between 1850 and 1879, 18 were on coastal sites—most of them links courses on the east coast of Scotland (Fig. 2.3). Courses at Prestwick (1851), Machrihanish (1876) and Troon (1878) heralded the expansion of golf around the shores of the Firth of Clyde. There were also signs of the first serious attempt to play golf at inland sites. Of particular interest is the opening of a course at Lanark in 1851. The course was located on a spread of fluvioglacial sand and gravel with an irregular surface topography of ridges, mounds and hollows. The site would have been well-drained and would have had many of the characteristics of true links land (see Chapter 3). Other inland courses existed at Perth (1858) on the gravel terrace at the North Inch on the banks of the Tay, at Haddington (1865), Stirling (1869), Forfar (1871), Hawick (1877), Airdrie (1877) and Ladybank (1879) in Fife. Little is known about the early character of these courses.

The first publication which lists Scottish golf courses is *The Golfers Manual* by 'A Keen Hand', published in 1857. It contains one or two pieces of information which indicate some of the problems faced by the golfers of this period. With reference to the Bruntsfield links in Edinburgh the author states: 'The Links, situated on the outskirts of Edinburgh, possesses a clay sub-soil, with grass which grows too luxuriantly for good play during summer, but during other seasons of the year, the course is in pretty good order.' Referring to the course on the North Inch at Perth the author states, '...from the thick growth of the grass, mole-heaps, and absence of hazards, the play is very monotonous. The principal time for play is autumn and spring.' This publication also provides information about the dates on which medal competitions were played on each of the courses. The most common months for such competitions were April, May, September and October. On some of the links courses, medal competitions were also held in July and August. It must be remembered that golf courses of the period were more or less in their natural state. The fine grasses of the links land, cropped by rabbits and sheep, could be played on throughout the year but would be at their best in spring and autumn. The turf of inland courses would produce longer grass and would be less suitable for play in July and August. On many courses there was little formal management of the fairways and greens. Old Tom Morris was appointed Green Keeper to the Royal and Ancient in 1865, a hole cutter was patented in 1869 and iron bands were purchased for the holes on the Elie course in 1874. The committee of the Earlsferry and Elie Golf Club authorised, on 17 August 1877, the purchase of a lawnmower for the putting greens (A. M. Drysdale, 1975). This was a major investment because the total income of the club for 1871–2 was £28.1s.0¼d, of which the wages of the greenkeeper accounted for £5. Expenditure was £27.9s.1d, leaving a surplus for the year of 11s11¼d.

It would appear that by the 1870s the first serious attempts at improving the conditions of both fairways and greens had begun. The part played by mowing machines in the improvement of golf courses is rather difficult to establish. The first grass cutting machine was invented in 1830 and the manufacture of such machines began in 1832. By 1852, Ransomes had produced some 1,500 machines, although in a publication describing the history of the company they state, 'Surprisingly, mechanised grass cutting was not generally accepted by golf courses until about 1890.' They produced their first horse-drawn machine in 1870. It would appear that the Elie Golf Club committee were a very progressive group.

There are letters in the Royal and Ancient archives from the early 1890s from the Town Clerk of St Andrews offering the pasturage of the Links to the Secretary of the Royal and Ancient (himself!). It would appear that sheep grazing plus rabbits were the main means of keeping the grass short throughout the period 1850–79. However, there are signs that both grass cutting by hand and by machine, along with other improvements in the course, had begun to take place. The management of both greens and fairways was a greater requirement on the inland courses than on the coastal links land.

By 1879 there were at least 48 golf courses in Scotland and some 50 golf clubs with some 4,000 members (including at least two ladies' clubs—St Andrews Ladies 1867 and Dunbar Ladies 1873). The first golf books had been published: *The Golfers Manual*, 1857; *Golfers Year Book*, 1866; *Golfers Handbook*, 1880. The Royal and Ancient had built its clubhouse, appointed its first professional/greenkeeper and was beginning to develop its role as the administrator of the game of golf. The game had started to be played on inland sites and the foundations had been laid for the rapid expansion of the game which would take place during the next three decades (Table 2.3).

THE FIRST GOLF BOOM 1880-1909

This was the period of great expansion of golf in Scotland (Fig. 2.5). Two hundred and forty-two golf courses (45 per cent of all of today's Scottish courses) were opened. The distribution of these golf courses (Fig. 2.6) was such that apart from the Western Grampians and North-West Highlands, all other parts of the country had at least one golf course within a 25-mile radius of any major settlement. The largest increase in the number of golf courses was in west central Scotland where 86 courses were opened between 1890 and 1909. More specifically, there were 47 new courses opened in and around Glasgow and 18 in and around Edinburgh.

Two distinct aspects of this rapid expansion require discussion. Firstly, this period saw the movement of golf away from predominantly coastal locations to inland sites. Of the 242 new courses, 157 were on inland sites and 66 on coastal sites. Secondly, the growth of the urban population in Scotland by nearly one million between 1870 and 1909 led to a great demand for suburban golf courses. The population of Scotland increased by one million between 1881 and 1911 with the population of Glasgow almost doubling (587,000 to 1,000,000) and Edinburgh's population increasing by 30 per cent (295,000 to 400,000) during the same period. By 1901 Scotland's urban population was

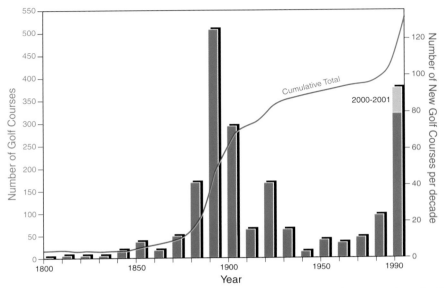

FIG. 2.5 *Course openings per decade (1800–1999) and the cumulative number of golf courses.*

2.9 million (65 per cent) with 44 per cent of the total population living in west central Scotland. It is therefore not at all surprising that the provision of golf courses in and around these rapidly growing areas was a major characteristic of the growth of golf in Scotland during this period. Although the majority of the new courses were related to the foundation of new members golf clubs primarily catering for the upper middle and upper classes, some 22 municipal courses existed in Scotland by 1909.

The growth of the urban centres of Greater Glasgow and Edinburgh was only partly responsible for the distribution pattern on Figure 2.6. It is not surprising that with the development of both rail and ferry networks, numerous courses were opened around the Firth of Clyde. Similarly, the development of tourism in Dumfries and Galloway, the Borders (particularly the Tweed valley) and in the Grampians (particularly the Tay, Dee and Spey valleys) led to the creation of new golf courses.

The rate of growth in the number of golf courses opened between 1880 and 1909 was not even (Table 2.3). The major expansion took place between 1890 and 1899 with 127 new courses, with a further 73 being opened between 1900 and 1909. The largest number of new courses opened in any one year was 17 in 1895.

Certain important growth points in Scottish golf were established during this period. The large number of courses established in and around Glasgow and Edinburgh has already been noted. East Lothian doubled its number of courses, and St Andrews added two additional courses alongside the Old Course. The basis of the modern map of

Scottish golf courses had been clearly established by the end of the first decade of the twentieth century.

The expansion of the inland courses not only reflected a major increase in demand for courses, but a major improvement in the ability of greenkeepers to control the condition of the course. It was not necessary to be totally dependent on rabbits and sheep to keep the fairways and greens in reasonable playing condition. No longer was it necessary to be totally dependent on the dune ridges, intervening hollows, sand spreads and other natural phenomena for the creation of a golf course. The coastal links land was relatively well-drained, but many inland sites required some drainage. While the position of tees and greens had evolved over many years on the old links courses, many of the new courses had various possibilities to offer in layout, landform modification, removal of trees and bushes and the creation of hazards. Such decisions were to be made by experienced and successful players of the game. The winners of championships became the designers of the new golf courses. The profession of golf course designer was beginning to emerge. F. W. Hawtree (1983) in his book *The Golf Course—Planning, Design, Construction* provides an interesting account of the history and philosophy of golf course design. He clearly establishes that, at least until the 1920s, all golf course designers accepted the natural landforms of the site chosen for a new course—the art consisted of making the best use of the natural landscape for the enjoyment of the game of golf. He states (p. 6), 'Before horses and scoops were called in, all insisted that their first duty was to employ fully all the natural features of the site.'

Since the game of golf had developed almost entirely on coastal links land up until 1880 it is not surprising that on many of the inland courses at least some of the characteristics of those links were 'transported' to inland sites. Specifically, the creation of sand-filled bunkers became a part of the inland golfing landscape even if they were entirely artificial.

A wide variety of landforms was utilised by the designers of the new inland courses between 1880 and 1909 (see Chapters 3 and 4). It is probable that very little modification of the natural contours took place, and we know little of the way in which actual sites were chosen. Presumably a group of golfers would decide to establish a club and try to obtain, either by lease or purchase, the most suitable available piece of ground in their neighbourhood. They themselves might decide on the positioning of tees, fairways and greens, or they might invite a golf 'professional', on the basis of his wide experience and proven golfing skills, to advise on the best layout. Two names dominated golf course design in Scotland at the turn of the century—Tom Morris ('Old Tom') 1821–1908, and Willie Park Jnr, 1864–1925.

Thomas Morris was born in St Andrews in 1821 and was apprenticed to Allan Robertson at the Old Course from 1839 to 1851. He had a major dispute with Robertson over the use of the gutta percha ball, so he moved to Prestwick as greenkeeper and professional, where he remained until 1865. He then returned to St Andrews, where he was the first professional appointed by the Royal and Ancient, which he remained until

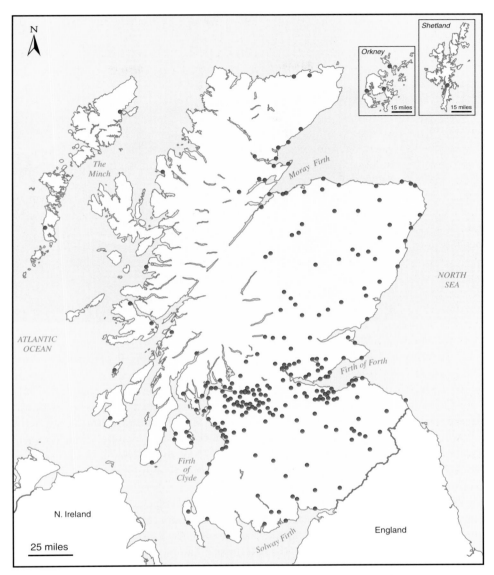

FIG. 2.6 *The location of golf courses opened between 1880 and 1909.*

Ph. 2.1 'Ransome's Motor Mower' on the Old Course, St Andrews, 1911. Note the sheep grazing the fairways (courtesy of Textron Golf, Turf and Speciality Products).

his retirement in 1904. Morris won the Open Championship on four occasions (1861, 1862, 1864 and 1867). His son 'Young Tom' also won the Open four times before he was 22 years old, but he died at the age of 25. 'Old Tom' Morris advised on the design of the following Scottish golf courses: Askernish (South Uist), Barry, Carnoustie, Crail, Dornoch, Dunbar, Elie, Glasgow Killermont, King James VI Perth, Ladybank, Luffness New, Machrihanish, Muirfield, Prestwick, Royal Burgess Edinburgh, St Andrews New, Stirling and Tain.

Willie Park Jnr was born in Musselburgh in 1864 and died at the age of 61 in Edinburgh. From 1880 to 1894 he served as assistant greenkeeper and professional with his uncle, Mungo Park, at Ryton in England. He then returned to Musselburgh to join his father (Willie Park Snr who had won the first Open Championship in Prestwick in 1860) in the club and ball making firm of W. Park & Son. He won the Open Championship in 1887 and 1889 and was runner up in 1898. He subsequently designed courses in England (Sunningdale and Huntercombe) and in the United States (1895–8 and 1916–24). Sir Guy Campbell called him the doyen of course architects and credited him with setting the standards for the many designers who followed him. He designed over 70 courses in the USA and Canada and over 100 in Britain, including the following in Scotland: Baberton, Barnton, Bathgate, Biggar, Bo'ness, Bridge of Weir, Bruntsfield Links,

Burntisland, Carnoustie, Crieff, Dalkeith, Duddingston, Forres, Gailes, Glasgow Killermont, Glencorse, Grantown-on-Spey, Gullane, Innellan, Innerleithen, Jedburgh, Kilspindie, Melrose, Monifieth, Montrose, Murrayfield, Luffness New, Selkirk, Shiskine, St Boswells, Torwoodlee, Turnhouse.

Another great name in Scottish golf at this time was James Braid. Born in Earlsferry in 1870, he won the Open Championship in 1901, 1905, 1906, 1908 and 1910. He went on to make a major contribution to golf course design in the 1920s and 1930s, which will be discussed in the next section.

Undoubtedly, the condition of golf courses began to improve during the last decade of the nineteenth century. The employment of greenkeepers and general workmen along with the use of grass cutting machines and other implements must have radically changed the condition of golf courses. Ransomes were selling lawnmowers to golf clubs through-out the United Kingdom during the 1890s. Initially they were designed for use on the greens and tees, but from 1870 horse-drawn mowers were available which may have been used to cut fairways. A horse-drawn machine, specially designed for cutting rough golf courses, was introduced by Ransomes in 1905. Ransomes also produced the world's first petrol-driven lawnmower in 1902, and by 1903 they were producing four models—one with a 30-inch cut which was described as 'a specially powerful machine for steep inclines and golf links'. The Royal and Ancient had purchased one of these motor mow-ers in 1911 (Ph. 2.1). Behind this machine can be seen the bridge over the Swilken Burn and there are numerous sheep grazing the fairway.

Not only had a great expansion of golfing facilities taken place at the turn of the century, but the quality of those courses must have improved dramatically as both man and machine were put to work both during construction and subsequent maintenance. Golf was no longer a casual game played on common lands. The era of the golf club committee, the club secretary and of income and expenditure accounts had arrived. Although still very dependent on the natural contours of the land, course design and course management had begun to change the character of the game of golf. Many of the suburban courses had to be designed to fit relatively small areas: quite often a single farm of approximately 100 acres would be purchased, and in order to provide 18 holes the lay-out required parallel alignment of fairways. In other circumstances, such as the utilisation of the parkland of a large mansion, a more expansive approach was possible. Already the debate had begun as to whether inland courses could ever be regarded as a true test of golfing skill since they were so obviously different from the classic coastal links.

CONSOLIDATION 1910–49

There were 78 new courses opened during this 39-year period (Table 2.3 and Fig. 2.7) and there were three distinct phases of development with two periods of stagnation.

The expansion in the number of golf courses which characterised the turn of the

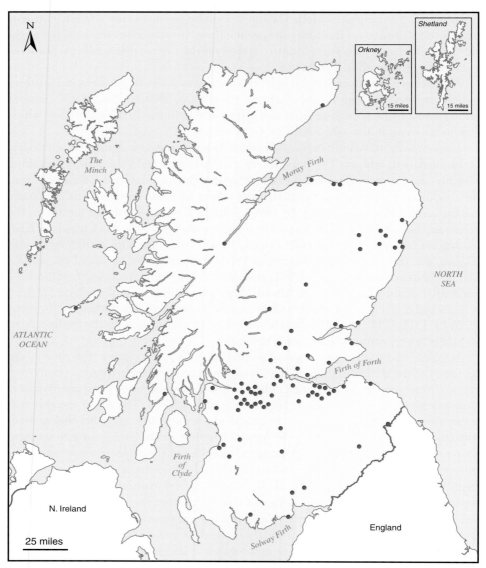

FIG. 2.7 *The location of golf courses opened between 1910 and 1949.*

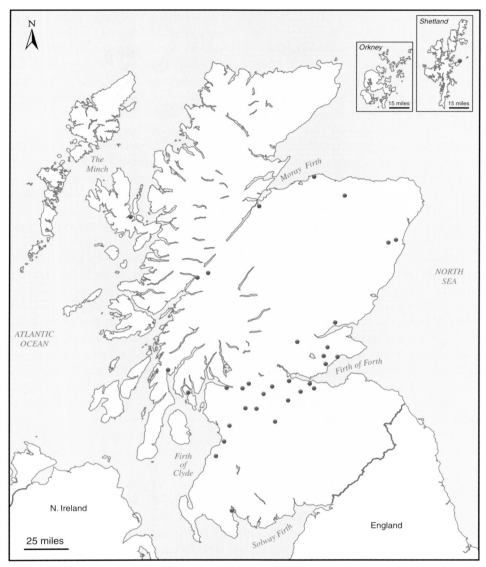

FIG. 2.8 *The location of golf courses opened between 1950 and 1979.*

century continued between 1910 and 1913, when a further 16 courses were opened. The period of the Great War (1914–18) saw no new courses and several courses went out of existence. Parts of many other courses were used for agriculture. Between 1920 and 1930, 42 new courses were opened, 22 of these between 1926 and 1930. A further 16 courses were added between 1932 and 1938. The advent of the Second World War (1939–45) meant that no new courses were opened until 1947. The pattern of this growth in the number of golf courses was very similar to that identified for the period 1880–1910. Of the 78 courses only ten were at coastal locations, with a large proportion (50 per cent) of the others being in the urbanised central belt—20 new courses in and around Glasgow and 12 new courses in and around Edinburgh. The demand for golf courses in suburban locations was still growing but total population growth had begun to lessen, and the effects of two World Wars and the financial depression of the nineteen-twenties and early nineteen-thirties obviously took its toll.

It was during this period that the concept of the golf resort was introduced to Scotland. In one sense, St Andrews was the forerunner of this type of development, but it had developed in association with a public links course of great antiquity and tradition. Hotels had already been built by the turn of the century in St Andrews, as had also the New and Jubilee courses. The Eden course was added in 1912. The four courses and the general character of the university town began to attract many visitors. The first purpose-built golf resort was developed at Turnberry by the Glasgow and South Western Railway. A branch line was opened from Ayr, allowing frequent train services from Glasgow and a direct sleeper service from London. By 1907 Turnberry had become a recognised golfing centre with a first class hotel. During both World Wars the golf courses were requisitioned for military use. A similar development was undertaken at Gleneagles by the Caledonian Railway Company. The construction of the Gleneagles Hotel began in 1914 but was interrupted by the First World War. Work was resumed in 1922, with James Braid designing both the King's and Queen's courses which were opened in 1924. It is perhaps surprising that other golf resorts on the scale of Turnberry and Gleneagles have not yet been developed in Scotland.

One name above all others dominated the profession of golf course design during this period. James Braid was born in Earlsferry, Fife, in 1870. He became an apprentice carpenter in St Andrews, played his first professional tournament in 1894 and was appointed Professional at the Romford Golf Club in England in 1896 before moving to Walton Heath Golf Club in 1906. Braid, along with Taylor and Vardon, were the 'Great Triumvirate' of competitive golf during the first 20 years of the twentieth century. After winning five Open Championships, Braid devoted a great deal of his time to golf course design but, because he hated travelling, many of his designs were based on the analysis of topographic maps from which he produced detailed and accurate working drawings. He designed some 60 courses in England and the following 38 courses in Scotland: Airdrie, Ayr Bellisle, Ayr Seafield, Balmore, Blairgowrie, Blairmore & Strone, Boat of Garten, Brechin, Brora, Carnoustie Burnside, Cawder, Cowal, Crieff, Crow Wood,

Dalmahoy, Deaconsbank, Dullatur, Edzell, Elie, Forfar, Forres, Glenbervie, Glencruitten, Gleneagles (King's and Queen's), Greenock, Hayston, Hilton Park, Kingsknowe, Kirkintilloch, Monkton Hall, Murcar, Nairn, Powfoot, Rothesay, Routenburn, Preston Grange, Stranraer and Turnhouse.

The number and distribution of golf courses in Scotland had been largely established by the beginning of the twentieth century. In 1900 there was one course for every 15,000 people in Scotland. This had only changed to one for every 13,000 by 1950 and one for every 10,000 by the end of the millenium. The great diversity in golf course types will be discussed in subsequent chapters. The game of golf remained accessible to a very wide cross-section of the Scottish people. Large numbers of golf clubs in rural areas provided very cheap golf in relatively unsophisticated circumstances. Numerous municipal courses in the large cities provided similar golfing opportunities in the urban and suburban setting. At the same time, high quality courses associated with sophisticated clubhouse facilities were developed by some private clubs and by resort developers. This wide range in the character of golf courses remains one of the most distinctive features of Scottish golf. It is also a striking feature of Scottish golf courses that although during the period 1910–49 developments in earth-moving equipment gave much greater scope to the golf course designer to make changes in the land surface on which courses were being laid out, the vast majority of Scottish courses show little sign of landform modification. While the detailed morphology and position of tees, greens and bunkers may reflect the work of man and machine, most Scottish golf courses owe their general character to the long history of geological and biological processes which had created the landscapes utilised by golf course designers.

STEADY GROWTH 1950–79

There were 31 courses opened in Scotland during this period, spread fairly evenly over the entire country (Fig. 2.8). This was a period of slow but steady growth. There were no new courses opened in and around Edinburgh, and only one in Dumfries, Galloway and the Borders. There were ten new courses opened in and around Glasgow—four of them associated with the new town developments at East Kilbride and Cumbernauld. The new towns at Glenrothes and Livingston also had golf courses constructed. Two courses (the Princes and Glen Devon) were added to the Gleneagles golf complex, and additional courses were opened at St Andrews (Balgove) and Carnoustie. Industrial developments at Fort William and Invergordon saw courses opened close to each of these towns and attempts to encourage additional tourism saw courses opened on Mull, Skye and in the Spey Valley. Two hotel-based projects were opened during this period—one at Gleddoch House (1974) to the west of Glasgow, and the other at Murrayshall (1980) to the east of Perth. It is interesting to note that 12 of the 46 new courses were public courses primarily provided and administered by municipal authorities.

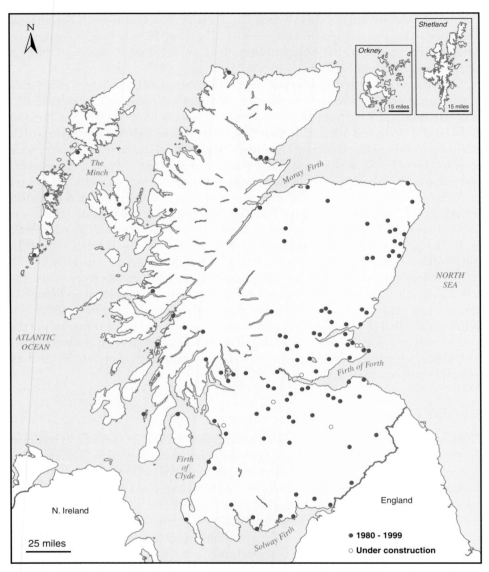

FIG. 2.9 *The location of golf courses opened between 1980 and 1999 and those under construction.*

THE SECOND GOLF BOOM 1980–2001

The second golf boom in Scotland began slowly in the seventies, with 12 new courses, and the eighties, with 24 new courses (Table 2.3). In the last decade of the century 79 new courses were opened for play with a further 14 opened or under construction in 2000–2001. Approximately 23% (117 courses) of the total stock has been created during the last twenty years. Half of these courses were of nine holes. Thirty-six were members club courses, sixteen of which were either 9- or 18-hole extensions to existing facilities. Of these 9% were municipal facilities and 60% were developed by commercial companies.

Fig. 2.9 shows the distribution of golf courses opened since 1980, and those under construction. Out of these 10% are located in Edinburgh and the Lothians, 14% in the Borders, Dumfries and Galloway, 10% in Fife, 10% in Perth and Kinross, 12% in Aberdeenshire and 20% in the Highlands and Islands.

In the 1980s there were numerous proposals for multi-million pound golf-related property developments in Scotland. Championship golf courses, five-star hotels with leisure and conference facilities, up-market housing and holiday chalets, and in a few cases marinas were proposed, often by developers who had no knowledge of the Scottish golf and housing markets. Fortunately, few of these projects were actually started and only four (Letham Grange, Brunston Castle, Loch Lomond and Westerwood) encountered serious financial problems.

The quality of the 103 new courses varies greatly. A small proportion are first-class championship courses designed by internationally recognized golf course architects (e.g. Loch Lomond, Carnegie Club, Gleneagles Monarchs, The Dukes, The Roxburghe and Kingsbarns), each of which cost several million pounds to construct. Fifty percent are basic 9-hole facilities costing between £50,000 and £300,000.

Another recognisable trend in these new golf courses is that 60% of the courses opened since 1980 were developed by commercial companies. The proportion increases to 72% if only those courses opened in the last decade are considered. Many of these courses are of good, members club standard (e.g. Kings Acre, Strathmore Golf Centre, Glenisla, Elmwood, Drumoig, Whitekirk, Charleton and Kames Golf and Country Club). The construction of these courses involved minimal earth movement, and they were designed by local golf course architects. Each course has an adequate clubhouse to accommodate a membership of 300–500 and to provide food and beverage sales for members and visitors. The members of the clubs (recognised by the SGU) attached to these facilities purchase an annual season ticket (typically £350–£450 per year) but have no say in the management of the facility. The facility, in most cases, is primarily operated as a 'pay and play' business. Most of these facilities cost between £600,000 and £1,200,000 to construct (excluding the cost of the land) and are highly dependent on a large number of visitor rounds, at weekday green fees of between £15 and £25, to be viable businesses. Unfortunately, largely due to the price of land, most of these new 'pay and play' facilities are located in rural areas rather than in urban or suburban locations where the demand for access to golf courses is greatest.

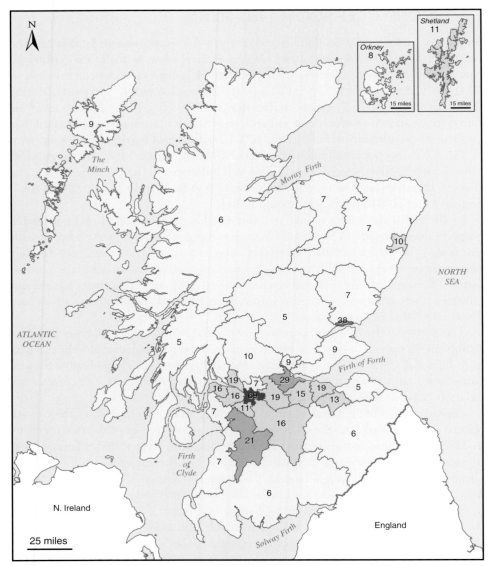

FIG. 2.10 *Population (thousands) per 18-hole unit in 2000.*

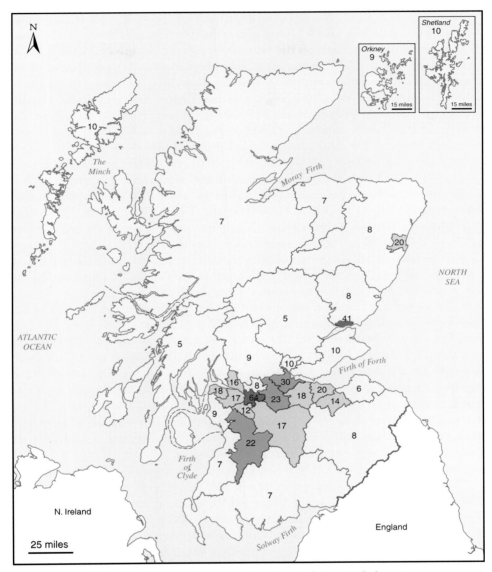

FIG. 2.11 *Number of adult golfers (hundreds) per 18-hole unit.*

SCOTLAND'S GOLF COURSES

There have been three types of capital investment into Scotland's golf facilities, during the last decade, which have led to significant improvements in existing facilities and the creation of new facilities. In 1994 Scottish members clubs received a total of £26 million in the refund of VAT payments which had been incorrectly charged on membership fees. This money was not returned to individual members, but invested in clubhouse refurbishment, extensions or replacements, course improvement and extensions and drainage and irrigation schemes. Since 1995 the Lottery Sports Fund has made 70 awards totalling £8.5 million to various golf development projects which had a total project value of £25 million. The third source of capital investment was the private sector, which invested some £50 million building new commercial golf courses and clubhouses. In total, over the last decade, these three sources invested sums of the order of £80 million in the improvement and creation of golf facilities in Scotland. It is interesting to note that between 1989 and 1993 Bord Fáilte (The Irish Tourist Board), in its Operational Programme for Tourism, estimated that £200 million was invested by the golf industry in 28 new commercial golf courses and 18 clubhouses in Ireland.

As a measure of golf course accessibility, a map (Fig. 2.10) showing the population per 18-hole unit (i.e. a 9-hole course = 0.5 units) in each of the 32 unitary authority regions, has been produced. The national average is 10,000 people per each 18-hole unit. Twelve regions, mainly in the central belt plus Dundee, have levels of provision well below the national average (15,000 to 69,000 persons per 18-hole unit). The Borders, Dumfries and Galloway, and the entire area north of a line from Aberdeen to Helensburgh, have high levels of provision (5,000 to 10,000 persons per 18-hole unit). Access to a golf course is not only a question of location, but it is also related to the management policy of the owner/operator of the facility. A resident in Edinburgh or East Dunbartonshire may live quite close to three or four golf courses, but if all are operated as members clubs and have long waiting lists, access is not readily available. If you are female and live next door to an exclusively male members club (a few still exist), then you cannot even place your name on the waiting list.

Measuring demand for golf is a difficult exercise. Statistics provided by the Golf Unions indicate that there are approximately 200,000 golf club members in Scotland (73% male, 15% female, 11% male junior and 1% female junior). The highest concentration of club members is in Greater Glasgow with 44,000, Edinburgh and the Lothians 26,000 and Fife 22,000. If it is assumed that each club member plays 40 rounds of golf per year (Scottish Sports Council Report, 1992, p. 42), eight million rounds of golf are played by club members each year.

If it is assumed that each 18-hole unit has an annual capacity of 32,000 rounds, then the spare capacity of Scotland's golf courses which could be available to non-club members is of the order of six million rounds. A significant proportion (estimate: 3 million) of these rounds are sold to visiting parties, individual Scots and golf tourists from the rest of the UK and other countries.

Another method of assessing demand for golf facilities from the resident population is to use participation rates. The Scottish Sports Council Report (1991, p. 1) stated that 15% of the adult population had played golf in the previous 12 months. The EMAP Golf Futures Report states that 12.7% of Scotland's adult population play golf. The mean of these two figures is 13.8%, and this figure has been used to calculate the number of adult golfers per 18-hole unit in each unitary area (Fig. 2.11). There are large rural areas where there are fewer than 800 golfers per 18-hole unit, and in much of the central belt (excluding East Dunbartonshire) there are between 1,700 and 2,300 per 18-hole unit, but Falkirk has 3,000, Dundee 4,100 and Glasgow City 6,400.

Accurate data on the usage levels of Scottish golf courses does not exist. Lack of waiting lists for club membership, active advertising by both members clubs and commercial facilities and discounting of green fees would suggest that, in some areas in Scotland, supply exceeds demand. While the data is weak, it is likely that without demand from visiting golfers, areas such as Perth and Kinross, Dumfries and Galloway, the Borders, parts of Fife, Ayrshire and Highland have an over-supply of golf facilities.

THE FUTURE

In the first edition of this book I was rash enough to forecast that 12 new golf courses would be constructed in Scotland during the nineties and I was wrong by a factor of seven. There are currently eight courses under construction and at least another ten submitted for planning approval. It would appear that the stock of Scottish golf courses is set to grow further.

The provision of golf facilities and their management constitute a service industry which occupies 50,000 acres, directly employs at least 6,000 people and has an annual turnover of over £100 million. The management structures are changing and will change further as the course providers adapt to the requirements of new generations of golfers. If the stock of golf courses is to continue to grow, then greater attention must be paid to attracting more female golfers and to encouraging juniors. The major untapped markets are in the urban areas of the Central Belt where unfortunately land values are highest. In order to develop new golf facilities in these locations a national strategy is required similar to that which produced the urban municipal golf courses during the first golf boom (1890-1910).

The Scottish Executive is currently developing a new strategy for the Scottish tourism industry, part of which will address the issue of golf tourism. During the last decade Scotland has been overshadowed by Ireland as a golf tourism destination. The dominance of members clubs as the principal operators of many of Scotland's best golf courses (Muirfield, Gullane, Royal Troon, Blairgowrie, Nairn, Royal Dornoch) makes for a potential clash between members' interests and tourist demand. While members clubs benefit greatly from income received from visitors, they must, if they wish to continue to benefit from these revenues, accept the responsibilities of being part of a service industry in terms of the quality and price of the service they sell to the visitors. Charging members the equivalent of £8 per round (for 40 rounds per year) and visitors £40 or even £70 per round does leave a bad impression on visitors. At the same time, if such a members club has a long waiting list for new members, should it be making large profits from visitors in order to keep annual membership fees low, while denying local residents access to the same facilities? During the next decade it will be necessary to address the many contradictions which exist in the provision, management and marketing of all sectors of the Scottish golf industry (Price 1998, Price 2000).

🌿 Three
Golfing Environments

Although a golf course only occupies 50 to 150 acres of land, its character is greatly influenced by the physical environment of its particular location. This physical environment consists of rocks, landforms, soil, vegetation and weather. The golf course designer may have created a few bunkers or mounds and constructed elevated tees or plateau greens, but the general character of a golf course is usually strongly related to its natural environment. Many of Scotland's golf courses were laid out before mechanical earth-moving equipment was available and therefore tend to incorporate many natural features. Not only the course itself but the surrounding scenery (or landscape) and the weather conditions all contribute to the golfing environment. This chapter is concerned with how these golfing environments originated and how they vary within Scotland.

Despite being a small country, Scotland (total area 28,000 square miles) has a great many different physical environments and therefore there is considerable variety in the available golfing environments. To understand how these environments have been created it is necessary to look back into the geological history of Scotland because the present environment has evolved over many millions of years. The early geological history of the country was responsible for the arrangement of rock types and structures which constitute the basic framework of the country. The erosional work of rivers carved valleys in the upland areas while the same rivers transported the eroded material to the lowlands and the coast. Major changes in the landforms of Scotland were brought about, during the past two million years, by the events collectively known as 'The Great Ice Age'. On numerous occasions the climate of Scotland cooled to such an extent that glaciers developed and merged into great ice sheets which buried the land surface. The last glaciers only disappeared some 10,000 years ago, and the erosional and depositional activities of glacier ice and its associated meltwaters were responsible for many of the landforms and surface deposits seen in Scotland today. As the ice sheets expanded and retreated, relative sea level around the Scottish coastline rose and fell by as much as 300 feet and the position of the coastline changed. After the last ice sheet retreated the new land surface was colonised by plants and animals. By 9,000 years ago much of Scotland was covered by forests—birch and oak in the lowlands and in the south and west, and by pine and birch in the north and on high ground. The earliest evidence, in Scotland, of man's colonisation of the natural environment dates to about 8,000 years ago. In the subsequent period both natural and man-induced changes have led to the destruction of much of the natural woodland and to the creation of vast areas of peat and heather moorland (Price 1983).

Before examining how the geological and vegetational history of Scotland has influenced the character of its golf courses it is necessary to clarify the meaning of several terms. The natural environment is produced by the operation of natural processes. The types of natural processes which operate in any area are largely controlled by the climate of that area. The climate determines the type of geological processes which create landforms and the range of animal and plant species which occupy an area. Together, the surface forms, drainage and natural vegetation comprise the natural landscape. When a natural landscape is occupied and used by man it can be extensively modified and the adjective 'natural' has to be removed. Scotland's present landscapes are far from natural. Even though the landforms, which constitute a major part of any landscape, are entirely the product of natural processes there are few parts of Scotland where man's use of the land has not modified the vegetation, the soil and the general appearance of the landscape.

THE GEOLOGICAL FRAMEWORK

There is a strong north-east to south-west trend in several important geological structures in Scotland (Fig. 3.1). These structures are related to the Caledonian earth movements which occurred some 500 million years ago. Three major faults divide the country into four distinct geological regions: the Southern Upland Boundary Fault, the Highland Boundary Fault and the Great Glen Fault.

Much of the area to the south of the Southern Upland Boundary Fault consists of closely folded sedimentary rocks which have been eroded to produce the smooth, rounded slopes of the Southern Uplands. There are also important masses of granite in the southwest.

The so-called 'Midland Valley' of Scotland is bounded by major faults both to the north and south. This geological region is not one single valley as its name implies, but consists of a series of sedimentary basins, mainly of Carboniferous (coal bearing) and Devonian age which form both lowlands and plateaus, separated by upland areas consisting of volcanic rocks. The volcanic rocks (mainly basalt) of Carboniferous age underlie the upland areas to the south and southwest of Glasgow and form the Kilpatrick and Campsie Hills. Volcanic rocks of Devonian age form part of the Pentland Hills, Ochil Hills and Sidlaw Hills.

North of the Highland Boundary Fault the geology is very complicated. Large parts of the Highlands are underlain by very ancient metamorphic rocks which, when eroded, tend to produce rather rugged scenery. There are important granitic masses in the eastern Grampians (e.g. the Cairngorms) and important areas of relatively recent volcanic rocks (Tertiary age: dating from about 60 million years ago) in the west on the islands of Skye, Mull and Arran. The far north-west of Scotland and the Outer Hebrides are

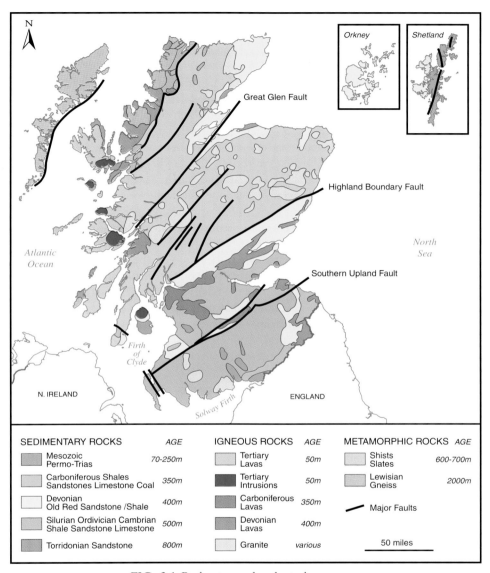

FIG. 3.1 *Rock types and geological structures.*

underlain by very ancient Lewisian metamorphic rocks. In great contrast to both the ancient metamorphic and more recent volcanic rocks are the stratified sandstones of Devonian age which underlie much of Caithness, Orkney and the areas around the Moray Firth.

Only in certain very specific circumstances can the solid rocks underlying a golf course directly influence the character of that course. The vast majority of golf courses are influenced by the unconsolidated sediments which usually cover the underlying solid rocks. However, in upland areas where glacial erosion has often laid bare the underlying solid rocks the character of those rocks certainly does influence the golfing environment. There are several courses in the Highlands where the tough metamorphic rocks give a rugged appearance to both fairways and rough. The most dramatic effect of a particular rock type on the character of golf courses is to be found in areas where the courses are built on land underlain by volcanic lavas. These lavas have a very distinctive 'layered' appearance and give the landscape a 'stepped' character. Because of the chemical characteristics of these lavas and their land-use history, golf courses built on these lavas are of the moorland type. Many such courses are to be found on the Clyde 'plateau basalts' around Glasgow. A most remarkable golf course built on the Tertiary lavas at Tobermory on the island of Mull makes full use both of the relatively flat surfaces of individual lava flows and the steep cliff-faces produced by subsequent glacial erosion of the lavas.

It is in terms of the general landscapes in which golf courses are located that the underlying solid geology and structural history are of significance. Few golfers are so absorbed in their game that they are not aware of the scenery which surrounds them. The superb views from the Tobermory course along the Sound of Mull or up Loch Sunart are very much a product of the geological history of that area—largely a volcanic landscape. The courses laid out on the sands and gravels of the Spey Valley have the marvellous backdrop of the granite massif of the Cairngorms. In the Southern Uplands many of the courses are to be found on valley-floors or valley-sides and yet it is the rounded hills so characteristic of much of this region which provide the scenic setting. Even on links courses it is the rock type and geological history of the landward margin of the wind-blown sand which give such courses their broader landscape characteristics.

THE IMPACT OF THE ICE AGE

No other geological event had a greater influence on golfing environments than the Ice Age. During the past two million years there have been major changes in Scotland's climate. We now live in an Interglacial Period which, if geological history repeats itself, is coming to an end. There may have been as many as 20 glacial periods each lasting about 100,000 years, separated by interglacial periods each lasting about 10,000 to 15,000 years during the last two million years. During the glacial periods, average January and July temperatures in Scotland at sea level were lowered by at least 10° centigrade. Such changes in climate allowed much more precipitation to fall as snow, and therefore glaciers

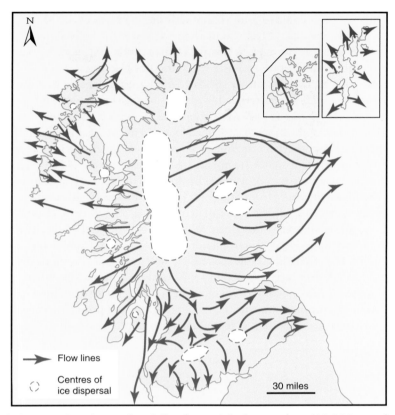

FIG. 3.2 *Centres of ice dispersal and flow lines of the last ice sheet (18,000 years before the present).*

were able to develop and expand into ice sheets. The last great ice sheet to develop in Scotland began to form about 27,000 years ago and finally melted away about 10,000 years ago. As the last ice sheet destroyed much of the evidence of its predecessors we know more about the impact of the last glaciation than we do about the many earlier ones. Because the last ice sheet had such a major effect on the Scottish landscape, and therefore on the character of the land used for golf courses, it is necessary to examine the history of the environmental changes brought about by that ice sheet.

The existence of a great ice sheet which covered Scotland in the recent geological past has been known since the middle of the last century (Price, 1983). Individual glaciers began in valley heads (corries) and expanded down valleys as snow accumulation increased. The main centres of ice accumulation were in the western Highlands and Islands, the western Southern Uplands and eastern Grampians (Fig. 3.2). Individual valley glaciers became thicker and longer and eventually over-topped the interfluves, spread out across the lowlands, and developed into a major ice sheet. It is highly likely that the surface of this ice sheet attained a maximum altitude in excess of 5,000 feet, and over central Scotland the ice was probably more than 4,000 feet thick. By about 20,000 years ago the entire mainland and most, if not all, of the islands and much of the area now covered by less than 300 feet of sea water was buried by glacial ice.

Glacial ice moving forward under the force of gravity is capable of a great deal of erosion. Valleys that have been occupied by glaciers tend to be straight and steep-sided—such glacial troughs are widespread throughout the Highlands and Southern Uplands. The material eroded by the moving ice is incorporated in the ice and transported some distance only to be deposited as a sediment, known as till, when the ice melts. Much of the till, consisting of angular rock fragments in a clay/silt matrix, is deposited beneath the glacier or ice sheet during ice wastage (melting). Till is a very widespread surface material in Scotland. It ranges from one to fifty feet in thickness and covers much of the lowlands and valley sides. Under certain circumstances the till deposits are built into hummocks or ridges known as moraines. When till is deposited while the ice sheet is still moving forward, a very distinctive landform known as a drumlin (Ph. 3.1) is created. A drumlin is a streamlined hill shaped like half an egg. These elongated mounds are usually 30 to 100 feet high and 200 to 1,000 yards in length. They often have steep slopes facing the former direction of ice movement and gentle streamlined tails. Drumlins often occur in groups or swarms (Fig. 3.3) and therefore produce a very distinctive landscape with a strong lineation, quite steep slopes and often poor drainage conditions

Ph. 3.1 *A typical drumlin, north-east Glasgow.*

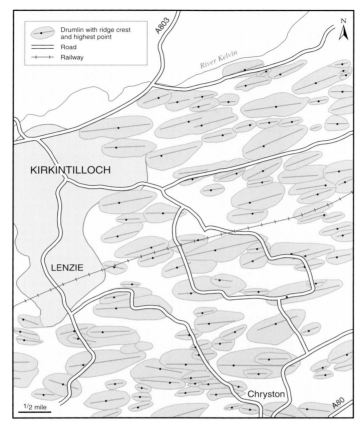

FIG. 3.3 *Drumlins near Glasgow.*

(heavy soils). There are numerous golf courses in drumlin landscapes around Glasgow (see Chapter 4).

A period of glaciation means that large quantities of water are locked up in the glaciers and ice sheets. When the climate begins to warm, vast quantities of meltwater are released in a relatively short period of time. These meltwaters are capable of eroding deep channels in solid rock and transporting large quantities of rock debris entrapped in the ice. This debris is released as the ice melts and the rapidly flowing meltwaters modify the rock debris to produce rounded gravel and sand. Large areas of Scotland are covered by these sand and gravel deposits (fluvioglacial deposits). These deposits have a variety of forms depending on how and where they were deposited (Fig. 3.4). Where valley systems debouch onto the lowlands, large fans of fluvioglacial sand and gravel have been deposited (e.g. near Blairgowrie). These gently sloping fans are known as outwash fans or sandar (an Icelandic term: singular = sandur). When the flow of meltwaters was confined by steep valley sides the floor of the valley became choked with sand and gravel which were later eroded by the river to produce river terraces. In some locations, fluvioglacial sands and gravels were deposited between a valley glacier and the valley side. When the glacier melted, the valley-side terrace was left abandoned—these features are known as kame-terraces. Both on outwash fans and kame-terraces large blocks of glacier ice were sometimes buried by the fluvioglacial deposits and, when the ice melted,

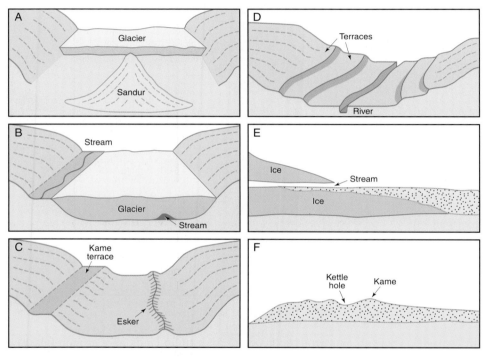

FIG. 3.4 *Landforms produced by the meltwaters of the last ice sheet.*

A. *The formation of an outwash fan (sandur) in front of a glacier.*

B. *Meltwater streams flowing along the lateral margin and in tunnels under the ice.*

C. *Lateral stream deposits (kame terraces) and tunnel deposits (esker ridges) after the glacier has melted.*

D. *River terraces produced by river cutting into sand and gravel deposits laid down on the valley floor by meltwaters.*

E. *A stream issuing from a glacier and depositing sand and gravel both on top of, and in front of, the ice.*

F. *When the ice melts the spread and sand and gravel contain depressions (kettle holes) and mounds (kames).*

Ph. 3.2 *Kames (mounds) and kettle holes (depressions) in sand and gravel.*

large enclosed depressions—kettle holes—were produced. When large masses of glacier ice were buried by sand and gravel the subsequent melting of the buried ice produced a chaotic assemblage of mounds, ridges and depressions known as kame and kettle topography (Ph. 3.2). Some large meltwater rivers were confined to tunnels in the glacier ice. When these tunnels became choked with fluvioglacial sand and gravel, long sinuous ridges known as eskers were produced (Ph. 3.3). They are literally fossil river channel deposits which emerge after the glacier ice has melted.

These spreads, mounds, terraces and ridges, produced by the meltwaters of the last ice sheet to cover Scotland, have been extensively used as sites for golf courses. They represent the nearest inland equivalent to the classic links ground of the coastal golf courses. The similarities between windblown-sand landforms (links) and fluvioglacial sand and gravel landforms (sandar, kames, terraces, eskers) are numerous. Both sets of landforms are well-drained and support firm turf. Both sets of landforms are characterised by ridges and hollows and by short, steep slopes which frequently change direction. Both sets of landforms consist of materials (sand and gravel) easily worked by man either with or without mechanical assistance. As was shown in Chapter 2, many of the early inland golf courses in Scotland were established on these relatively easily-managed fluvioglacial deposits. It would appear that golfers and golf course designers have a considerable affinity for fine-grained, unconsolidated sediments whether they are deposited by wind or water.

Reference has already been made to the fact that a period of glaciation results in the

Ph. 3.3 *Eskers—ridges of sand and gravel.*

'locking up' of large quantities of water (precipitation) in the ice sheet. This water is extracted from the oceans and since it is stored in the ice sheet for long periods before being returned to the oceans, there is a worldwide fall in relative sea level (up to 300 feet) during periods of glaciation. However, the development of an ice mass, several thousand feet thick, on a land mass results in increased weight on the earth's crust beneath the ice sheet, which in turn produces a depression in the crust and a rise in local relative sea level. The manner in which these opposing tendencies operate, during a period of glaciation, to affect local relative sea level changes, need not concern us. The geological record around Scotland's coastline clearly demonstrates that such glacially-induced sea level changes have taken place. During the wastage of the last ice sheet (14,000–10,000 years ago) much of the land area of Scotland was still depressed by the weight of the last ice sheet and some of the oceanic waters of the world were still locked up in the large ice sheets which still existed in Northern Europe, North America and Antarctica. Relative sea level in the Firths of Moray, Tay, Forth and Clyde stood some 50–120 feet above present sea level. Marine cut platforms in Fife (Ph. 3.4), bear testimony to these former higher stands of sea level. Relative sea level continued to fall from these higher altitudes until about 8,500 years ago, when the world's great ice sheets began to melt at such a rate that worldwide sea level began to rise rapidly. This sea level rise was sufficiently fast that it overtook the still rising land of Scotland and relative sea level rose around much of the Scottish coastline, reaching a maximum about 6,500 years ago. The relative rise in sea level was of the order of 15 to 40 feet depending on location. This rise in sea level, followed by the subsequent fall to present levels, had a profound effect on the character of much of Scotland's coastline and on the provision of land subsequently used for golf courses. During the high stand of sea level, low lying areas, particularly in the estuaries of the Tay, Forth, Clyde and Solway, were inundated and large quantities of marine clays were deposited. When sea level later fell these marine clays were exposed to form the extensive flat-lands (carse lands) which now border the present shores of the Scottish estuaries. On more exposed coasts the high stand of the sea cut new cliff-lines and deposited raised beaches of sand and gravel (Ph. 3.5). As the sea retreated from this old coastline (a process that began 6,500 years ago) large sandy beaches (strands) were exposed. These intertidal sands became the source of vast quantities of sediment which could be picked up and transported by the wind to a new location further inland. The windblown sand was then spread across older raised platforms or raised beaches and frequently shaped into dune systems (Ph. 3.6). One of Scotland's most distinctive golfing environments—the links—was therefore a product of changing sea levels which were in turn brought about by a period of glaciation.

Blown sand in the form of coastal dunes and 'links' (machair) occupy about 300 miles of Scotland's coastline (Fig. 3.5). The total length of the Scottish coastline (including the islands) is about 7,500 miles, so the links only occupy four per cent. Although a small percentage, the links occupy four distinct regions, in only three of which they have been developed as golf courses. From North Berwick to Fraserburgh, links form a very

Ph. 3.4 *Raised marine platforms—Kincraig, Fife.*

53

Ph. 3.5 *Post-glacial raised beach and shoreline, Girvan.*

Ph. 3.6 *Dune ridge (with marram grass), inter-dune flat occupied by fairway and former coastline (abandoned cliff behind white houses), Turnberry.*

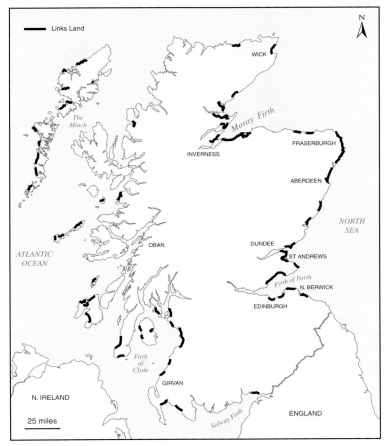

FIG. 3.5 *The distribution of 'links land' (accumulations of wind-blown sand).*

significant part of the coastline and golf has a long history on many of them (St Andrews, Carnoustie, Aberdeen, Elie, Leven, Gullane). The second most important region is around the shores of the Moray Firth. The third region is in south-west Scotland around the shores of the Solway Firth and the Firth of Clyde. The fourth region is made up primarily of the Inner and Outer Hebridean Islands, and although there are many miles of links (known locally as machair), only in a few locations (Islay and South Uist) have they been used for golf courses.

Scottish links land occupies a relatively narrow zone along the coast. Since the source of the sand is the adjoining beach and the mode of transport is on-shore winds, the distance the sand extends inland is not great. It tends to accumulate in dune ridges which are usually 10 to 30 feet high, and, on average, blown sand rarely occurs higher than 75 feet above present sea level. There are limited cases, however, where blown sand occurs

55

between 200 and 300 feet above sea level. The links land is, therefore, a narrow zone paralleling the present coastline where sand has accumulated in the form of ridges, hummocks and spreads. The zone is usually about half-a-mile wide and the ridges rarely more than 30 feet high. These sand accumulations are the product of aeolian transportation and subsequent deposition. The cause of deposition is related to a reduction of wind velocity as a result of the presence of colonising plants such as marram grass (*Ammophila arenaria*) and sea lyme (*Elymus arenarius*). The morphology of a links area is affected by the character of the depositional area (which is often a raised beach or raised marine-platform), wind strength and direction, the source and volume of blown sand, the nature of the vegetation cover and the local surface and subsurface drainage conditions. A typical links area has the following characteristics (Fig. 3.6). Above the line reached by high water Spring tides is the back shore, where pioneer species begin to colonise the sand accumulations. The coastal dune, which is aligned parallel to the coastline and covered by long dune grasses (marram), may attain heights of between 10 and 40 feet in Scotland. It usually has a steeper seaward-facing slope. The coastal dune may be succeeded inland either by a 'slack', separating it from an older dune ridge, or by a gently undulating surface or 'links plain'. In some localities there may be more than one 'old dune' ridge or there may be areas of sand hills or hummocks when dune ridges have migrated inland as a result of erosion in blow-outs. Since many of the links areas in Scotland are the product of the general fall in relative sea level, there is a series of parallel dune ridges, with the oldest (and often lowest) ridge being on the landward margin of the system. Golf course designers have often taken full advantage of the sequence of ridges and depressions to be seen on links land. The fairways and greens are found on the short grass of the inter-dune areas (slacks or valleys) while the dune ridges and their tough marram grass form areas of 'rough'.

Links land has provided an ideal combination of variety of surface form and vegetation, which together accommodate fairways and greens on firm turf (short grass) interspersed by rough grass (or heather or gorse) which may or may not be on steeper slopes. It is perhaps tempting to think of links land as a natural environment. However, the coastal links have been occupied by man for over 5,000 years, and grazing of animals, the collection of whins, and in some cases intensive cultivation have led to extensive modifications to this environment. The golfers of the seventeenth and eighteenth centuries also acted as agents of erosion and no doubt initiated 'blow-outs' in dune ridges. It is often claimed that little modification by golf course designers and greenkeepers has taken place on these 'natural' links when laying out golf courses. However, it should be remembered that even without mechanical aids the landforms of the links, which consist entirely of sand, were easily reshaped. At a very minimum, plateau tees and greens were constructed, bunkers excavated and in some cases dune ridges either removed or modified. Areas of rough grass, whin, heather and scrub were either trimmed or removed and new species of grass planted on tees and greens. One wonders just how much the present Old Course at St Andrews has changed since the eighteenth century.

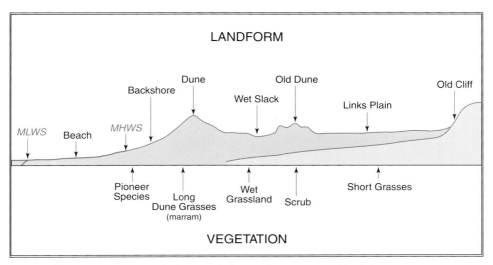

FIG. 3.6 *The morphology and vegetation of 'links'.*

SCOTLAND'S VEGETATION

Although changing sea levels associated with the wastage of the last ice sheet in Scotland played a major role in determining the character of coastal golf courses, other changes in the natural environment which followed the return to Interglacial (i.e. much milder climate) conditions were also significant. Within a thousand years of the last glaciers melting in the Highlands, much of Scotland was covered by trees. The forests in the south and in the Midland Valley were mainly of oak and birch. The forests at higher altitudes and throughout much of the Highlands were of birch and pine. There is no doubt that the earliest known human occupants of Scotland found it to be a wooded country even up to altitudes of 2,500 feet. Based on botanical records in the form of different species of pollen recovered from lake sediments and peat, it has been established that during the past 5,000 years a transformation in the vegetation of Scotland has taken place—the forests were gradually replaced by moorlands (heathlands), grassland, and arable land. Although there is much debate as to whether these vegetational changes were initiated by climatic changes (e.g. increased wetness), or by human activity in the form of creating woodland clearances for agriculture, or a combination of both, there can be little doubt that the forest cover declined in favour of the expansion of moorlands.

The decline of forests and increase in moorland is frequently associated with signs of human settlement and land cultivation. The Neolithic, Bronze Age and Iron Age populations certainly had an impact on the extent of forest cover in Scotland. Forests survived longest in the more remote regions. Further forest clearance was undertaken at the time of the Viking invasions in the first and second centuries AD and again in the sixteenth, seventeenth and eighteenth centuries when timber was in demand as charcoal

Ph. 3.7 *Moorland—Tobermory, Mull.*

Ph. 3.8 *Parkland—Pollock Golf Club, Glasgow.*

for iron smelting. In the eighteenth and nineteenth centuries the increasing acreage of open country attracted sheep farmers and this development led to the final act of forest destruction. The grass moors and heather moors are now a major feature of the Highlands, Islands, and Southern Uplands (Ph. 3.7).

There are a few golf courses in Scotland where natural woodlands, either of oak or pine, are still present to give a distinctive character to the golfing landscape. There are many courses where the golfing landscape is dominated by heather moorland. It has also been common practice during the past 100 years to plant extensive acreages of imported pines. The fairways of many Scottish golf courses are lined by pine plantations or mixtures of Scots Pine, imported pines and birches.

After the major transformation from forest to moorland and/or cultivated land had largely been completed, it became fashionable for Scottish landowners to develop parklands around their large country houses in the eighteenth and nineteenth centuries. The essential characteristics of an area of parkland are that the area was enclosed by a fence and that there was a mixture of pasture land and woodland. Wealthy landowners employed landscape architects to plan their parklands so that pastures, elegant deciduous and coniferous trees, roadways lined with shrubs, lakes, lawns and flower gardens blended together to produce beautiful vistas. Enclosure was the dominant idea, so that in southern Scotland a fenced field of any description is often called a 'park'. The mixture of meadows and isolated trees (often oaks, elms or horse chestnuts) produces a landscape ideally suited to inland golf courses. Even where golf courses have been laid out in grassland (and even on moorland courses) trees have often been planted in an attempt to create a parkland landscape. However, the classic parkland courses are to be found in the grounds of large estates where changes in land use resulting from economic and social changes have led to the break up of the estate. In some instances fine Georgian or Victorian houses have been converted to golf clubhouses. Such parkland courses may now be found in suburban locations (Ph. 3.8).

With few exceptions, the majority of inland golf courses in Scotland owe their landscape characteristics as much to their vegetation as to the landforms upon which they are built. Sixty-one percent of Scotland's golf courses (330) may be described as parkland courses.

The 154 coastal courses are primarily on links land, but some are on high coastal platforms which have either a very thin cover of blown sand or none at all. In such circumstances a moorland vegetation with extensive areas of heather has developed. The vegetation of the coastal links courses has also been much modified by human interference. This has not always been a destructive influence because the addition of new grasses for greens and tees, the provision of fertilisers, irrigation and drainage, have all helped to stabilise some dune systems. Since most Scottish dune systems are less than 6,000 years old and since the dunes were often used as settlement sites by early man, it is likely that there has always been some human interference in the dune environment. Dunes are very rich in species of plants and animals. A survey of natural and introduced vascular plants on 43 of the more important dune systems in Britain showed that over 900 species occur on them (more than half of these species being introduced directly or indirectly by man). Because of the wide variety of habitats in a dune system there are quite rapid changes in vegetation across the system (Fig. 3.6). There is little evidence of extensive natural woodlands on Scottish dunes, but there have been numerous attempts at afforestation during the past two hundred years. Essentially the dune vegetation consists primarily of a variety of grasses and herbs, plus some scrub woodland.

From the few descriptions of the character of the early links golf courses there can be little doubt that they were very different to the manicured modern equivalents. Gorse and heather, marram grass and marsh plants have been controlled to constitute reasonable 'rough' and the tees and greens much improved by drainage, weeding, irrigation and re-seeding. The modern links course is hardly a part of nature's wilderness!

Although all aspects of the vegetation on Scotland's golf courses have been much modified by man, the trees, shrubs, grasses and herbs which do occur give particular characteristics to the courses. The rolling links land, where fairways of close-cropped grasses and herbs are separated by mounds or dunes covered by long marram grass, heather or gorse, are in great contrast to the inland parklands and moorlands. These vegetation patterns are themselves often related to variations in altitude which in turn produce some remarkable contrasts in local climate.

GOLFING WEATHER

Scotland has a cool, humid, temperate climate. At low altitudes extremes of heat or cold are rare and there are marked contrasts between the western and eastern parts of the country in wetness. A major characteristic of the Scottish environment is the variability in weather conditions from day to day, and even on some occasions from hour to hour. There are few days in the year when a golfer can safely set out for a round of golf with the appropriate clothing for the conditions on the first tee, and be certain that he will neither have to remove nor add items of clothing to adjust to changing weather conditions during the next three hours. A set of adequate rainwear and an umbrella are as important to a Scottish golfer as a set of golf clubs.

Golf is played throughout the year on most Scottish golf courses. The relatively mild and humid climate sustains the turf of fairways and greens throughout the year. The links courses of Ayrshire, East Lothian, Fife and north-east Scotland remain in the best condition, and only periods of snow cover and/or intense frost cause the closure of such courses. Even in periods of heavy rain the sandy soil of these courses allows water to drain away fairly quickly. Inland courses may become waterlogged during periods of heavy rain and become unplayable. Courses at higher altitudes—there are some 50 golf courses above 600 feet—have shorter playing seasons due either to excessive wetness,

TABLE 3.1

Climatic Data for a Selection of Scottish Locations

	Temperature Av. daily max °C		Gales	Bright Sunshine	Snow Lying	Precipitation mm.			
			Av. no.	Hours per					Two Driest
	JAN	JULY	Days	Year	Days	JAN	JULY	YEAR	Months
AYR	6.1	17.9		1333	6.1	83	81	918	Mar, Apr
GLASGOW	5.5	18.6	5.8	1266	9.7	94	74	982	Mar, Apr
LANARK	4.9	18.0		1277	28.0	67	73	813	Apr, June
EDINBURGH	5.9	18.6		1332	16.1	52	75	661	Mar, Apr
DUNBAR				1515	7.0	46	55	571	Mar, Apr
PERTH	5.3	19.2		1301	18.3	70	74	778	Mar, Apr
ST ANDREWS			9.5	1427		61	65	682	Mar, Apr
ABERDEEN	4.8	17.1		1376	3.8	80	83	847	Mar, Apr
NAIRN	5.7	17.7		1285	19.6	45	61	613	Mar, Apr
FT. WILLIAM	6.2	17.0		1055		191	149	2049	May, June
WICK	5.1	15.4	12.2	1264	19.2	82	63	788	Apr, May
TIREE	6.9	15.9	35.2	1420	4.5	115	85	1129	Apr, May

frost or snow. The Scottish climate deteriorates rapidly with increasing altitude, and the maintenance of golf courses which are between 500 and 1,000 feet above sea level is both more difficult and more costly.

In addition to the condition of the course, weather conditions also determine the overall enjoyment of a game of golf and greatly affect the difficulty of the courses. Wind strength and direction are perhaps a greater influence on the character of a golf course than the landforms on which it has been built or the ideas of the golf course designer who built it. Since both wind strength and wind direction change from day to day or even within the period of one round of golf, the vagaries of weather add to the character of Scottish golf courses. On many links courses a relatively easy, par three hole of 175 yards may require only a seven iron in calm conditions, but a three wood or even a driver when a strong wind is blowing in the golfer's face.

There are eight weather elements of particular interest to Scottish golfers: temperature, precipitation, hours of sunshine, fog, wind strength and direction, frost, and snow cover. Because there are some significant regional variations in each of these elements, a brief analysis of their characteristics will be given.

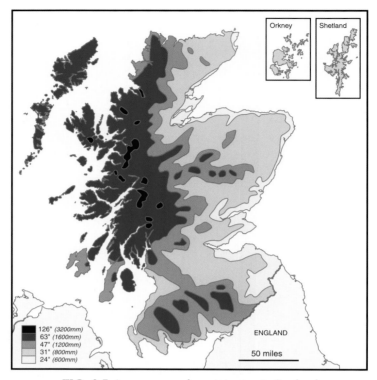

FIG. 3.7 *Average annual precipitation in Scotland*

Temperature

The average daily maximum temperature in July at low altitudes is generally between 17°C and 19°C (Table 3.1). In January mean daily maxima range between 6° C on the west coast and 5°C on the east coast. Winter golf can be quite pleasant so long as it is not raining, there is little or no wind, and the sun is shining.

Precipitation

There are some very marked regional contrasts in total precipitation received by different parts of Scotland, with a distinct west to east gradient (Table 3.1 and Fig. 3.7). The western parts of Scotland receive between 800mm (31 inches) and 3,000mm (120 inches) per year, with only the Ayrshire coast and the Solway Firth coast receiving less than 1,200mm (47 inches). Large parts of the eastern half of the country receive between 800mm (31 inches) and 1,200mm (47 inches) but the east coast lowlands receive only 600–800mm (24–31 inches). Throughout the country the three driest months are usually March, April and May.

Hours of Sunshine; Fog

Scotland can hardly claim to be a sunny country (Table 3.1 and Fig. 3.8). Much of the country records less than 1,400 hours of bright sunshine per year. In January nearly all of the country receives, on average, less than one and a half hours of sunshine per day and this rises to between four and five hours per day in July. The sunniest places in Scotland are Dunbar (1,515 hours per year), St Andrews (1,427 hours per year) and Tiree (1,420 hours per year), while west coast locations tend to receive between 1,000 and 1,300 hours per year. Many east coast locations would record much higher sunshine figures if it were not for the development of coastal fog (locally known as haar) during periods of calm, warm summer weather.

A feature of the summer in Scotland is the long period of twilight. On the longest day there is no complete darkness in northern Scotland. For example, at midsummer, places in the Moray Firth area have more than 18 hours of daylight compared with about 16 hours at places in southern England. Throughout Scotland it is possible to play 18 holes of golf after 6 p.m. during the months of May, June, July and August.

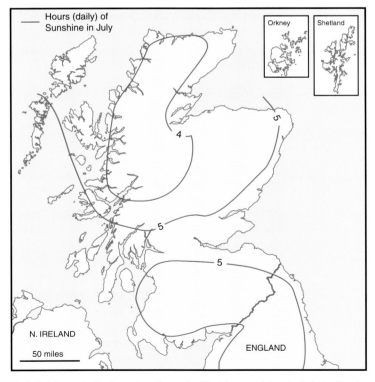

FIG. 3.8 *Mean daily duration (hours) of bright sunshine in July in Scotland.*

Wind Strength and Direction

Over large areas of Scotland the average wind speed is about 8 to 10 knots (10 to 12 miles per hour) but along the west coast, in the Western and Northern Isles and at high altitudes, there is a much higher frequency of strong winds and gales. The strong winds are usually associated with the passage of winter depressions: even in the west and north of the country, prolonged periods of strong winds are unusual in summer. Gale force winds are recorded on average on six days per year in Glasgow, nine days per year in St Andrews, 12 days per year in Wick and 35 days per year on Tiree. At most locations the winds have a westerly component for about 50% of the time and an easterly component for about 35% of the time.

Frost

Frozen ground not only changes the character of a golf course but it inhibits plant growth, and greens can be damaged by excessive use when they are frozen. Over much of Scotland, excluding the Western and Northern Isles, the coasts of the Firth of Clyde and the entire length of the east coast, frosts can occur at any time between mid-September and mid-May. The incidence of frost increases with altitude, so that relatively high (over 300 feet) inland golf courses can experience frozen ground conditions for over half the year. When frost occurs on coastal links courses, which are generally very well-drained, it may only last for a couple of hours after sunrise.

Snow Cover

With the exception of coastal lowlands (less than ten days per year) and areas of high ground over 2,000 feet (over 40 days per year) snow cover is experienced in Scotland on between 10 and 40 days per year. The majority of golf courses are located in areas of relatively low frequency of snow cover—10 to 20 days per year.

Scotland contains a greater variety of golfing environments than any other country. The 538 golf courses reflect the complex environmental history of the country. Landscapes produced by ancient geological events contrast with those which were produced as a result of the events of the last Ice Age, which only happened 'yesterday' in geological terms. Scottish golf owes much to the advance and retreat of the last ice sheet and the associated sea level changes. With human occupation of the recently deglaciated and newly forested landscape beginning some 8,000 years ago, man's impact was soon to modify nature's handiwork. Forests were cleared, farming began and eventually in the eighteenth and nineteenth centuries an urban industrialised society would evolve. Golf courses are to be found on wild moorlands, wind-swept links, elegant parklands, surrounded by housing estates and factories, and in suburban and periurban environments.

The combination of nature and man has produced a remarkable variety in the environments available to the golfer in Scotland.

ENVIRONMENTAL MANAGEMENT

During the past decade considerable interest has arisen, particularly as a result of the golf boom in England, in conservation issues related to golf course development and management. The Nature Conservancy Council published a monograph, 'On Course Conservation', in 1989 and a research paper, 'Nature Conservation and the Management and Design of Golf Courses in Britain', in 1990. In 1994 the European Golf Association Ecology Unit was established and has subsequently produced a series of publications on conservation issues (1996, 1997). While there was considerable concern about the development of large golf complexes in England and on the European continent, the lack of large property developments in association with new golf courses in Scotland led to a greater interest in the sensitive management of existing facilities. The Scottish Golf Course Wildlife Initiative was launched in 1992 and in 1996 the SGU appointed a Wildlife Adviser (Mr Jonathan Smith) to work with the Scottish Golf Course Wildlife Group. Funding for this appointment was provided by the SGU, Scottish Natural Heritage, the Scottish Greenbelt Foundation and the R&A. In 1997 the SGCWG published 'Golf's Natural Heritage—An Introduction to Environmental Stewardship on the Golf Course'. In the introduction to that monograph Jonathan Smith states:

> Debate over golf's relationship with the environment has been ongoing for some time, and it is now widely recognised that golf courses can play an important role in the conservation of Scotland's native flora and fauna. In short, golf courses have the potential to be a valuable environmental asset in both rural and urban areas.

It would appear that the relationship between conservationists and the golf facility owners/operators in Scotland has benefited from mutual consideration. The tendency for new developers to accept and even improve the landscape on which they build golf courses, along with the relatively low levels of irrigation and artificial fertilisation required in Scotland, have resulted in little conflict between conservationists and developers. The willingness of long-established golf clubs to adopt modern 'environmentally friendly' maintenance methods has also been beneficial.

🌾 Four
The Classification of Golf Courses

It is possible to classify Scotland's 538 golf courses in a variety of ways. The tables in the Appendix provide a range of data upon which objective classifications can be based, and these are summarised in Table 4.1.

Golf in Scotland is often strongly associated with coastal links land. Only 28% of golf courses are located along the coastline and only 17% are true links courses, laid out across wind-blown sand. Of all the courses in Scotland, 72% are at inland locations and 50% are in urban/suburban environments.

Because of the age of so many of Scotland's golf courses, one-third are less than 5,700 yards in length and 82% are less than 6,400 yards. Many of the courses laid out prior to 1920 occupied 100-acre properties and there are only short distances from one green to the next tee. This explains why the average Scots golfer expects to play a two-ball match over 18 holes in three hours. There are only eight courses in Scotland which are longer than 7,000 yards. The powered golf cart is still a rare sight on Scottish courses, whereas modern course designers from the USA and Australia have ignored the desirability of walking 18 holes and being in the clubhouse bar within three and a half hours.

There are no generally accepted criteria by which the quality of a golf course can be judged. Subjective assessments frequently place twenty of Scotland's courses in the top one hundred courses in the UK. Using two objective criteria, the standard scratch score and the weekday green fee charged to visitors, this writer (Price, 2000) developed a classification of Scotland's golf facilities.

The standard scratch score (SSS) is the score which a scratch player is expected to return in ideal conditions over a measured course. In the case of a nine-hole course it represents two rounds. The SSS is determined on the basis of the length and perceived difficulty of the course, and it ranges between 60, for short and relatively easy courses, to 74 for long (over 7,000 yds) difficult courses. In terms of establishing a classification system it has the major advantage that it is one aspect of the challenge/difficulty of a golf course determined by an outside agency.

For those golf facilities which permit visitors to play on their course(s)—98%—the published weekday green fee represents what the operator believes to be the value of the golfing experience and the price which the customer is willing to pay.

This classification system seeks to identify the golf facilities which are excellent and of world-class significance as 5-star; very good facilities, 4-star; good facilities, 3-star; basic facilities, 2-star; and very basic facilities, 1-star. Nine facilities, including the five

TABLE 4.1

Classification of Golf Courses
Percentage in Each Category
(538 Courses)

Location		Altitude (ft)		Length (yds)	
Coastal		0–49	20%	4000–4399	2.4%
Non–links	11%	50–99	13%	4400–4999	12%
Links	17%	100–199	17%	5000–5699	22%
Inland	72%	200–299	14%	5700–6399	46%
Urban	50%	300–399	10%	6400–6999	16%
Rural	50%	400 –599	16%	over 7000	1.6%
		600–799	7%		
		800–999	2%		
		over 1000	1%		

Landform		Vegetation		Weekday Green Fee	
Undulating	33%	Parkland	61%	<£9	13%
Hillside	15%	Woodland	1%	£10–£19	54%
Drumlin	6%	Moorland	17%	£20–£29	21%
Esker/Kame	3%	Links	21%	£30–£39	7%
Kame Terrace,				£40–£49	1%
Sandur, River				>£50	4%
Terrace	15%				
Raised Beach,					
Raised Marine					
Platform	11%				
Links	17%				

Management Type		Course Quality—Stars	
Members Club	72%	1-Star	33%
Municipal	13%	2-Star	24%
Commercial	15%	3-Star	33%
		4-Star	8%
		5-Star	2%

Open Championship venues, plus Gleneagles, Carnegie Club, Kingsbarns and Loch Lomond, each have five stars. All of these facilities have weekday visitor green fees in excess of £70. There are 37 (8%), 4-star facilities, all with green fees between £30 and £69. There are therefore only 46 golf facilities (10%) which have at least one golf course which can be described as very good or excellent. Out of the total, 33% of courses are of good quality (3-star) and 57% are of basic or very basic quality.

The management type and philosophy influences the accessibility of golf courses.

SCOTLAND'S GOLF COURSES

Although 72% of courses are operated as members clubs, a high proportion welcome visitors, although in some cases a handicap certificate is required. All the municipal (13%) and most of the commercial courses (15%) welcome visitors. No longer are all of the municipal courses cheap to play, and those at St Andrews (particularly the Old Course) and the championship course at Carnoustie, are in great demand. Of the commercial courses, Loch Lomond and the Carnegie Club are only available to members and their guests.

The cost of golf, measured in terms of average weekday green fees, has increased by 150% in the last decade. However, there are still some 70 courses where a round costs less than £10 and only on 65 courses does a weekday round cost more than £30.

The classification of golf courses used in this book is based on the landscape characteristics of the courses themselves. A landscape consists of the rocks, soils, landforms, vegetation and man-made structures. The previous chapter demonstrated that much of the landscape of a golf course is determined by the geology and landforms on which it is located along with its vegetation. The character of a golf course is the product of the morphology, soils, drainage and vegetation of the fairways and greens; the general landscape characteristics of the entire course (e.g. undulating parkland, moorland plateau or sand dunes/links) and the general scenic setting. The geological and botanical history, plus the history of land use by man, all contribute to the present landscape characteristics of a course. The surface geology is most important in determining the landforms, the soils and drainage of golf courses. The events associated with the last glaciation either directly or indirectly were responsible for creating the distinctive character of over 60% of Scotland's golf courses—directly through the deposition of glacial and fluvioglacial deposits or indirectly by marine and aeolian processes associated with changes in relative sea levels.

The altitude of a course can be significant in determining its character—this is particularly true for those at low altitudes on the coast (mainly links courses) and those at inland sites at high altitude (mainly moorland courses). Table 4.1 shows the percentage of golf courses at various altitudes. One-third of Scotland's golf courses are below 100 feet above sea level, while 20% (mainly the links courses) are below 50 feet. Some 50% of all courses are below 200 feet. A further 40% are between 200 and 600 feet, with only 10% above 600 feet. Surprisingly, Scotland's highest golf course is not in the Highlands but in the central Southern Uplands at Leadhills (1,200 feet). Other high altitude courses occur at the head of the Dee Valley at Braemar (D18), in Glen Shee (C44) and in the Spey Valley at Aviemore (D10), Kingussie (D63), Carrbridge (D23) and Newtonmore (D85).

The 50 courses at altitudes above 600 feet have relatively short playing seasons either because of snow, frozen ground or heavy rain and strong winds. They also present particular problems for greenkeeping staff. On a less severe level, similar problems occur on those 80 courses which are at altitudes between 400 and 600 feet. High altitude should not be correlated with steepness of slope. The courses at Braemar, Glen Shee, Carrbridge, Aviemore and Newtonmore are located on valley-floor sands and gravels. However, high altitude may be correlated with high quality surrounding scenery because many such courses have spectacular views.

Another simple means of classifying golf courses is to distinguish coastal and inland courses. Approximately 30% of Scotland's golf courses (160) are located on the coast and their distribution is highly correlated with raised beaches and/or blown sand, all below 100 feet above present sea level. Not all of these courses are classic golf links, as some have parkland or moorland characteristics.

The classification of golf courses used in this book is primarily based on two quite separate sets of criteria: landforms and vegetation. It should be pointed out that two courses built on the same type of landforms may have different vegetation or conversely one vegetation type (e.g. parkland) may be associated with a variety of landforms. Table 4.1 lists the landform and vegetation types used in the classification.

LANDFORMS

Any classification of the landforms occupied by golf courses will be determined by the fact that an 18-hole course only occupies between 100 and 150 acres and therefore, within the confines of any one course, it is often difficult to recognise any one landform or group of landforms. Fig. 4.1 shows, in profile, the range of landforms upon which golf courses have been built in Scotland. The broad classification of landforms into mountains, valleys, plateaux and lowlands does not necessarily reveal the landscape characteristics of individual golf courses because there are numerous and significant

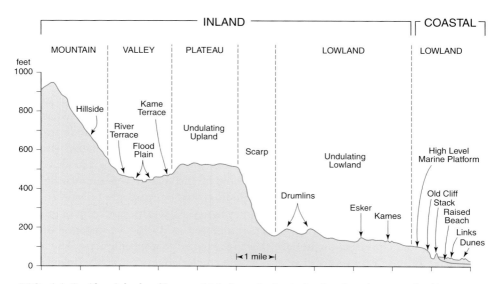

FIG. 4.1 *Profile of the landforms which form the basis for the classification of golf courses.*

69

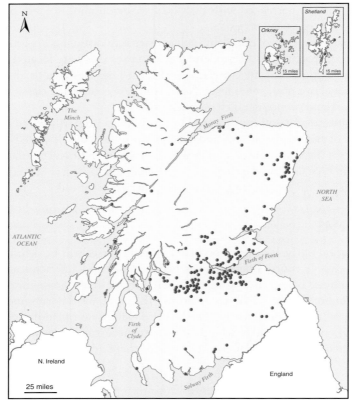

FIG. 4.2 *The location of 'undulating' golf courses.*

landform variations within these broad units. Even within the next level of classification (e.g. hillside, river terrace, drumlin, raised beach, links) an individual golf course may be built across more than one type of landform. In assigning an individual course to a particular class, the dominant or most common landform type on that course has been used (Table 4.1). Forty-eight per cent of Scotland's golf courses occur on landform units which are larger than the individual courses and they have been classified either as 'undulating' or 'hillside' courses. Depending on the definition of these two classes, courses which occur on kames, eskers or links land could be included in the 'undulating' class and certain courses located on the sides of drumlins could be classed as 'hillside' courses. However, for the purpose of this classification, whenever a specific landform or group of landforms within a golf course have been recognised as distinctive in terms of their morphology and constituent materials, they are assigned to a specific class. The 'undulating' and 'hillside' courses are distinctive in their own right but cannot be linked to any one group of geological processes.

Undulating

Thirty-three per cent of Scotland's golf courses fall into this classification (Fig. 4.2). These courses have no distinctive landform characteristics other than that they consist of assemblages of low angle slopes and have no great range in altitude (usually less than 75 feet) within the course (Ph. 4.1). Such courses can occur at relatively high altitudes on plateau surfaces or on lowlands. In lowland locations many of these courses have been built across areas covered by glacial till (a mixture of boulders and pebbles in a sand-clay matrix). This glacial deposit has buried many of the irregularities of the underlying rock surface. The main concentration of these courses is in the Central Lowlands of Scotland, with 29% of Region B's courses falling into this category. Many of the landscape characteristics of these courses are determined more by their vegetation than by their landforms—they are either moorland or parkland courses. One distinctive sub-group of undulating upland courses consists of those courses which occur on the plateau lavas (mainly basalts). These volcanic rocks have a very distinctive layered appearance and they have often been eroded into minor cliffs and crags. Many of these courses have a moorland vegetation because of their high altitude, the chemical characteristics of their soils and their land-use history. Examples of this type of course are: Old Ranfurly (B1 31), Paisley (B1 32), Cathkin Braes (B1 35).

Ph. 4.1 *An 'undulating' golf course: Kirkintilloch, Glasgow.*

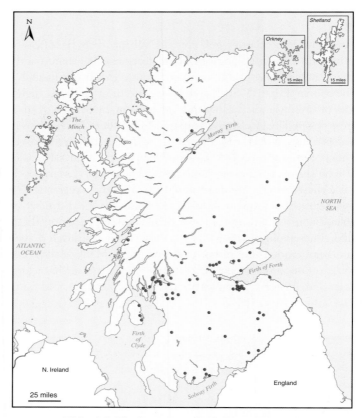

FIG. 4.3 *The location of 'hillside' golf courses.*

Hillside

Fifteen per cent of Scotland's golf courses are located on hillsides (Fig. 4.3). Many of these hillsides are in fact valley sides, which provide fine views along the strath, glen or sea loch from the higher parts of the courses (Ph. 4.2). The difference in altitude between the highest and lowest points on such courses can be as much as 500 feet, and to play them the golfer not only needs skill but stamina. It has also been suggested that on such courses having one leg longer than the other is a distinct advantage! Specific examples of courses dominated by steep slopes are those at Hawick (A43), Strathpeffer (D109), Tobermory (B156), Braid Hills (A3, A4) and several courses around the Firth of Clyde.

Drumlins

Drumlins are elongated, streamlined hills, 30–100 feet high and 300–500 yards long, having the shape of an upturned spoon (Fig. 4.4). They tend to occur in 'swarms' and

Ph. 4.2 *A 'hillside' golf course: the Braid Hills, Edinburgh.*

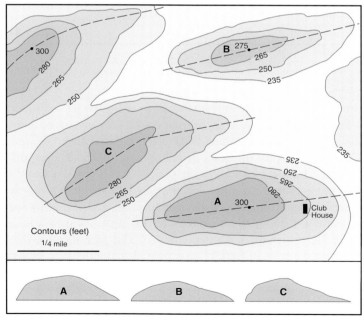

FIG. 4.4 *Contour map and profiles of drumlins: Mount Ellen Golf Course.*

73

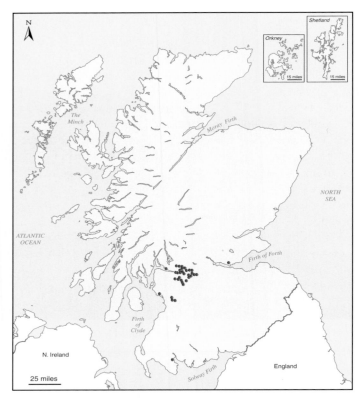

FIG. 4.5 *The location of 'drumlin' golf courses.*

were produced by the passage of the last ice sheet to cover Scotland (15,000–20,000 years ago). They are often not simple features, as small drumlins have been superimposed on larger ones. They vary greatly in terms of their constituent materials. Some consist entirely of glacial till, while others contain beds of fluvioglacial material (sand and gravel) often with a covering of glacial till. Some drumlins have solid rock cores with only a thin cover of glacial till. Drumlins are interesting sites for golf courses in that they provide a variety of slope angles, slope directions and slope lengths within a relatively small area.

Of the 34 golf courses (6%) located on drumlins (Fig. 4.5), 33 are in Region B, with the majority of these being in the Greater Glasgow area. Glasgow could well be described as the 'Drumlinoid City' as much of the late nineteenth- and early twentieth-century expansion of the city took place across a drumlin field produced by the last ice sheet. Examples of golf courses on drumlins are: Balmore (B8), Bearsden (B10), Clober (B38), Clydebank (B39, 40), Crow Wood (B49), Kirkintilloch (B102), Lenzie (B112), Lethamhill (B113) and Mount Ellen (B128). Other drumlin courses occur in Ayrshire and Dumfries and Galloway.

Eskers and Kames

Accumulations of sand and gravel deposited in close association with the glacier ice of the last ice sheet provide the nearest inland equivalent to coastal links land. When the last ice sheet melted, vast quantities of meltwater were released and these waters picked up and transported much of the rock debris which was on and in the ice. Transportation of the rock debris by the meltwater streams caused rounding and sorting of the rock particles and the debris was deposited as stratified sand and gravel. There are very large areas in Scotland covered by these sands and gravels and some of these deposits have very distinctive landforms associated with them. Because some of these deposits were accumulated actually in, on top of, or against glacier ice they acquired distinctive forms (Fig. 4.6). As the ice sheet was melting, large volumes of water flowed in channels on the ice surface, in tunnels in the ice, along the side of the ice mass and away from the ice front. When debris choked the tunnels in the ice mass, new routes were found and when the ice eventually melted completely these tunnel deposits were left as upstanding ridges of sand and gravel. These ridges are known as eskers and they can occur either as single features or as a series of sub-parallel ridges (Ph. 4.3), but they all represent the former courses of meltwater streams. They range from five to 50 feet in height, often have irregular crestlines and sometimes merge with chaotic mounds or spreads of sand

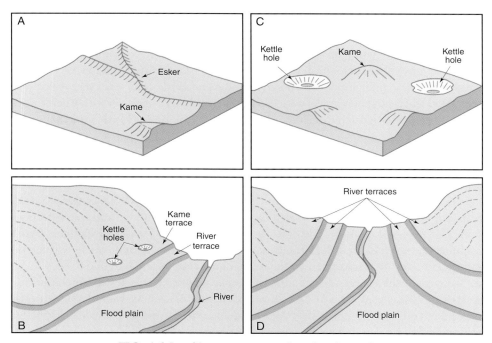

FIG. 4.6 *Landforms consisting of sand and gravel.*

75

Ph. 4.3 *Esker ridges on either side of the 15th fairway, the King's Course, Gleneagles.*

and gravel. Isolated mounds of sand and gravel are known as kames and may represent the deposits laid down in an individual cave under the ice. More commonly, sand and gravel occur as a series of mounds of various sizes and shapes interspersed with enclosed hollows. Such accumulations are known as kame and kettle complexes (Fig. 4.6C) and originated when sand and gravel were laid down over blocks of glacier ice. When the ice blocks melted they left large enclosed depressions (kettle holes) which sometimes contain small lakes.

Ridges (eskers) and mounds (kames) of sand and gravel provide well-drained 'heath' land which has a morphology highly suited to the game of golf. There are many similarities between these areas and the ridges (dunes), hummocks and spreads of sand that form the traditional links land where so many of Scotland's early golf courses were located. Fourteen golf courses (3%) are located on fluvioglacial sand and gravel in the form of kames or eskers (Fig. 4.7). The courses at Dumfries (A25), Castle Douglas (A12), Lochmaben (A59), Carnwath (B32), Lanark (B106) and Muckhart (C93) are located on kame complexes with associated kettle holes. Three courses at Alyth (C6, C68, C118), on the edge of the Highlands, are built on kames. However, it is at the famous golfing centre of Gleneagles (C65, C66, C67), where three courses have been developed on a large esker and kame complex, that these sand and gravel deposits provide a distinctive golfing landscape. The ridges are 20 to 50 feet high, steepsided (20–25°) and are separated by elongated troughs or enclosed hollows (kettle holes). The ridge system splays

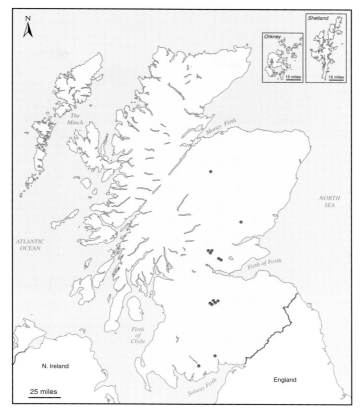

FIG. 4.7 *The location of golf courses on eskers and kames.*

out at its eastern end with larger flat areas separating the ridges. The golf course design-ers (J. Braid, J. Nicklaus) have utilised the ridges for 'rough' and tees and the inter-ridge troughs and hollows for fairways and greens (see Chapter 7).

Kame Terraces, Sandar, River Terraces

Kame terraces and sandar (outwash fans) are landforms resulting from large quantities of sand and gravel being deposited by glacier meltwaters alongside (kame terrace) or in front of (sandar) a wasting ice mass (Fig. 4.6). Kame terraces are very similar to river terraces, except that their scarp faces may be highly irregular and the upper surface may be pocked by kettle holes as a result of the burial of blocks of ice during their formation (Ph. 4.4). Most river valleys in Scotland were choked by deposits of sand and gravel at the end of the last Ice Age. During the past 6,000 years (a period of falling relative sea level) rivers have cut down into these deposits and in so doing produced a series of

77

Ph. 4.4 *Kame terrace with kettle hole (depression): Fort Augustus.*

Ph. 4.5 *River terrace at Braemar (© Angus McNicol).*

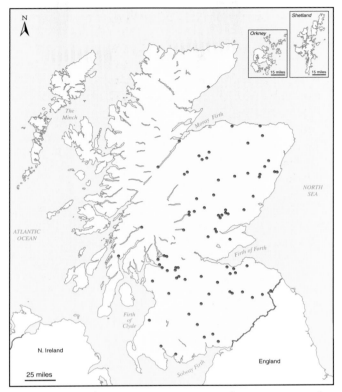

FIG. 4.8 *The location of golf courses on river terraces, kame terraces and outwash fans (sandar).*

terraces representing former higher flood plains (Fig. 4.6D). Where there has been a considerable amount of postglacial erosion, only the highest parts of a kame terrace may have survived, with normal river terraces occupying the lower levels of the floor of the valley (Ph. 4.5). For this reason kame terraces and river terraces are classed together as golf course sites. At Newtonmore (D85), for example, several holes of the golf course are located on an upper kame terrace which contains kettle holes, while the majority of the course is laid out on the river terrace cut during post-glacial times by the River Spey.

In locations where meltwater deposition was not confined by valley walls, great fan-shaped spreads (sandar or outwash fans) were deposited. Such large sandar are not common in Scotland, but the three courses at Blairgowrie (C17, C18, C19) are located on such a feature. Its low angle slopes and free-draining soils are ideally suited to golf course construction. The old meltwater routeways (channels) across the sandar surface can be seen and there are a few kettle holes which have resulted from the melting of buried blocks of ice.

All three landforms (kame terrace, river terrace, sandar) consist of silt, sand and

79

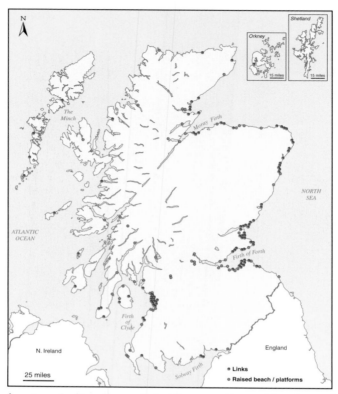

FIG. 4.9 *The location of golf courses on links (blown-sand), raised beaches and raised marine platforms.*

gravel and make excellent sites for golf courses. Eighty courses (15%) are located on these landforms (Fig. 4.8), which are characterised by large areas of low-angle slopes separated by short steep slopes (terrace scarps). Although such courses are usually well-drained, any parts of courses sited on the present flood plain can obviously be subject to flooding. Golf courses located on terraces are widespread in Scotland, but there are significant concentrations of such courses in the valleys of the Tweed, Tay, Dee and Spey.

Raised Marine Platforms and Raised Beaches

One hundred and fifty-four golf courses (28%) are located on the Scottish coastline (Fig. 4.9). They all occupy sites which have been created as a result of the relative changes in sea level which occurred during the Ice Age—mainly during the past 14,000 years (see Chapter 3). Marine erosion has produced a series of coastal platforms of unknown age at altitudes between 100 and 150 feet above present sea level. Another series of platforms at 50 to 120 feet above present sea level are believed to have been formed as the last ice

Ph. 4.6 *High level marine platform, abandoned cliff and sea-stacks, and raised beach covered by blown-sand: Cullen.*

sheet wasted away (14,000 to 10,000 years ago) and a period of relatively high sea level about 6,000 years ago trimmed existing platforms and cliff lines up to altitudes of 40 feet above present sea level. Some of the higher marine platforms have little or no marine or aeolian sand on their surfaces, while most of the marine platforms below 100 feet have both marine sands and gravels and wind-blown sands on their surfaces. The almost flat or gently undulating surfaces of high-level marine platforms are in great contrast to the steep cliffs which border them or the steep valley sides of streams which cross them. A series of well-developed high-level marine platforms occur on the northern coast of Moray and are sites for the golf courses at Hopeman (D51), Buckpool (D20), Cullen (D27) and Royal Tarlair (D99). The course at Cullen is a good illustration of the variety of coastal landforms which can be found in this type of environment (see Chapter 8, Fig. 8.6 and Ph. 4.6).

Along many parts of the Scottish coastline, raised-beach deposits form relatively narrow zones beneath former coastal cliffs (Fig. 4.10A/B). The material in these beaches may be cobbles (e.g. Spey Bay Golf Course—D104) or gravel and sand (Brodick B20), and usually their surfaces are flat or gently undulating. Courses located on raised beaches have many of the characteristics of true links courses except that they do not have the distinctive dune ridges or hummocks. In a few locations (e.g. Spey Bay) abandoned storm-beach ridges of gravel or cobbles do provide a strong linear element to their morphology. Sixty golf courses (11%) occupy raised beaches or raised marine platforms

81

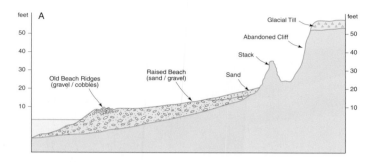

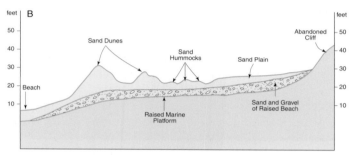

FIG. 4.10 A. *Section of raised-beach deposits backed by abandoned stack and cliff.*
B. *Section of wind-blown sand forms (dunes, hummocks, plains) covering
raised-beach deposits resting on a raised marine platform.*

Ph. 4.7 *Links land at Machrie, Islay.*

which have little or no wind-blown sand on their surfaces. Courses located on high-level marine platforms are often windswept and have a moorland vegetation.

Links

The typical Scottish links course is located on a raised beach or raised marine platform produced or at least trimmed by the relatively high sea level attained about 6,000 years ago (Fig. 4.10B). The majority of these beaches or platforms are between 10 and 35 feet above present sea level. The raised beach or platform is backed by an abandoned cliff-line cut in either glacial drift (till or fluvioglacial sand and gravel) or solid rock. On top of the raised beach or platform is a covering of wind-blown sand (Ph. 4.7) either in the form of dune ridges, dune hummocks or as a gently undulating sand-spread (sand plain). The landward dunes and hummocks along with the sand plains are usually stabilised. The youngest dune ridges or hummocks are nearest to the present high water mark and may be still growing and subject to blow-outs (erosion). The dune ridges have been used for 'rough' and inter-dune troughs (slacks) have been used for fairways and greens for several centuries by Scottish golfers. Similarly, the minor undulations associated with sand spreads over raised-beach deposits have also been traditional golfing areas. Many of Scotland's most famous golf courses—St Andrews, Carnoustie, Muirfield, Troon, Prestwick and Turnberry—make use of these natural links. Such links land was often 'common land'. It was relatively easily cleared of shrubs, and rabbits and sheep produced close-cropped turf. It is interesting that the game of golf began and flourished on the youngest and in some ways most delicate of Scotland's land surfaces. Dune areas are highly unstable. They can develop very rapidly (in geological terms) over a few hundred years, and even after long periods of stability as a result of the development of a good grass cover, can easily become unstable with further sand movement. They have three characteristics which make them highly suited to the game of golf. They have a variety of slope angles and slope lengths in a small area. They are usually well-drained and they support an easily managed grass/herb/shrub vegetation.

It is perhaps a gross over-simplification to put all links courses into one class. They range from courses built on raised beaches and raised platforms with only a thin, almost flat, sand cover, through courses built on a combination of sub-parallel dune ridges and associated undulating sand spreads, to courses built entirely on sand dune ridges and hummocks. It is the morphological variety both within and between links courses that makes them so attractive to the golfer. There are 92 links courses (17%) in Scotland.

No other country of similar size contains 538 golf courses which, within their 50,000 acres, incorporate such a variety of landforms. The morphology and general scenic setting of these courses owes much to the direct and indirect effects of the environmental changes which took place during and since the last period of glaciation. The glacier ice and meltwaters moulded much of the scenery and created many of the landforms within the confines of individual golf courses. The fluctuations in relative sea level which accompanied the growth and decay of the ice sheet were responsible for all of the landforms occupied by golf courses around the Scottish coastline. It is therefore most reasonable to base a classification of Scottish golf courses primarily on their landform characteristics.

VEGETATION

Six thousand years ago virtually all of Scotland below 2,000 feet was covered by trees— oak and birch in the south and west, pine and birch in the north and north east, and birch in the far north and on the Western Isles. With the exception of the coastal links land (all developed during the last 6,000 years) the vegetation of the areas utilised for golf courses in the nineteenth and twentieth centuries was much modified from its original state by man's agricultural and industrial activities. The vegetation of golf courses falls into four classes: woodland, parkland, moorland and linksland (grass, herbs, shrubs). Many golf courses have elements of all four classes. For example, many courses are combinations of woodland, grassland and moorland vegetation. By definition, a parkland course is a combination of grass and trees, and few golf courses are only grassland, there being always some attempt to introduce either trees or shrubs. For this reason the grassland classification is not used in this book, it being replaced by parkland.

Woodland

The areas of extensive natural woodlands remaining in Scotland are very limited and none of them contain golf courses. However, there are a few golf courses on which most of the fairways are lined by trees. The most obvious examples are at Blairgowrie, where three courses (C 17, C18, C19) have been laid out through pine and birch forest (Ph. 4.8). Even on these courses there are more open areas which are better classed as parkland. A similar set of circumstances can be found at Dougalston (B56) near Glasgow. There are many courses on which pine plantations give a woodland character to at least part of the course (e.g. Forfar C61, Alyth C6).

Parkland

Three hundred and thirty three (61%) of the golf courses in Scotland are classed as parkland. (Fig. 4.11). The classic parkland course consists of mainly deciduous trees (oak, elm, horse chestnut, birch) forming a distinctive landscape which was designed as a part of the policies of a large estate (Ph. 4.9). The golf course designer simply inherited the characteristics given to the site by landscape architects employed by the former landowner. Excellent examples of such planned parkland courses are: Ratho Park near Edinburgh (A89), Glenbervie (C64), Murrayshall (C95), Taymouth Castle (A121), Pollok (B133) and Loch Lomond (B117). At the other end of the spectrum even the most recent parkland courses laid out within the confines of a few grassland fields usually have some

Ph. 4.8 *A woodland course: Rosemount, Blairgowrie.*

Ph. 4.9 *A parkland course: Ratho Park.*

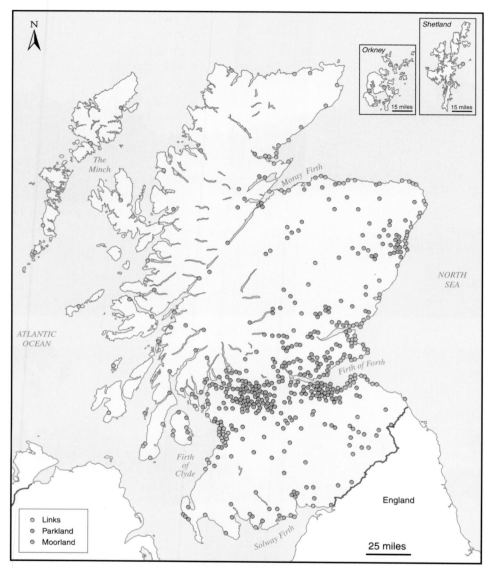

FIG. 4.11 *The location of links, parkland and moorland golf courses.*

planted trees along the sides of fairways. Between these two extremes fall the majority of parkland courses which are characterised by a mixture of grassland and trees. The trees may be either old established oaks, elms and birch, or may be relatively new plantations of pine or birch. The more rapidly growing conifers have often been used by golf course designers in Scotland to develop the parkland character relatively quickly. On many parkland courses both rhododendrons and gorse bring great spreads of colour during spring and early summer (e.g. Gleneagles) and introduce added problems to the golfer whose shots stray from the fairway.

The trees on parkland golf courses fall into two distinct categories. There are those that are integral parts of the course, in that they either line the edges of fairways or are in the fairways and form golfing hazards, and those which are set back from fairways or are around the periphery of a course and add to its landscape setting. Some golf course designers have incorporated trees into the playing area, and therefore they can rightly be regarded as hazards. Generally, however, trees simply add to the scenic attractiveness of a golf course.

Moorland

As was explained in Chapter 3, large areas of Scotland which were formerly forest have degenerated into moorland. This is particularly true of the uplands (land over 1,000 feet), but also applies to certain areas between 500 and 1,000 feet. Typical moorland vegetation consists of tough grasses and heather plus gorse, willow and occasional trees such as birch, juniper and rowan (Ph. 4.10). Even on some typical moorland courses, plantations of conifers have been used as windbreaks and to add variety to the landscape. There are 91 (17%) moorland courses in Scotland (Fig. 4.11). Most of them are over 300 feet above sea level and many of them (50) occur on outcrops of basalt lavas. There are numerous examples of moorland courses on the plateau basalts around Greater Glasgow (see Chapter 6). The fairways and greens on moorland courses are usually located on peaty soils which have poor drainage. Coarse grasses and mosses have been improved by seeding. The rough is generally heather and/or coarse grass with gorse. In recent decades the replanting of moorland areas with commercial coniferous woodland has changed the general scenic setting of many moorland golf courses.

Links

The vegetation of sand dunes, sand spreads and raised beaches is essentially grassland. The very existence of dune systems is related to the presence of tough grasses (e.g. marram grass) which not only survive in this very dry environment but assist in the trapping of sand in the dune system. Because most of Scotland's sand dune systems post-date the arrival of man in Scotland and were often the sites for early human occupation, we have little knowledge of how the dune vegetation would have developed without any human

Ph. 4.10 *A moorland course: Selkirk, the Borders.*

interference. Whether or not, without human interference over a long period, natural woodland would have developed on coastal dunes is a matter of conjecture. Certainly, coniferous plantations have been used in the last 100 years by man to stabilise dune areas (e.g. Cuilbin Sands and Tentsmuir Forest). However, over the past 5,000 years the 'natural' vegetation (including human influences) has been grasses, herbs and scrub (buckthorn and gorse). The contrast between the tough, long grasses of the active dune system (marram grass) and the short grasses and herbs of the inter-dune areas (slacks) or sand plains was accentuated by the grazing habits of cattle, sheep and rabbits. The development of modern greenkeeping methods further modified the vegetation into fairways and rough. On some links land, heather and gorse has also added to the variable character of the rough. The great diversity of landforms within an area of links land produces a variety of environments in which different types of vegetation will develop. It is this great variability in vegetation within the area of a links course which produces such a challenge to the golfer.

Throughout the rest of this book, golf courses will be classified primarily on the basis of the dominant landforms and vegetation within the confines of a course. Apart from the rather obvious difference between inland and coastal courses (most coastal courses are on links land but a few have parkland or moorland characteristics) there are certain other important variables which should be borne in mind. There are some noticeable differences in the general environmental quality of rural golf courses compared with those located in suburban and urban environments. Poor general scenic setting, high noise levels, industrial smells and vandalism all tend to be associated with golf courses in an urban environment. However, some rural courses in Scotland (e.g. St Andrews, Carnoustie, Lossiemouth, Nairn) also have noise problems associated with low flying military aircraft. On the other hand there are some delightful parkland courses which are oases of peace in the heart of urban areas.

Wherever it is located, and whatever its landscape characteristics, the golf course is for many people the closest they get to the 'natural environment' at any time in their lives. Although tees, fairways and greens may be man-made, the general landscape produced by geological processes and the vegetation and animal life of the golf course are vital ingredients of the game of golf. It would be an interesting exercise to classify Scottish golf courses on the basis of their environmental attractions. However, for a resident of Tokyo, to play even a nine-hole course in the centre of Glasgow would be valued highly compared with the use of a driving range for a couple of hours per week. For Scottish golfers the fresh air (often too strong!) of a links course with countless seabirds on the foreshore, or the sounds of grouse or curlew or deer on a high moorland course, provide 'added value' to a round of golf. One of the great attractions of the game of golf is that it can be played in such a variety of environments.

🌿 Five
South and South-east Scotland (Region A)

The south of Scotland has a great variety of scenery and golfing landscapes. The area can be divided into three parts (Fig. 5.1): Dumfries and Galloway, the Borders, Edinburgh and the Lothians. The earliest courses were established in and near Edinburgh in the eighteenth century, but between 1880 and 1909 some 50 golf courses were established throughout the region. During the last 20 years 24 new courses have been built (50% of which were of nine holes) and only five of these (The Roxburghe A93, Craigielaw A17, Cardrona A10, Whitekirk A113 and Kings Acre A51) can be described as good-quality facilities. Ten of the new courses in the Borders and Dumfries and Galloway are commercial facilities, mainly of nine holes.

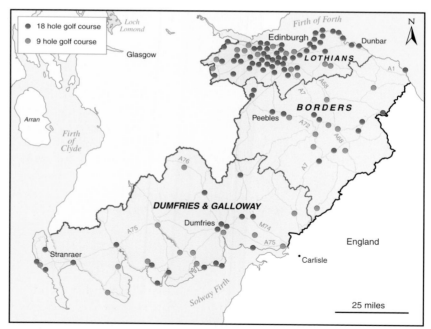

FIG. 5.1 *The location of 9-hole and 18-hole courses in South and South-east Scotland.*

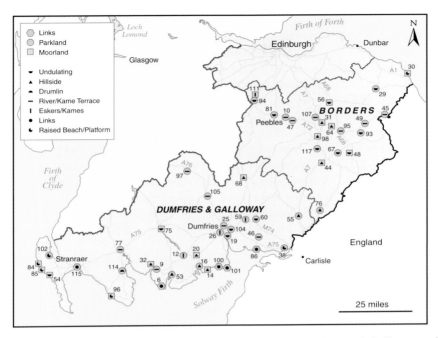

FIG. 5.2 *The landforms and vegetation of golf courses in Dumfries and Galloway and Borders.*

DUMFRIES AND GALLOWAY

There are eighteen 18-hole and fourteen 9-hole courses in this area (Fig. 5.1). With the exception perhaps of Southerness (A101), which is a classic links course of championship standard (the Scottish Amateur Championship was played here in 1985), none of the courses is particularly famous or of very high quality. However, the variety of golfing landscapes and challenges to be found in this region is quite remarkable. Many of the courses are set in beautiful scenery with views of the Solway Firth to the south and the mountains of the western Southern Uplands to the north. The climate for golf is also relatively mild and the cost of a round of golf on many of the courses is between £10 and £20.

Coastal Courses

There are only five links courses (Fig. 5.2) in this region: Wigtownshire County at Glen Luce (A115), Southerness (A101), Powfoot (A86), Solway Links (A100) and Brighouse Bay (A6). Wigtownshire County is very flat, built on a raised-beach only 10–25 feet above sea level. Southerness was the first course to be built in Scotland after World War

II (Ph. 5.1). It is also built on a raised beach between 20 and 35 feet above sea level. It is a course which requires accurate driving because of the presence of heather and gorse rough. Its exposed position means that wind direction and strength play an important part in determining the course's difficulty. A mere five miles to the north of the course, the granite mass of Criffell rises to 1,868 feet. Powfoot (A86), some four miles west of Annan, is an undulating links course. The outer sand ridge reaches altitudes of between 23 and 46 feet above sea level, and the course is built on an undulating sand plain with a relief of between 6 and 12 feet. The rough consists largely of gorse. The course was laid out by James Braid in 1903. Solway Links is a very basic holiday 'pay and play' course of 11 holes (3,062yds). The clubhouse is a converted farm cottage and there is no bar or catering, although the local guide to golf facilities does state that, '...a kettle is provided and all the necessary items for making tea or coffee—biscuits can also be purchased.' Brighouse Bay was originally developed as a 9-hole course in association with a holiday park. The course was extended to 18 holes in 1999. There is an adjacent Leisure Club with bar, catering and swimming pool.

Although the courses at Stranraer (A82), Portpatrick (A84), Lagganmore (A54) and St Medan, Port William (A96), are on the coast, they each have landscape characteristics which are associated with inland locations. The course at Stranraer, which was the last one designed by James Braid, is an undulating parkland course between 15 and 70 feet above sea level, built on dissected raised-beach sand and gravel. It is a good-quality parkland

Ph. 5.1 *Southerness* (© *M. Williamson*).

course which owes its landscape characteristics to the fact that the isthmus between Loch Ryan and Luce Bay was once an arm of the sea, and much of the land around the present shores of Loch Ryan, up to an altitude of about 100 feet above present sea level, is covered by marine sand and gravel.

There are two courses at Portpatrick (A84, A85)—one of 18 holes and the other of 9 holes. They are both built on a rolling upland between 150 and 200 feet above sea level. Although next to the coast they are essentially moorland courses. The most spectacular hole is the 283 yards par four, where one drives from a tee, high up on the cliff edge, to a green far below. Portpatrick is an excellent centre for a golfing holiday. One mile east of Portpatrick, at Lagganmore (A54), is a new 18-hole 'pay and play' facility, which has a driving range and clubhouse with a bar and catering. The course is on undulating moorland and is very basic.

Another moorland course by the coast is that at St Medan (A96), some three miles south-east of Port William. This 9-hole course has fine sandy beaches on two sides, but it is built between an old degraded cliff and a small rounded hill on a promontory. There are no trees and very little rough on the course. The fourth hole, the Well, is 274 yards from the tee on top of a hill down to the green amongst sand dunes some 70 feet below. The fifth, sixth and seventh holes are links holes constructed on a raised beach covered by blown sand.

Although the courses at Wigtown (A114), Gatehouse of Fleet (A32), Cally Palace (A9), Craigieknowes (A16), Kirkcudbright (A53), Colvend (A14) and Gretna (A38) are all within a mile of tidewater, they are all classed as inland courses.

Inland Courses

There are 23 inland courses in Dumfries and Galloway of which 17 are classed as parkland and five as moorland.

One of the most distinctive courses is that at Wigtown (A114). It is a 9-hole parkland course built on the side of drumlins (see Chapter 4). The parkland courses at Newton Stewart (A77), Castle Douglas (A12), Thornhill (A105), Sanquhar (A97) and Lochmaben (A59) are all on undulating areas of sand and gravel, as are also the three 18-hole and one 9-hole parkland courses at Dumfries (A25, A19, A26, A104). The 18-hole course at Kirkcudbright (A53) is built on a steep hillside. Of these parkland courses the three 18-hole courses (A25, A26, A104) at Dumfries and the courses at Thornhill (A105) and Lochmaben (A59) are the most attractive.

The five courses classed as moorland—Gatehouse of Fleet (A32, Ph. 5.2), New Galloway (A75), Dalbeattie (A20), Colvend (A14), and Moffat (A68)—all present problems of classification. Only that at Moffat, which is at an altitude of between 550 and 675 feet, is a true moorland course. There are magnificent views of the Annan Valley, the Tweedsmuir Hills and the town of Moffat from the eighteenth tee. This 271-yards par four is a spectacular finishing hole with a drop from tee to green of some 75 feet. There is a

Ph. 5.2 *Gatehouse of Fleet.*

similar final hole on the 9-hole moorland course at Gatehouse of Fleet (A32), but this course is only between 100 and 300 feet above sea level. The courses at Dalbeattie (A20) and Colvend (A14) are less spectacular moorland courses.

Two new 18-hole parkland courses have been opened in this area. In the grounds of the Cally Palace Hotel at Gatehouse a beautiful golf course has been created, laid out around the Cally Lake and on the raised beach of Fleet Bay. It is the fine mature trees to be found on the course which make it so attractive. There are some challenging golf holes, but it is the fine landscape which makes a round on this course so memorable. The Cally golf course has no club membership nor day visitors, and is exclusive to residents of the McMillan Hotels, the Cally Palace, the North West Castle at Stranraer, the Kirroughtree at Newton Stewart and the Fernhill at Portpatrick. In contrast, the new 18-hole 'pay and play' course at The Pines, on the north-east side of Dumfries, is easily accessible to visitors. The course, which opened in 1998, is 5,850yds in length, is laid out on undulating land within woodland and has some significant water features.

The 9-hole parkland courses at Hoddom Castle and Gretna are basic commercial facilities. The course at Hoddom Castle is on a flat river terrace and is associated with a large caravan park. The Gretna Golf Club and driving range has a 9-hole course (SSS 72) and a modern clubhouse.

THE BORDERS

Although this region is more famous for its rugby pitches than its golf courses, the 21 golf courses provide some interesting golfing landscapes. Fourteen of the courses were established during the last quarter of the nineteenth century, but those at Minto (A67) and Coldstream were founded in 1926 and 1948 respectively. Nine of them are of nine holes and twelve are 18-hole courses. On most of them a round of golf costs between £10 and £20. Until the opening of the Roxburghe (A93) near Kelso in 1997, there were no first-class courses in this area, which is in marked contrast to the adjacent East Lothian region. However, the occurrence of 17 very different golf courses within a 20 mile radius of St Boswells or Melrose makes these towns excellent centres for a golfing holiday. The Tweed Valley and its tributaries, the Ettrick and Teviot, provide delightful background scenery and many sites of historical interest. Although the courses may not be of the highest quality, the cheapness of the green fees, the delightful countryside and interesting towns of this area make this one of Scotland's most attractive golfing prospects. It should also be pointed out that the challenging courses of Gullane, North Berwick and Dunbar are only 35 miles away. All of the courses, apart from the one at Eyemouth (A30, coastal moorland) are inland courses. They fall into two clear categories—seven courses (A44, 48, 98, 31, 64, 56, 111) are moorland courses often located on steep hillsides at altitudes of between 600 and 800 feet above sea level, and thirteen courses are parkland courses. The parkland courses can be further subdivided between those located on the flood plains and river terraces of the river Tweed (A47, 107, 95, 49, 45) and those located on rolling uplands above the valley floors (A67, 81, 29, 12, 93).

Moorland Courses

The boundary between cultivation and rough grazing/heather moorland has varied considerably throughout history and varies from place to place within the Southern Uplands. The availability of modern machinery means that a golf course which has moorland characteristics may now be surrounded by arable land or coniferous plantations. This contrast of a moorland course with both coniferous plantations and ploughed fields around it is seen at Melrose (Ph. 5.3). This course (A64) is located on the north-west flank of the Eildon Hills. The smooth conical and heather-clad summits of these hills are formed of hard volcanic rocks, sheets of lava having invaded the bedding-planes of the Old Red Sandstone sediments (see the red soil in the field to the north-east of the golf course). The Eildon Hills were made famous by the writings of Sir Walter Scott whose home at Abbotsford is only a few miles away. Although Melrose Golf Course has conifer plantations both on the course and around its edges, it still has many characteristics related to the heather moorland which covers the higher parts of the Eildon Hills.

The three 9-hole courses at Melrose (founded 1880), Selkirk (founded 1883) and Jedburgh (founded 1892) were all designed by Willie Park. They are all of similar length, but the course at Selkirk (A98) is perched on the side of a glacially scoured hill consisting

Ph. 5.3 *Melrose*.

of volcanic rock. The north-east to south-west trending hill upon which the Selkirk course is built consists of a vertical sheet of volcanic rock (a dyke) intruded into Silurian shales. The north-west face of this hill has been eroded by glacier ice moving from south-west to north-east and consists of a series of minor ridges and depressions which have been utilised in the construction of the golf course. The view from the ninth tee to the ninth green demonstrates the significance of the heather-clad minor ridges in the character of this course (Ph. 4.10). The course at Jedburgh (A48) is less spectacular in its morphology but is also built on the side of a hill and is an enjoyable test of golf.

There are three 18-hole moorland courses in the Borders. Those at Hawick (A44) and Galashiels (A31) are both constructed on steep hillsides with spectacular views of the surrounding countryside. Both the Ladhope course at Galashiels and the course at Hawick have some tees and greens which are perched on hillsides. The moorland course at West Linton (A111) in the far north of the district, is largely built on fluvioglacial sands and gravels and has relatively gentle undulations. There are some fine views of the Pentland Hills from this course.

Parkland Courses

There are thirteen parkland courses in the Borders region, eight of them being of 18 holes. Three of the courses are on rolling uplands—Peebles (A81), Minto (A67) four miles north-east of Hawick, and Duns (A29). There are some fine views of the Border Hills and the Tweed Valley from the Peebles course but the course at Minto is in classic deciduous parkland.

Perhaps the most distinctive type of golf course in the Borders is that built on the gravel terraces of the Tweed and its tributaries the Leithen Water, Gala Water and Leet Water (A47, 10, 107, 95, 48, 45). During the wastage of the last ice sheet, some 15,000 years ago, these river valleys were choked with sands and gravels deposited by the meltwaters from the melting ice. Subsequently the rivers have cut down into these gravels leaving flat or gently undulating terraces which have proved excellent sites for golf courses. The 9-hole course at Innerleithen (A47) is built on flat land immediately adjacent to the river and at the foot of the smooth, rounded slopes which lead up to moorland. In great contrast is the parkland course at Torwoodlee, Galashiels (A107). This is one of the most beautiful courses in the Borders with some fine individual trees on the course which is built both on the flat flood-plain and on higher river-terraces. Another pleasant 9-hole parkland course is that at St Boswells (A95) on the banks of the Tweed. The 18-hole course at Kelso (A49) is to be found in the centre of a racecourse and is a flat, featureless course with but few planted trees. Further down the Tweed Valley at Coldstream (A45) is a very pleasant parkland course built in the grounds of the Hirsel, the former home of Sir Alec Douglas-Home.

During the past decade there have been two significant additions to the commercial golf facilities in the Borders. The Roxburghe (A93) course at Kelso (Ph. 5.4), designed by Dave Thomas, is a first class golf course in a beautiful setting and adjacent to a high quality hotel. The new course at Cardrona (A10) also designed by Dave Thomas, which is currently under construction on the Tweed River terraces, is part of a new village and hotel project. Together these courses will add significantly to golf-related tourism in this region. In the north of the region, south-west of West Linton, a more basic golf facility was opened in 1998 at Rutherford Castle (A94). It is an 18-hole parkland course.

THE LOTHIANS AND EDINBURGH

Although only containing 64 golf courses, this area is one of the old heartlands of Scottish golf. Students of the history of the game in Scotland savour the names of the Royal Burgess Golfing Society of Edinburgh (founded 1735) and the Honourable Company of Edinburgh Golfers (founded 1744) which established the original 13 rules of golf. Edinburgh, therefore, claims to be the 'Golf Capital of the World' on the basis of its historical links with the game and the fact that it has 26 courses within its city limits and that there are 80 courses within 20 miles of Princes Street. One of the earliest golf courses was at Bruntsfield Links in the heart of the city of Edinburgh, where the original six holes are now part of a 'short' course on common land where golf is still played immediately in front of the Golf Tavern (established in 1456). The other early site of golf in Edinburgh was at Leith Links which are now used as public playing fields. Although it is perhaps sad

Ph. 5.4 *The Roxburghe (courtesy of the Roxburghe Hotel and Golf Course).*

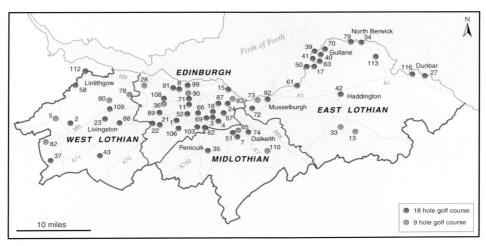

FIG. 5.3 *The location of 9-hole and 18-hole golf courses in Edinburgh and the Lothians.*

that golf is no longer played on Leith Links, the overcrowding of those links and also of the Bruntsfield Links led to a movement of the game outside of the city, first to Musselburgh (1836) and then to Muirfield, just outside Gullane, which became the home of the Honourable Company of Edinburgh Golfers in 1891.

This sub-region consists of four unitary authorities (Fig. 5.3), East Lothian, Midlothian, West Lothian and Edinburgh. The distribution of golf courses is rather uneven with the main concentration being in Edinburgh (26 courses) and along the East Lothian coast between Musselburgh and Dunbar (16 courses). There are three inland courses in East

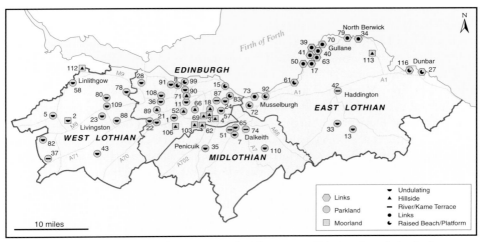

FIG. 5.4 *The landforms and vegetation of golf courses in Edinburgh and the Lothians.*

Lothian, seven in Midlothian and twelve in West Lothian. The majority of the courses are of 18 holes (12 are of nine holes) and, apart from the 12 links courses between Dunbar and Musselburgh (Fig. 5.4), six moorland courses on the south side of Edinburgh and two moorland courses in West Lothian, the majority of the courses are inland parkland.

EAST LOTHIAN

Coastal Courses

The 20-mile stretch of coastline on the south side of the Firth of Forth, between Musselburgh and Dunbar, contains some classic golf courses steeped in history. They all owe their existence to changes in relative sea level along the coastline during the past 6,000 years. About 6,000 years ago sea level stood some 25 feet higher against the land than it does at present. Old cliff lines and beaches associated with that higher stand of sea level have since been abandoned and large quantities of blown sand have accumulated to form dune systems and sand spreads (links). It is these blown-sand accumulations and the underlying raised-beach deposits which have provided such good golfing country.

Golf was played on the links at Musselburgh as early as 1672 and the earliest known trophy for stroke play was competed for by members of the Thorn Tree Golf Club on that course in 1774. Six Open Championships were played at Musselburgh links but the Honourable Company of Edinburgh Golfers, who moved to Musselburgh from Leith in 1836, later moved again to Muirfield and took the Open Championship with them.

As was pointed out in Chapter 1, the date of foundation of Golf Clubs does not necessarily indicate the first date at which golf was played on a particular course. It is believed that golf has been played on Gullane Hill for over 300 years, but Dirleton Castle Golf Club was founded in 1854, Luffness Old in 1867, Kilspindie in 1867, and Gullane Golf Club in 1882. The North Berwick Golf Club was founded in 1832 and Dunbar in 1856.

There are two courses at Dunbar. The original 15 holes on the East Links (A27) were designed by Tom Morris and a further three holes added in 1880. This course is a combination of coastal links and 'inland' parkland. Holes 1, 2, 3 and 18 are in the Old Deer Park of the Duke of Roxburgh's estate, while the other 14 holes are on links land. In 1968 the Schweppes PGA Championship was held on this course. With the increase in demand for golf in the 1930s, a second course was established to the west of the town (A116) at Winterfield in 1937. The course is built on a raised marine-platform covered with sand.

There are also two golf courses at North Berwick. The North Berwick Golf Club, founded in 1832, plays over the west links (A79). A raised-beach is overlain by blown sand that forms undulating links land between 10 and 30 feet above sea level (Ph. 5.5) and provides some classic links golf. Neil Elsey, writing about the course, states:

Ph. 5.5 *North Berwick.*

Measuring 6,317 yards it's no monster in length but such is its trickery that it demands a full repertoire of shot-making. Every hole here is memorable (two of them, the 382 yards 14th named 'Perfection' and the 192 yards 15th called 'Redan' have been copied at courses all over the world) and you almost get the feeling of stepping back in time as you tackle its idiosyncrasies. There are blind shots, drives over walls and burns, shots across the bay and bunkers in which you can disappear from view. So this is how golf used to be played!

The East Links or 'Glen' course (A34) at North Berwick was originally laid out as a 9-hole course by James Braid and Ben Sayers in 1894 and extended to 18 holes in 1906. The 1st and 18th holes are on low lying links land developed upon a raised beach with a fossil cliff some 75 feet high on the landward side. Holes 2 to 17 are above the cliff and provide a course of gentle undulations, on an old marine platform covered with blown sand. There are excellent views across the Firth of Forth to the Kingdom of Fife and to the Bass Rock with its colony of gannets.

In 1995 an 18-hole commercial facility was opened at Whitekirk (A113) on high ground three miles to the south-east of North Berwick. Wind is a crucial factor in determining the difficulty of this moorland course. There is a fine clubhouse and restaurant (Ph. 5.6).

Ph. 5.6 *Whitekirk.*

Ph. 5.7 *Gullane.*

The small village of Gullane has been a major golfing centre for over 100 years—records show that the Dirleton Castle Golf Club played over Gullane Hill in 1854 (Ph. 5.7). There are three courses at Gullane (A39, 40, 41), two at Aberlady (A17, 50) and one at Muirfield (A70) and Luffness New (A63). Again, blown sand plays a major part in producing the character of all these courses but variations in relief, morphology and the underlying solid geology produce variations on the links theme. Gullane Hill consists of Carboniferous sediments into which volcanic rocks (dolerite sills) have been intruded. Its summit stands 200 feet above sea level and its higher parts have a distinctly moorland appearance. However, on its northern, western and south-eastern flanks the hill has a covering of blown sand up to about 120 feet above sea level and large parts of the three courses (Fig. 5.5) have been laid out on the links land. The Luffness New course was opened in 1893 and incorporates the original nine holes of Luffness Old which was

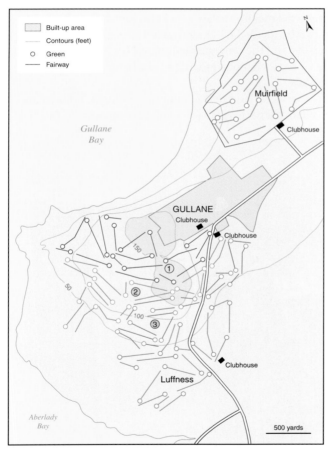

FIG. 5.5 *The golf courses at Gullane, Luffness and Muirfield.*

founded in 1867. It is a comparatively flat course built on postglacial marine sediments and blown sand on the south-western flanks of Gullane Hill. The greens on this course were reputedly described by Gerald Micklem as the finest in Scotland. This course is used during the Oxford and Cambridge Golfing Society's Scottish tour and is also used as a qualifying course for the Open Championship.

From the top of Gullane Hill there is an excellent view northeastwards towards Muirfield (A70). On the skyline are the distinctive volcanic hills of Bass Rock and North Berwick Law, while in the foreground is Gullane Beach backed by the high (45 feet) coastal dune ridge. Gullane Bay has a variety of dune forms and there is an extensive area of blown sand some half a mile in width underlying Muirfield golf course, upon which is a series of old dune ridges aligned west-south-west to east-north-east.

Although the links at Muirfield have been the home of the Honourable Company of Edinburgh Golfers only since 1891, the minute records of the club go back to 7 March 1744, at which time the members played on Leith Links. They moved to Musselburgh in 1836 and then to Muirfield. The Honourable Company drafted the original 'thirteen rules of golf' in 1744 and the original parchment on which these rules were written is in the Honourable Company's archives with a copy hanging in the Smoking Room of the Muirfield clubhouse.

The course is relatively flat, but the numerous hillocks, hollows and bunkers (a total of 151) and the relatively narrow fairways and fearsome rough together put a premium

Ph. 5.8 *Craigielaw.*

on length and accuracy. The ninth hole was once described by R. T. Jones Jnr as the best hole he knew in golf. The concentric circulatory layout of the course (the back nine holes are located inside the front nine) make it an ideal course for the spectator, with even the furthest points on the course being only a few minutes walk from the clubhouse. Muirfield has been the venue for fourteen Open, seven Amateur and six Scottish Amateur Championships as well as for Ryder, Walker and Curtis Cup matches.

Near Aberlady is the Kilspindie golf course (A50). Although the club was founded in 1867, the present course, which was designed by Willie Park, was opened in 1898. It is a flat links course sitting on a raised beach between 10 and 20 feet above sea level. A new links course of 6,600 yds has been constructed inland of the Kilspindie course. Craigielaw Golf Club (A17, Ph. 5.8) is a high-quality commercial facility which opened in 2001, welcomes visitors and will add further to the attractiveness of East Lothian as a golf tourist destination. The 54 holes at Gullane, with their own visitors' clubhouse, attract many thousands of visitors each year, as do the links at North Berwick and Dunbar. While Muirfield has an international reputation, it is difficult to access and expensive to play. There are plans to build two new golf courses on the adjacent property of Archerfield House.

The Longniddry golf course (A61) is rather different from the other links courses in East Lothian. Although it sits on a sand-covered raised beach and is backed by the fossil cliff line of the postglacial sea (formed about 6,000 years ago), there are sections of the course which are of a parkland character with some fine Scots pines and various deciduous trees. Longniddry has a fine stone-built clubhouse overlooking the course and the Firth of Forth.

The site of the Royal Musselburgh golf course (A92) at Preston Grange is difficult to classify. It is within half a mile of the coast, is built on a raised-beach and yet has all the characteristics of an inland parkland course. The forerunner of this club was the Thorn Tree Club which played on the links in Musselburgh—their 'Old Club Cup' for match play dating back to 1774. The present course was laid out by James Braid and opened in 1926.

The 9-hole course (A73) in Musselburgh, mostly located within the horse racecourse, is perhaps of more interest in a historical context than in its present golfing landscape. Golf was being played on these links as far back as 1672. This course was one of the original venues for the Open Championship, along with Prestwick and St Andrews, and it remained on the rota until 1891. During the mid-nineteenth century these rather inconspicuous nine holes were the focus of Scottish golf—the Honourable Company of Edinburgh Golfers, the Royal Musselburgh Golf Club, the Royal Burgess Golfers and the Bruntsfield Golfing Society all played here. Musselburgh produced champion professionals and became the centre of the golf ball and golf club manufacturing industry. Men of Musselburgh spread the game far and wide as they sought employment as golf professionals, course designers and club and ball manufacturers in many parts of the world. It was at Musselburgh that a tool to cut a standard 4¼ inch hole on the putting green was introduced in 1829. Because of the new hard-paved roads to the right of the first few holes, a metal plate was fitted to produce the 'brassie' wooden club (1888) for use on these hard surfaces. The over-crowding of the links and the availability of rail transport led to the movement away from Musselburgh of the prestigious Edinburgh clubs and to the decline of Musselburgh as a major golfing centre.

Inland Courses

About a mile south of the town of Musselburgh, on the banks of the River Tyne and bisected by the main Edinburgh to London railway line, is the Monktonhall course (A72). It is a parkland course on undulating land. This new home for the Musselburgh Golf Club was laid out by James Braid and opened in 1938.

Three other parkland courses, at Haddington (A42), Gifford (A33) and Castle Park (A13) add variety to the predominantly links courses of East Lothian. The 18-hole course at Haddington is located in 130 acres of fine parkland on the gravel terraces adjacent to the River Tyne. In great contrast is the 9-hole course at Gifford which sits on a rolling till-covered upland adjacent to the picturesque village with its wide main street and fine old buildings. Lord Tweeddale leased a part of his estate for the construction of the course and the course was designed by the famous golfer and landscaper, Willie Watt of Royal Epsom. A fine beech hedge and mature woodland surround the course. It is indeed an interesting course, not least because it is in great contrast to the more famous links on the East Lothian coast. A 9-hole course was opened at nearby Castle Park in 1995 and there are plans to extend the 'pay and play' facility to 18 holes in the near future.

MIDLOTHIAN

All the golf courses in Midlothian are parkland courses. Perhaps the least interesting is the rather flat course at Bonnyrigg (A77). To the south-east of Dalkeith is the beautiful mature parkland of Newbattle Abbey, within which is to be found Newbattle Golf Club (A74). Much of the course is built on the terraces of the River South Esk with the river itself coming into play on the 2nd and 17th holes. Glencorse Golf Club near Penicuik (A75) is partly built on the terraces of the River North Esk and also on an area of undulating upland and it therefore presents a variety of landscapes to the golfer.

Two recent commercial additions to the golf facilities of Midlothian have been constructed near Lasswade. The Melville Golf Centre (A65) consists of a driving range, putting and pitching practice areas and a 9-hole course of 3,834 yards. This is a first-class facility for people of all ages to learn and practice the game of golf. The 18-hole parkland course at nearby Kings Acre (A51) was opened in 1997. The course is of high quality with a variety of holes both on undulating upland and in dramatic river terrace settings. The most attractive clubhouse and first-class practice facility is used by the club members and many visitors (Ph. 5.9).

Ph. 5.9 *Kings Acre* (© *M. Williamson*).

WEST LOTHIAN

Many of the communities of West Lothian were associated with coal and oil shale min-
ing during the nineteenth and early twentieth centuries. In this industrial background
there are six parkland courses: Fauldhouse-Greenburn (A27), West Calder (A88),
Linlithgow (A58), Livingston Deer Park (A23), Pumpherston (A88) and Uphall (A109).
The 9-hole course at Pumpherston has recently been renovated and extended to 18 holes.
Deer Park is a commercial facility which also developed from an original 9-hole course.
The Harburn Club at West Calder is at the high altitude of 800 to 900 feet and has some
characteristics of a moorland course despite the planted trees. The courses at Bathgate
(A3) and Boness (A4) are moorland courses, the latter having spectacular views over the
Firth of Forth.

EDINBURGH

This historic city has a long association with the game of golf. The 26 courses (only four
of them being of nine holes) within the present boundaries of Edinburgh (Fig. 5.3) provide a variety of golfing landscapes with the notable lack of any true links courses. Golf
was probably played within a mile of Edinburgh Castle on common land at Bruntsfield
Links (not a true links course) in the fifteenth century (Fig. 5.6). It was there that two of

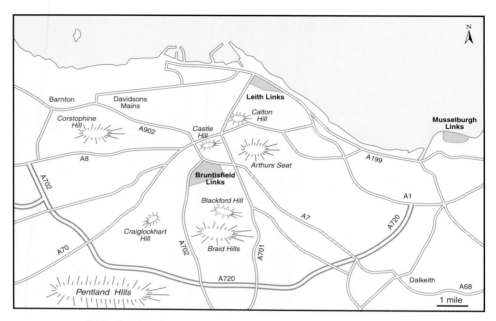

FIG. 5.6 *The location of the early golfing grounds of Edinburgh.*

the oldest clubs in the world were established—the Royal Burgess Golfing Society (1735) and the Bruntsfield Golfing Society (1761). Edinburgh's third famous club, the Honourable Company of Edinburgh Golfers (1744) played over Leith Links. Neither the Bruntsfield Links nor the Leith Links accommodated these clubs for very long—the Royal Burgess Club moved first to Musselburgh (1836) and then to its present location at Barnton in 1895. The Bruntsfield Golfing Society also moved to Musselburgh in the 1870s and then to its present site at Davidson's Mains in 1895, while the Honourable Company of Edinburgh Golfers moved from Leith to Musselburgh in 1836 and then on to Muirfield in East Lothian in 1891. The earliest Edinburgh clubs have therefore had associations with the flat links courses at Leith and Musselburgh before either returning to fine parkland sites to the west of the city or moving further afield, in the case of the Honourable Company, to the links at Muirfield.

Including the three famous old clubs of Edinburgh, which all moved to their present locations in the 1890s, the big expansion in the number of golf courses within Edinburgh occurred between 1890 and 1912, sixteen courses being opened during this period. A further six courses (A21, 22, 57, 87, 89, 103) were opened between 1920 and 1930. The concept of providing golf 'for the people' became a strong idea at the turn of the century—courses were to be owned and run by the City Fathers in contrast to the somewhat exclusive clubs which catered for the upper classes. The earliest municipal course was opened at Craigentinny (A15) in 1891 to be followed by the two courses on the

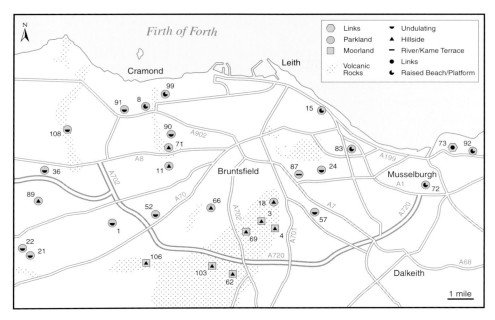

FIG. 5.7 *The landforms and vegetation of the golf courses of Edinburgh.*

Braid Hills (A3, 4) in 1893-4 and courses at Carrickvale (A11) in 1930 and Silverknowes (A99) in 1947. The course at Portobello (A83) which dates back to 1853 is also now a municipal course. This means that nearly a quarter of Edinburgh's golf courses are 'public' courses freely accessible to the visitor at a cost of £8 to £10 per round.

Two types of golfing landscape are to be found in Edinburgh, moorland and parkland courses (Fig. 5.7). The city of Edinburgh is built around a series of volcanic hills and uplands. The city centre is dominated by the 'crag and tail' of Castle Rock and the Royal Mile. Arthur's Seat and Salisbury Craigs also bear witness to ancient volcanic action. None of these locations provide sites for golf courses. However, to the south of the city, the steep craggy slopes of the Braid Hills and Pentland Hills produce not only sites for distinctive moorland golf courses but also magnificent views across the city to the Forth Estuary and beyond to the north. There are three courses on the north face of the Pentland Hills (A62, 103, 106). Lothianburn (A62), which was redesigned by James Braid in 1928, has been described as a good example of mountain golf—the par four ninth hole providing a particular challenge. The course at Swanston (A103) is less spectacular, but that at Torphin Hill (A106) has several steep climbs with the highest part of the course rising to over 800 feet. All three courses provide spectacular views across the city of Edinburgh to the Firth of Forth. The Braid Hills are the location of three excellent courses—the two municipal courses of Braids United (A3, A4) and Mortonhall (A69). The Braids United courses have been described as an excellent combination of hill walking and golf with drives from high crags down or across intervening valleys.

Volcanic rocks also underlie Craigmillar Park (A18), Merchants (A66), Murrayfield (A71), Ravelston (A90) and Turnhouse (A108), but none of these sites are as craggy or are at as high an altitude as the courses on the Pentland or Braid Hills. They still tend to be hilly courses but have a parkland character. Craigmillar Park golf course is situated near the Royal Observatory on Blackford Hill. This hill is a 'crag and tail', and the course is laid out along the tail and up onto the higher slopes of the volcanic crag. The Merchants course (A66) is built around ridges and valleys cut into volcanic rocks and is also quite hilly. The name of the club relates to the time when the city was divided into districts of merchants' associations. This club is proud of the fact that two of its members were awarded Victoria Crosses—one in the 1914–18 war and one in the 1939–45 war. The club records show that in 1936 James Braid redesigned four holes on the course for the sum of £5. The Murrayfield (A71) and Ravelston (A90) courses are adjacent to each other on the 'dip' slope of a volcanic sill—Corstorphine Hill. Both are hilly, parkland courses. Ravelston is a 9-hole course and once was described by a *Sunday Times* correspondent as the finest 9-hole course in Britain. The course at Turnhouse (A108) is also partly built on volcanic rock and it is adjacent to the busy Edinburgh airport.

Several of the Edinburgh courses were built in the grounds of large and distinguished 'country houses' around the periphery of the city. Baberton (A1) is an undulating parkland course originally planned by Willie Park. The club house building dates back to

Ph. 5.10 *Dalmahoy.*

1622. This club is also associated with the introduction of the steel-shafted golf club. Thomas Horsburgh, who was club captain from 1914–17 and 1929–31, made a patent application for a steel-shafted club in 1894, but it was not until November 1929 that the Royal and Ancient finally approved steel shafts. Liberton (A57) golf course was laid out around an eighteenth century mansion, Kingston Grange, which is now the clubhouse. Just a short distance from Liberton are the ruins of Craigmillar Castle, which was once the home of the first recorded lady golfer, Mary Queen of Scots. On the south side of Arthur's Seat is the Prestonfield Golf Club (A87) which has a fine parkland course adjacent to Holyrood Park and Prestonfield House (now a hotel) which dates from 1687. A similar parkland course is to be found at Duddingston (A24). These courses offer high-quality golf in a beautiful and historic setting in the heart of Edinburgh.

James Braid was associated with the design or alteration (redesign) of ten of Edinburgh's golf courses. Two of his finest courses are to be found at Dalmahoy (A21, 22) and a third just across the road at Ratho Park (A 89). Dalmahoy, some seven miles to the west of the city centre, has two 18-hole courses (opened in 1927) in 1,000 acres of undulating parkland (Ph. 5.10). They form part of a large hotel and sporting complex with facilities for swimming, squash, riding, trout fishing, archery and clay pigeon shooting. The east course is a fine test of golf and has been used for many championship events. A year after Dalmahoy opened, James Braid played a match against Harry Vardon on the nearby Ratho Park course which he had laid out among the beautiful trees in the grounds of the Georgian mansion built in 1824. This must be one of the most beautiful courses in Scotland.

Within a one mile radius of Davidson's Mains on the west side of Edinburgh and adjacent to the shore of the Firth of Forth are to be found the two faces of Edinburgh golf. Two world-famous clubs, the Royal Burgess Golfing Society (A91) and the Bruntsfield Links Golfing Society (A8), brought their eighteenth-century traditions to beautiful parkland locations in the 1890s. Both clubs maintain first-class courses and treasure their great history. Just half-a-mile towards the banks of the Forth from the Bruntsfield course is to be found one of Edinburgh's municipal courses, Silverknowes (A99). It is a good test of golfing skills and although it does not have the great traditions of its illustrious neighbours it makes an important contribution to the Edinburgh golfing scene.

Edinburgh frequently claims to be the Golfing Capital. While other towns or cities may wish to dispute this claim, there can be no doubt that for over 300 years golf has been played in and around the city. If Edinburgh is chosen as a centre for a golfing holiday, not only do the 26 courses of Edinburgh have much to offer, but within easy access are the links of East Lothian and the numerous courses across the Forth estuary in the Kingdom of Fife.

✿ Six
West Central Scotland
(Region B)

Until the reorganisation of local government in 1996, this region was administered as a single authority known as Strathclyde Region. In the reorganisation, twelve local authorities were created. Region B stretches from Loch Ryan in the south to the island of Coll in the north (over 200 miles) and from Biggar in the east to Islay in the west. Although this region contains nearly half of Scotland's population (2.3 million), 1.6 million of the region's population is concentrated in the Greater Glasgow conurbation, so that many other parts of the region have very low population densities. This region has a great variety of landscapes ranging from the urban canyons of central Glasgow to the rugged mountains of the south-west Grampians and the windswept shores of the Inner Hebridean Islands.

Region B contains 173 golf courses, only **44** of which are of nine holes. For ease of reference the region is divided into seven sub-regions (Table 6.1 and Fig. 6.1). Greater Glasgow consists of the City of Glasgow and its suburbs and surrounding areas from Dumbarton and Lochwinnoch in the west to Kilsyth, Cumbernauld, Airdrie and Wishaw

		Population (000)	No of Courses 18-hole	No of Courses 9-hole	No 18-hole Units	Pop. per 18-hole Unit
	TABLE 6.1 *The Population, Number of Courses and Population per 18-hole Unit in the Seven Sub-regions of Region B*					
1	**Greater Glasgow**	1,600	71	8	74.5	21,000
2	**Firth of Clyde**	180	14	8	18	10,000
3/5	**Ayrshire & Arran**	237	32	10	37	6,000
4	**South Lanarkshire**	307	7	5	9.5	21,000
6/7	**Kintyre, Argyll Islay, Gigha, Coll Tiree, Mull**	90	5	13	11.5	6,000

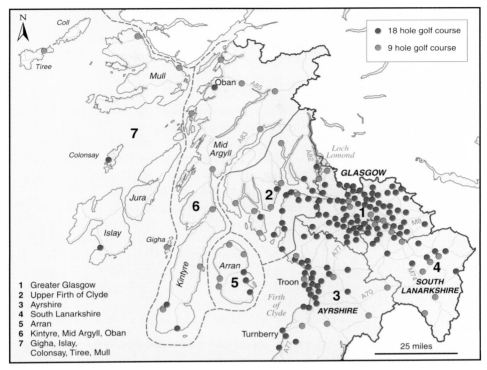

FIG. 6.1 *The location of 9-hole and 18-hole golf courses in the seven sub-regions of West Central Scotland.*

in the east, and from Milngavie in the north to Eaglesham, East Kilbride and Hamilton in the south. In this sub-region there are 80 golf courses within a 15-mile radius of the centre of Glasgow (George Square). Within 30 miles, or approximately one hour's drive by car from the centre of Glasgow, there are about 120 golf courses.

The distribution of golf courses in Region B is strongly concentrated in and around Glasgow, along the shores of the Firth of Clyde, and in Ayrshire. These sub-regions contain 143 out of the total of 173 golf courses.

Golf was played on Glasgow Green in the seventeenth century and the first Open Championship was played at Prestwick in 1860. Glasgow Golf Club celebrated its 200th anniversary in 1987. There is therefore a long tradition of golf in Glasgow, but prior to 1879 (Fig. 2.3) there were only five courses in existence. A major expansion took place between 1880 and 1909 (Fig. 2.6) when a further 86 courses were opened.

Apart from the classic links courses at Turnberry, Prestwick, Troon, Machrihanish and Machrie (Islay), the majority of the courses in Region B are inland, parkland or moorland courses. However, there is enormous variety within these two broad categories depending on the local geology, altitude and vegetation. The quality of the golf courses

113

ranges from those of championship standard at Turnberry and Troon to unsophisticated 9-hole courses either in the heart of the City of Glasgow or amid the beautiful scenery of Argyll or the Islands.

GREATER GLASGOW

The City of Glasgow lies at the centre of a basin, through which the River Clyde and its tributaries flow to the Firth of Clyde. This basin is surrounded by hills which rise to over 1,800 feet in the Kilpatrick and Campsie Hills to the north (Ph. 6.1), and to between 500 and 800 feet to the south-west and east of the city. There are five variables which strongly influence the character of golf courses in the Greater Glasgow sub-region: solid geology, glacial history, vegetation, land use and altitude.

About 300 million years ago central Scotland was located in the tropics some 600 miles south of the equator. A series of climatic changes from semi-arid to tropical resulted in the formation of the limestones and coals which were to play such a significant role in the development of Glasgow and other industrial towns in central Scotland during the nineteenth century. These sedimentary rocks underlie much of the Glasgow basin, while the high ground around the rim of the basin is composed of layer upon layer of volcanic rocks. The Clyde plateau basalts form a very distinctive upland landscape of rock steps and undulating plateau surfaces with a characteristic heather moorland vegetation.

Ph. 6.1 *The Campsie Hills (plateau basalts) and drumlins in the Kelvin Valley, Kirkintilloch Golf Course.*

During the past two million years, the Glasgow area has been inundated by glaciers on numerous occasions. The last great ice sheet covered the area completely 18,000 years ago and the last ice melted away about 13,000 years ago. A great glacier moved across the area from west to east, moulding the landscape by processes of erosion and deposition. The most distinctive features produced by the last ice sheet were the drumlins. These streamlined hills dominate the landscape of the lower parts of the Clyde Basin. They are a quarter to half a mile in length, 50 to 100 feet high, oval in plan shape, and usually consist of boulder clay or sand and gravel. There are some 800 drumlins in the Greater Glasgow area. After the glaciers melted away, the natural vegetation of the area would have been mixed deciduous woodland of oak, hazel, elm and birch. Little of this natural woodland survived the expansion of agriculture and industry. The deciduous trees which characterise so many parkland golf courses are the product of landscaping in the eighteenth and nineteenth centuries around large houses. Even the woodlands on the higher grounds were removed to permit grazing. Therefore, much of the present landscape of west central Scotland reflects the changing patterns of land use which occurred during the agricultural revolution of the eighteenth and early nineteenth centuries and the industrial development of the nineteenth and twentieth centuries.

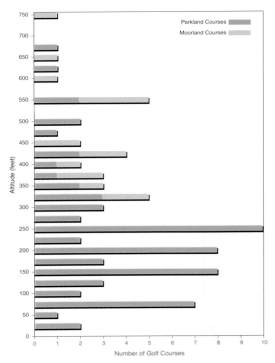

FIG. 6.2 *Number of parkland and moorland courses at various altitudes in West Central Scotland.*

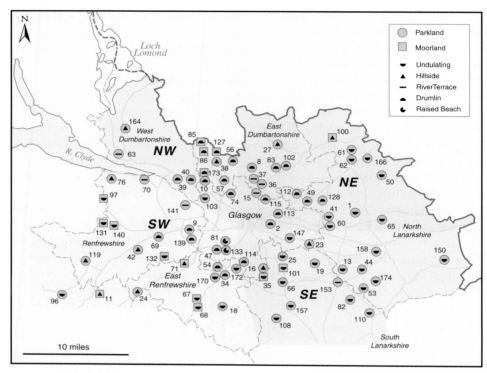

FIG. 6.3 *The landforms and vegetation of golf courses in Greater Glasgow.*

There is a certain degree of altitudinal zonation in the landscape of the Greater Glasgow sub-region. Below 100 feet the impact of glacial and fluvioglacial sedimentation, along with the occurrence of marine clays associated with the high stand of relative sea level about 13,000 years ago, produced relatively flat land. Between 100 and 300 feet above sea level, large numbers of drumlins produce a landscape which is strongly stream-lined and dominated by short steep slopes. Above 400 feet, steep slopes are associated with the outcrops of volcanic rocks while undulating plateaus have developed on the Carboniferous sediments (limestones, sandstone, coals).

The golf courses of the Greater Glasgow sub-region strongly reflect these varia-tions in altitude (Fig. 6.2). Only ten golf courses are at altitudes of less than 100 feet. These are all parkland courses built on either river terraces or raised marine clays around the upper Firth of Clyde in the vicinity of Renfrew, Paisley and Erskine. Twenty-eight courses are between 100 and 300 feet above sea level and most of these are built on the drumlins and associated glacial and fluvioglacial deposits. The drumlin land-scape produces an interesting variety of slopes in a relatively small area upon which the golf course designer can exercise his talents. There are 32 courses above 300 feet, of which 15 are classed as moorland courses. All of the moorland courses are sited on outcrops of volcanic lava and they provide a most distinctive golfing environment. Six of the courses are between 500 and 750 feet above sea level and they often provide the golfer with spectacular views while at the same time exposing him to the full fury of wind and rain.

Because of the large number of golf courses in the Greater Glasgow sub-region it is further sub-divided into four quadrants (Fig. 6.3)—north-west, north-east, south-east and south-west.

NORTH-WEST GREATER GLASGOW

There are 15 golf courses (two of nine holes) on the north-west side of Glasgow (Fig. 6.3). They range from Killermont (B74), the present home of the 200-year-old Glasgow Golf Club, to Knightswood (B103), a basic 9-hole municipal course. The Glasgow Golf Club began its life on Glasgow Green alongside the River Clyde in the eighteenth century. It moved to Queens Park in 1870, to Alexandra Park in 1874 and to Blackhill in 1895 before occupying its present site at Killermont in 1904. Such movements are typical of golf clubs situated in a rapidly expanding city. The present Hilton Park Golf Club (B85, 86) was originally the Glasgow North Western Golf Club, whose golf course was situated in the Ruchill district, but which was forced to give up its course because the ground was acquired by Glasgow Corporation for the purpose of building houses. At the same time the Bankhead Golf Club, whose course was at Scotstounhill, also had its ground bought by Glasgow Corporation for housing schemes. The officials of both clubs met and decided to purchase a large tract of hill land some nine miles north of the city. James Braid was commissioned to design two courses and they were opened in 1928. The migration of clubs and courses from city centre to suburban or rural sites, as a result of pressure on land for uses other than golf, has produced some fine clubs and courses. The two courses at Hilton Park command fine views across the city to the south as well as to the Highlands in the north. Since the highest part of the course is over 500 feet, the golfer can experience the full impact of a south-westerly gale.

Eleven of the 15 courses to the north-west of Glasgow have been built on drumlins (Fig. 6.4). They fall into two distinct groups. The group of four courses (Clober—B38; Milngavie—B127; Hilton Park—B85, 86) in the valley of the Allander Water to the north of Milngavie occur on drumlins which were formed by glacier ice which moved from north-west to south-east through a gap in the Kilpatrick Hills. Because of their high altitude (350—500 feet), the Milngavie and Hilton Park courses have a mixture of moorland and parkland, while the Clober course is parkland. The seven other drumlin courses (B40, 39, 10, 173, 56, 57 and 74) are all part of the main Glasgow drumlin field which has a general west to east alignment (Fig. 6.4). Although the main landform type upon which these seven courses are built produces a certain degree of similarity between the courses, they also have certain distinctive characteristics. Windy Hill (B173) is a moorland course perched high on a hillside (over 400 feet) and lives up to its name with

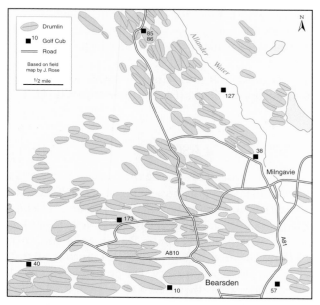

FIG. 6.4 *The drumlins and golf clubs of north-west Glasgow.*

Ph. 6.2 *Clydebank municipal course.*

strong westerly winds funnelling up the Firth of Clyde. The public course at Dalmuir-Clydebank Overton (B40) is built on two large drumlins some 75 feet high, and although the course is a parkland area (Ph. 6.2) it is surrounded by high-rise flats. The Clydebank and District course (B39) is at a higher altitude (250 feet) and is mainly built along the flanks of one long, narrow drumlin which has a distinctive west-east crest. The Bearsden (B10) and Douglas Park (B57) courses are similar in that they are both parkland courses built on west-east aligned drumlins with the Roman Wall (Antonine Wall) in close proximity. The newest course in this area, opened in 1978, is at Dougalston (B56). Although built across several west-east aligned drumlins, the drumlinoid aspect of the course is less apparent because many of the fairways have been cut through woodland. This is the only course in the Greater Glasgow area which is dominated by tree-lined fairways. Only the northern part of the fine course of the Glasgow Golf Club at Killermont is built on drumlins. Three-quarters of this beautiful parkland course to the west and south of the clubhouse is built on gravel terraces alongside the River Kelvin.

Only three courses on the north-west side of Glasgow are not on drumlins. The 9-hole municipal course at Knightswood (B103) is built on raised-marine sediments (an old raised beach) and is fairly flat. Similarly the flat, parkland course at Dumbarton (B63) is built across a river terrace on the floor of the Vale of Leven. The course at Alexandria (B164) is built on a hillside with fine views to the north.

The 15 courses on the north-west side of Glasgow mainly provide golf in urban or suburban environments. Even those courses beyond the built-up area (B127, 85, 86, 173) are dominated by views across the city. Only amidst the tree-lined fairways of Dougalston or on the parkland of Killermont is the presence of the city less pervasive. Even these two courses have the misfortune to be located below the main flight-path to Glasgow Airport.

NORTH-EAST GREATER GLASGOW

The 22 courses in this sub-region fall into three groups (Fig. 6.3): the courses on the higher ground to the north (at the foot of the Campsie Hills) and east; the drumlinoid courses; the courses in the Kelvin Valley.

Two courses (B27 and B100) have been built on the lower slopes of the south-facing escarpment of the Campsie Hills. They are on the edge of moorland, although the Campsie Course at Lennoxtown has a parkland character. The 'new town' of Cumbernauld, which was established in 1957, has seen the development of two new golf facilities and the transformation of a third (Dullatur Golf Club). In 1975 a municipal course was opened at Palacerigg. It is a parkland course at an altitude of 500 feet to the east of the town. To the northwest of the town the Westerwood Hotel, with a range of leisure facilities, was developed in the late 1980s. Seve Ballesteros worked with Dave Thomas on the design of an 18-hole championship course of 6,600 yards. The site was a difficult one, with heavy clay soils and incorporating an old quarry. The high altitude (400 feet), exposure, heavy

Ph. 6.3 *Westerwood, Cumbernauld.*

soils and length of the course did not make Westerwood an attractive venue for middle and high handicap players (Ph. 6.3). The facility went into receivership in 1999 and was subsequently purchased by the Morton Hotel Group.

Dullatur Golf Club was established in 1896 and for many years served the residents of the area well. It is located on the edge of Cumbernauld, and as the new town expanded Dullatur's waiting list for membership lengthened. In 1997 the club sold off a part of its property for housing development and was thus able to add a second 18-hole golf course and a large new clubhouse.

The industrial area of Coatbridge and Airdrie has four courses (B60, 41, 1 and 65). The Airdrie Club was established in 1871. The Coatbridge Townhead course, on the other hand, is a municipal course opened in 1970.

There are nine courses built on drumlins in this sub-region (B128, 49, 112, 115, 113, 2, 102, 83, and 8). Three of them are municipal courses: Alexandra Park (B2), Letham Hill (B113) and Little Hill (B115). All these courses are within the City of Glasgow and therefore surrounded by built-up areas. In considerable contrast are the fine parkland courses at Crow Wood (B49) and Balmore (B8). The most distinctive drumlin course is at Mount Ellen, where the drumlin form is easily visible. The course at Lenzie (B112) is built over a series of three large drumlins, each with a strong west to east alignment. The courses at Kirkintilloch and Hayston are built on a combination of drumlins and associated fluvioglacial sands and gravels. The drumlin forms are quite subdued and at least parts of these courses have been modified as a result of the removal of sand and gravel prior to their construction.

There are three courses (B15, 36, 37) in the Kelvin Valley, near Bishopbriggs, which owe their character to the glacial and postglacial history of this valley. Prior to the last glaciation this valley was much deeper than it is at present. A glacier moved up the valley from west to east and deposited large quantities of debris on the valley floor. The west-ward flowing River Kelvin has since cut into these gravel deposits and produced flat-topped river terraces upon which the Bishopbriggs course (B15) and the two courses of the Cawder Golf Club have been built. The Cawder and Keir courses are in fine parkland, but several of the holes are largely man-made on ground reclaimed after the commercial exploitation of sand and gravel.

While the north-east side of Glasgow cannot claim to have any courses of great distinction, there is much variety amidst the relatively large number of courses in this essentially suburban area.

SOUTH-EAST GREATER GLASGOW

The 19 golf courses (Fig. 6.3) in this sub-region (of which four are 9-hole courses) either occur in the industrialised Clyde Valley or on the high (500–600 feet) plateau which rises above the valley to the south-west. Six of the courses are municipal—Sandyhills (B129) and Linn Park (B114) in Glasgow, Torrance House (B5157 and Langlands B108) in East Kilbride, Strathclyde Country Park (B153) in Hamilton and Larkhall (B110). All but two of the courses are classed as parkland courses, although most of them are dominated by the urban environment which surrounds them. During the past 20 years the section of the Clyde Valley between Rutherglen and Wishaw has been transformed by the removal of much of the industrial blight which characterised this area following the decline of numerous heavy industries. The south-eastern urban boundary of the City of Glasgow is often remarkably sharp, the golf course at Blairbeth (B16) being bounded on the north by the housing estate of Castlemilk and on the south side by the wooded slopes of Cathkin Braes. The municipal course at Linn Park (B114), is built on drumlins, a small oasis of green amidst the urban landscape of Glasgow's South Side. A mere two miles to the south-east, the fine course of Cathkin Braes Golf Club (C35) sits high on the lava plateau at an altitude of 650 feet in a moorland environment. The Kirkhill Course (B101) at Cambuslang is another moorland course on the plateau.

With the exception of the 9-hole course at Calderbraes (B23), which is a hillside course, and the 9-hole course at Strathclyde Country Park (B153), which is built on river terraces, all the other courses in the Clyde Valley are undulating parkland. In terms of quality, most of them are undistinguished, although the Riccarton Course at Hamilton (B82), designed by James Braid, is both a well-kept and a challenging course.

The three courses near the New Town of East Kilbride are all located on the plateau surface at between 500 and 700 feet. The East Kilbride Club has played at Nerston (B66) since 1900 and long pre-dates the New Town development. Two municipal courses—Torrance House (B157) and Langlands (B75)—followed the expansion of the population in this area associated with the New Town development. The Langlands course was opened in 1983.

Two new commercial golf facilities have been developed near Motherwell. In 1998 the Dalziel Park Golf and Country Club was opened with a 9-hole parkland course (2,754 yards). A further nine holes are under construction and the facility includes a 15-bay driving range. Three miles northeast of Motherwell, at Newhouse, a major development is in progress which will include a hotel and conference centre and an 18-hole golf course. The facility is to be named Torrance Park in honour of Sam Torrance, who has been acting as an advisor to the project.

Apart from the two courses on the Cathkin Braes (Blairbeth and Cathkin Braes Golf Clubs), Torrance House, East Kilbride, Bothwell Castle and Hamilton Riccarton, the courses to the south-east of Glasgow are neither very attractive nor of high quality. This sub-region does not have the variety of golfing landscapes which occurs in the other three Glasgow sub-regions.

SOUTH-WEST GREATER GLASGOW

It is not surprising that the south-west quadrant of Greater Glasgow has the largest number of golf courses. The 26 courses are largely a response to the high quality of the suburban housing of the area, along with the good communications network linking much of Renfrewshire with the centre of Glasgow.

The golf courses of this sub-region are of four types (Fig. 6.3, Fig. 6.5).

1. Those built mainly on river terraces or raised marine sediments: Erskine (B70), Haggs Castle (B81), Pollok (B133) and Renfrew (B141).

2. Those built mainly on drumlins: Cathcart Castle (B34), Cowglen (B47), Deaconsbank (B54), Elderslie (B69), Barshaw (B9), Ralston (B139).

3. Those built on hillsides or undulating land but with strong parkland characteristics: Caldwell (B24), Cochrane Castle (B42), Kilbirnie (B96), Gleddoch Golf and Country Club (B76), Lochwinnoch (B119), Whitecraigs (B170), Williamwood (B172).

4. Those built at relatively high altitude (400–600 feet) on the plateau basalts and which have a distinctive 'craggy' appearance and a dominantly moorland vegetation: Fereneze (B71), Beith (B11), Old Ranfurly (B131), Ranfurly Castle (B140), Bonnyton (B18), East Renfrewshire (B67), Eastwood (B68), Kilmacolm (B97), Paisley-Braehead (B132).

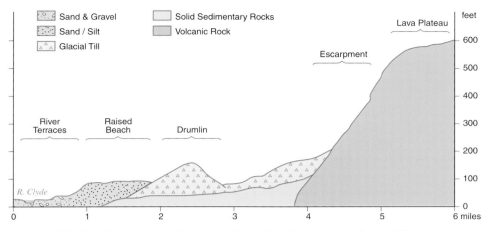

FIG. 6.5 *Cross-section of typical rocks and landforms in south-west Glasgow.*

In each of the above four types there are respectively four, six, seven and nine courses. Although the main contrast is between the parkland courses of types 1, 2 and 3, and the moorland landscapes of type 4, there is considerable variety within each type.

Four courses close to the River Clyde owe their character to the changing sea levels which affected this area after the last glaciers wasted away (see Chapter 3). A relatively high stand of sea level about 13,000 years ago allowed the deposition of marine clays in the areas around Renfrew, Paisley and Pollok, and these clays now underlie relatively flat land up to an altitude of about 100 feet above present sea level. In many locations the flat 'carse' lands (raised estuarine mud flats) lap against the relatively steep slopes of drumlins. Two fine golf courses were built on the relatively flat land between drumlin hills at Pollok (B133) and Haggs Castle (B169). The fine mature parkland of the Pollok estate provides a most attractive setting for a good golf course of 6,295 yards. Nearby are the attractions of Pollok House itself and the now world-famous Burrell Museum. The Haggs Castle course is a championship course (6,464 yards), which for several years hosted the PGA European Tour's Glasgow Open Championship.

As the River Clyde adjusted itself to the changing sea levels following the last glaciation, it cut terraces into the glacial, fluvioglacial and marine sediments which had choked its course to the sea. Two parkland golf courses have been developed on the Clyde terraces at Renfrew (B141) and Bishopton (B70). Both courses are of high quality.

The six courses built on drumlins in this quadrant (B34, 47, 54, 69, 9, 139) reflect the fact that the drumlins to the south-west of Glasgow tend to be larger but less numerous than those on the north side of the city and they are often surrounded by relatively flat land underlain by marine clays. The drumlin forms are often modified by the presence of outcrops of solid rock, but most of them have a strong north-west to south-east orientation. All of the golf courses built on drumlins are relatively short (circa 6,000 yards). The shortest course (4,800 yards) is that at Deaconsbank (B54). The most attractive course in this group is that of Cathcart Castle Golf Club (B34).

In the heart of south-side suburbia are located two fine parkland courses, Williamwood (B172) and Whitecraigs (B170), which are well-maintained and provide some interesting golf. They were designed respectively by James Braid and William Fernie, and opened during the first decade of the nineteenth century. The course at Cochrane Castle, Johnstone (B42), is of a similar type. The most recent golfing development in this sub-region took place at Langbank with the opening of the Gleddoch Golf and Country Club (B76) in 1974. It is a parkland course (6,375 yards) designed by J. Hamilton Stutt and built on a hillside with views across the Firth of Clyde.

There are six moorland courses in this sub-region, all of which are located on the Clyde plateau basalts (lavas) at altitudes of between 400 and 600 feet. All of these courses are characterised by their craggy outcrops and rough of heather and gorse. The course at Bonnyton (B18) and the two courses at Newton Mearns—East Renfrewshire (B67) and Eastwood (B68), are just beyond the suburban fringe of Glasgow and are of good quality. The two courses on the high lava plateau to the south of Paisley (Braehead B132 and Fereneze B71) provide spectacular views to the north-east while exposing the golfer to the full impact of inclement weather. There are two high-quality moorland courses at Bridge of Weir (B131 and 140) and another at Kilmacolm (B97). All of these moorland courses provide a distinctive golfing challenge, where weather conditions are of prime concern.

THE UPPER FIRTH OF CLYDE

The pattern of the coastline in the Upper Firth, between the Kyles of Bute in the west and Helensburgh and Greenock in the east, provides a very distinctive environment (Fig. 6.6). Only occasionally are the fine views obtainable from many of the golf courses spoilt by industrial or urban development. The West Kyle, Loch Riddon, the East Kyle, Loch Striven, the Holy Loch, Loch Long and Gare Loch are glacially-scoured valleys which have been invaded by the sea. Loch Lomond is also a glacially-scoured valley, which some 5,000 years ago was a marine inlet and part of the Firth of Clyde. Along the shores of these sea lochs the ground rises rapidly to altitudes of between 800 and 2,000 feet. To the south of Port Glasgow, Greenock and Gourock, the plateau lavas provide high moorlands (600–900 feet) and this high ground is continued to the coast between Skelmorlie and West Kilbride. Even the island of Bute attains altitudes between 600 and 900 feet. While the industrial significance of Greenock and Port Glasgow as ports and famous centres of ship-building are a part of the story of the past industrial prosperity of West Central Scotland, the rest of the Upper Firth has traditionally been a place of recreation. The development of steamer services as extensions of the rail network during the second half of the nineteenth century led to the development of places such as Dunoon, Kilcreggan and Rothesay. Summer residences and holidays 'doon the water' in turn led to the opening of numerous golf courses between 1890 and 1910.

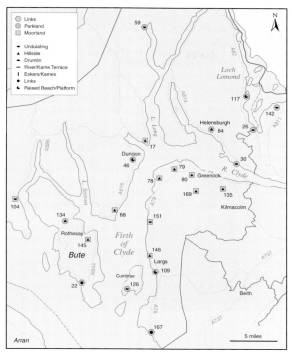

FIG. 6.6 *The landforms and vegetation of golf courses in the upper Firth of Clyde.*

There are 22 golf courses (Fig. 6.6) in this sub-region—seven of nine holes, one of 13 holes and 14 of 18 holes. The majority of the courses (12) are of a moorland character, but seven are parkland (B26, 30, 46, 59, 84, 117, 142) and three are links courses (B109, 176, 22). None are of championship standard, few are of high quality, but most of the courses are interesting and are surrounded by fine scenery.

All of the 12 moorland courses stand on relatively high ground (300–500 feet). The four courses at Port Glasgow (B126), Greenock (B79, 169) and Gourock (B78) are all built on the Clyde Plateau lavas and therefore have a rather craggy appearance. The views northwards from these courses towards the Highlands can be spectacular (Ph. 6.4). The 18-hole course at Skelmorlie (B151) has a moorland character with excellent views across to Bute and Arran. The course at Routenburn (B146) was designed by James Braid and is located along the hillside overlooking the Firth of Clyde. Some of the holes on this course have parkland characteristics. The two moorland courses on Bute, Port Bannantyne (B118) and Rothesay (B125) each have distinctive attributes. The Port Bannantyne course has 13 holes, so that holes one to five are played twice to make up an 18-hole round. While a round at the Rothesay Golf Course (B145) involves some stiff climbs, golfers are repaid by fine views and some very interesting golf. Each of

Ph. 6.4 *Gourock.*

the moorland courses at Tighnabruich (B104), Innellan (B88) and Blairmore and Strone (B17) are of nine holes and all are noted for their views while providing good 'holiday golf'.

The three parkland courses at Cardross (B30), Helensburgh (B84) and Dunoon (B46) are all of good quality and each has distinctive features. The Cardross course is in fine parkland with the lower holes crossing the raised beaches which occur on the north side of the Clyde Estuary. The inland part of the course is built across drumlins and there are famous downhill drives from the 7th and 18th tees. The Helensburgh course, designed by Tom Morris in 1893, is of good quality but difficult to classify, in that parts of it have a parkland aspect while other parts are moorland in character. From the higher parts of the course the Firth of Clyde can be seen to the south and Loch Lomond and the High-lands can be seen to the north.

The Cowal Golf Club at Dunoon (B46) plays on a course designed by James Braid and opened in 1890. Some of the holes cross raised-beach deposits and have an affinity with links land, while other holes have a more inland/parkland character.

The three courses around the shores of Loch Lomond are included in this section because in the recent geological past (i.e. since the last Ice Age ended 10,000 years ago) the Loch Lomond basin was, for two periods, invaded by the sea and the landforms and deposits produced during these marine incursions underlie the three golf courses. The 9-hole course at Ross Priory (B142) is attached to the University of Strathclyde staff club,

Ph. 6.5 *Loch Lomond.*

while the 9-hole course at the Cameron House Hotel (B26) is only available to hotel residents.

The new golf course on the west bank of Loch Lomond at Luss (B117) was designed by Tom Weiskopf and Jay Morrish (Ph. 6.5). Work commenced in 1990, but the initial developer had to place the project in administration. The project was completed and operated by the Cairns Hotel group, a wholly-owned subsidiary of the Bank of Scotland. The facility was subsequently purchased by Mr Lyle Anderson of Arizona. While the site consists of very fine parkland, the underlying geology is dense marine clays which, combined with high annual precipitation totals (in excess of 60 inches per year), did not provide an ideal location for a golf development. However, an excellent design and expensive engineering work has produced a first-class championship golf course which has rapidly obtained international recognition through professional tour championship events, held usually during the week prior to the Open Championship, and hosting the Solheim Cup in 2000. The facility is operated as an exclusive members club and plays little part in either domestic amateur golf or in the golf tourism industry. The facility is not available to casual visitors.

There are only three strictly coastal courses in the sub-region, even though nearly all the other courses are close to the sea. Even the course at Largs (B109) is difficult to classify, because although it is at a low altitude and is built across raised-beach sands and gravels and backed by a steep, wooded cliff, much of the course is of a parkland character.

There is a small, 9-hole links course at Kingarth (B22) on the west side of Bute. It has small, fenced greens and is in a delightfully isolated position. The West Kilbride Golf Club (B167) plays over true links land at Seamill and the course can be regarded as the northern outpost of the string of links courses that are to be found along the Ayrshire coast between Irvine and Ayr.

AYRSHIRE

The old county name of Ayrshire is still used in golfing circles. Although not possessing a well-documented golfing history prior to 1851 (the founding of the Prestwick Club) to match the history of golf in East Lothian or Fife, the golf courses of Ayrshire have made and continue to make very significant contributions to Scottish golf. The 35 golf courses in this sub-region (Fig. 6.7) fall clearly into two groups—the coastal courses and the inland courses (B3, 4, 7, 11, 21, 24, 28, 55, 96, 120, 125, 130). The 22 coastal courses occur along a stretch of coastline only 30 miles long, and over one stretch of 12 miles between Irvine and Prestwick there are 14 links courses. A good drive from the extremities of one course will usually reach the adjacent golfing ground! No other county can claim to contain three venues which have been used for the Open Championship—Prestwick, where the Championship began in 1860 and was played for on 24 occasions,

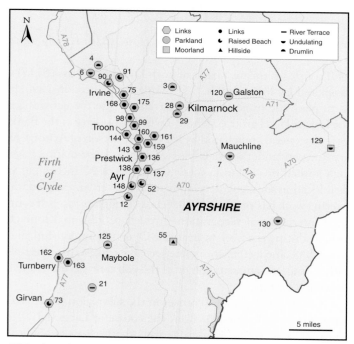

FIG. 6.7 The landforms and vegetation of golf courses in Ayrshire.

Troon and Turnberry. Although these championship venues naturally bring fame and fortune to the area, the 32 other courses offer a variety of golf to both locals and visitors. More golf is probably played in Troon on the five courses (three of the courses being municipal) than in any other town in Scotland—with the possible exception of St Andrews. In fact there are 12 municipal courses in the sub-region and it is probably easier to get a game of golf within a 20-mile radius of Prestwick than it is anywhere else in Britain.

Coastal Courses

The character and development of golf courses along the Ayrshire coast from Irvine in the north to Girvan in the south are the product of changing sea levels and the coming of the railway (Fig. 6.8). The broad bay between Ardrossan and the Heads of Ayr and the low-level coastal platforms near Turnberry and Girvan, have been affected by major changes in sea level during the past 8,000 years (see Chapter 3). Some 6,000 years ago sea level stood between 25 and 35 feet higher than at present, and as the sea fell to its present level, large areas of raised beach sands and gravels were left high and dry. Along much of the coastline strong winds drove the sand into dune ridges and mounds. At

FIG. 6.8 *The landforms of the golf courses between Ayr and Irvine.*

Ph. 6.6 *Prestwick.*

some locations, golf courses have been built on relatively flat spreads of gravel and sand, while in other places these raised beaches have been covered by blown sand and classic links and sand dunes have developed.

There is a remarkable concentration of links courses between Irvine and Prestwick. The urban development of this coastline was very much associated with the building of the railway in the mid-nineteenth century, thus linking it with Glasgow. Although relatively late starters compared with the links land of East Lothian and Fife, the Ayrshire links were to play a significant part in the development of golf in Scotland. While the links land between Irvine and Troon is of high quality and there are some fine views to the west, the industrial and urban development in this area detracts somewhat from the quality of the golfing environment.

The Prestwick Golf Club (1851) plays over what is now known as the Old Prestwick Golf Course (B136). This was the original home of the Open Championship (1860) and a stone cairn marks where the first tee used to be. From that tee, Young Tom Morris took three shots to cover 578 yards, holing out on what is now the 16th green, in one of his Championship rounds. It is interesting that the first golf course on the Ayrshire coast should be located on one of the most varied pieces of links land along this coastline (Fig. 6.8). A course of some 6,668 yards has been laid out between a high coastal dune ridge some 30 feet high and the railway. The ground varies between flat links, undulating links and hummocky dunes (Ph. 6.6). The Prestwick St Nicholas course (B138), half a mile to the south, is built over similar terrain; a fine challenging course, it was used for qualifying rounds prior to the 1982 Open Championship at Royal Troon. The third course at Prestwick, Prestwick St Cuthbert (B137), is very flat, being built on a raised beach with a thin covering of blown sand.

The Old Prestwick and Royal Troon courses are virtually continuous. In the 1920s, the ninth green at Troon was only a short distance from the Prestwick course; members of both clubs would play from Troon to Prestwick in the morning and, having had lunch at the splendid Prestwick clubhouse, would play back to Troon in the afternoon. The Old Course (B143) at Troon (Ph. 6.7) started as a five hole course in 1878. By 1883 the course had been extended to 12 holes and to 18 holes by 1886. The course is a combination of smooth undulating links on the landward side of a single dune ridge which merges into a series of dune ridges (15–30 feet high), towards the Pow Burn at the southern end of the course and a complex of hummocky dunes and undulating links in the south-east corner of the course. There are excellent views across the Firth of Clyde towards Goat Fell but the inland views are far less attractive. The Open Championship was first played here in 1923, and this course has the longest par five (577 yards, 6th hole) and the shortest par three (126 yards, 8th hole) on the Championship circuit. In the 1973 Open, Gene Sarazen had a hole-in-one on the 8th hole (the Postage Stamp) which was shown on television. The Royal Troon Club has a second course, the Portland (B144), which is a less stiff test of golf. It is built across undulating and flat links. There are also three

Ph. 6.7 *Royal Troon.*

municipal courses in Troon: Lochgreen (B159), Darley (B160), and Fullarton (B161). The Lochgreen course is the longest (6,765 yards, SSS 72) and has been used as an Open Championship qualifying course. The other courses are relatively flat and are less challenging.

On the northern edge of the town of Troon is the delightful links course of the Kilmarnock (Barassie) Golf Club (B98, 99). This course was built by Kilmarnock merchants in 1877 and has many similarities with Old Prestwick. It is maintained to a high standard and has been used for qualifying rounds of the Open Championship. The club has recently added a 9-hole course.

The Barassie course is the most southerly of three courses which occupy a stretch of links land around Irvine Bay. A series of dune ridges (15–20 feet high) run parallel to the shore of the bay for two and a half miles and they merge into smooth links which in turn merge landward into a flat raised beach covered with wind-blown sand. The Western Gailes Clubhouse (B168) stands on a terrace (the raised beach) overlooking the links where fairways are often separated by marram or heather covered dune ridges (Ph. 6.8). The course has no ladies' tees, there being no lady members. The course was built for Glasgow merchants, beside the railway line to Glasgow, and it is a fine example of a true links course. The club was host to the Curtis Cup in 1974, and thus allowed women into the clubhouse for the first time. Immediately to the north-east of the Western Gailes course is the Glasgow Gailes course (B75) of the Glasgow Golf Club. Somewhat less

Ph. 6.8 *Western Gailes.*

Ph. 6.9 *Turnberry.*

attractive than its neighbour, it is a good-quality course used by the members of the Glasgow Club based in the heart of Glasgow at Killermont. An 18-hole, 7,000 yard course is under construction at Southern Gailes. The architect is Kyle Philips and the course should be open for play in 2002.

The two courses at Irvine, Bogside (B90) and Ravenspark (B91), are on rather flat terrain consisting of raised-beach deposits covered with blown sand. The Ravenspark course is a municipal course.

The three courses in Ayr are all municipal courses and although they are near the coast and have been built on raised-beach deposits, they are all parkland courses. The mature deciduous parkland of Belleisle Park was utilised by James Braid to lay out the Belleisle (B12) and Seafield (B148) courses. The Ayr Belleisle Course has been described as the best public inland course in Scotland. It has hosted the British Ladies and the Coca-Cola championships, and in 1979 was a qualifying course for the European Open. The adjacent Seafield Course and the Dalmelling Course are both shorter parkland courses, but with green fees of less than £15 (in 1999), are pleasant alternatives to some of the more famous courses of this area.

Undoubtedly one of the most famous golf complexes in Scotland is to be found at Turnberry on the Ayrshire coast (Ph. 6.9). A first class hotel and two high quality courses, the Ailsa (B162) and the Kintyre (B163), formerly the Arran, in a magnificent scenic setting, place Turnberry high on the list of Scotland's golfing centres. Both courses are on

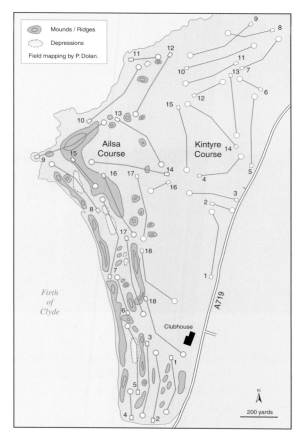

FIG. 6.9 *The landforms of the Turnberry golf courses.*

links land, but the championship course (the Ailsa) is partly built among the high dune ridges which fringe the bay. The Kintyre Course was less spectacular and is located on a gently undulating raised-beach surface with a thin covering of blown-sand. However, this course has been redesigned by Donald Steel as part of a £1.1 million project involving seven new holes. The new Kintyre Course is 6,785 yards (par 72) and is part of a major £20 million development programme by the new owners, Starwood Hotels and Resorts, which purchased Turnberry from a Japanese company in 1998. The Colin Montgomerie Links Golf Academy opened in April 2000 and the new Kintyre Course in 2001.

The original course at Turnberry was designed by Willie Fernie, and the Turnberry Golf Club was founded in 1902. The Arran Course was opened in 1912. The development of Turnberry by the Glasgow and South-Western Railway Company not only required the building of a first-class hotel, but also the construction of an expensive railway between Ayr and Girvan. Both the hotel and railway were opened in 1906.

Between 1920 and 1939, the rich and famous would travel to Turnberry by train and enter the hotel by a covered way leading from the station into the entrance lounge. Although not facing the courses and the sea, the railway entrance was known as the front of the hotel and remains so today, even though the station and line have long been closed.

During the First World War, Turnberry was used as a training station for pilots of the Royal Flying Corps and other Commonwealth Flying Units, and the hotel was converted to an Officers' Mess. The damage done to the golf courses between 1914 and 1918 was very limited compared to the impact of the construction of an aerodome for RAF Coastal Command during the Second World War. The construction of concrete runways, hangars and numerous buildings virtually destroyed much of the golf courses apart from the coastal dune ridges. The hotel was used as a hospital. At a meeting in the hotel in 1946 the directors concluded that Turnberry was finished as a golfing centre. However, Frank Hole, Chairman of British Transport Hotels, who then owned the complex, convinced them that, by using the compensation due from the War Office, the rehabilitation of the golf courses and hotel was possible. Mackenzie Ross was asked to design the layout and Suttons of Reading were awarded the contract. After demolition of runways and buildings, they moved vast quantities of sand, gravel and topsoil. Most of the Ailsa course was then completely re-turfed and was reopened in 1951. This course is now ranked in the top ten of the best 50 British courses by *Golf World* and has hosted every major championship except the Ryder Cup. It was used for the Open Championship for the first time in 1977 when the dramatic final hole battle between Nicklaus and Watson took place.

The Ailsa Course is 6,976 yards of windswept links land (Fig. 6.9). The course is dominated by a series of dune ridges which run parallel to the present shoreline and which reach heights of between 15 and 30 feet above the intervening hollows. Some of the fairways and greens are located in the inter-dune hollows and therefore have some protection from onshore winds. Even such locations can suffer from a funnelling of wind, particularly when winds are blowing from the north or south. Although the Ailsa course has essentially a north-south alignment, there are five holes transverse to this alignment and therefore the golfer has to face up to a variety of wind directions during any round of golf. As on all great links courses, weather plays an important part in determining its difficulty.

The southern outpost of the Ayrshire coastal courses is at Girvan (B60). It is a municipal course which has two distinct parts. Eight holes are located on a raised-marine platform covered with sand and these holes provide good links golf. Ten holes are on the flood plain adjacent to the River Girvan which crosses the course and provides a challenge at the 15th hole where a carry of 170 yards is required off the tee.

Inland Courses

The twelve inland courses in Ayrshire are not particularly attractive or challenging, with four exceptions. The municipal courses at Kilmarnock (Annanhill, B3, and Caprington,

B28) provide good parkland golf, and the course of the Loudon Gowf Club at Galston (B120) is in an attractive location along a series of river terraces. At Dailly, some six miles southeast of Turnberry, a commercial 18-hole golf facility, Brunston Castle (B21), was opened in 1992. The course, of 6,681 yards (par 73), was designed by Donald Steel and is in open parkland. This facility encountered financial problems and went into receivership, but has recently been purchased by a group of local businessmen.

SOUTH LANARKSHIRE

The twelve courses in this sub-region (Fig. 6.10) have one thing in common—they are all over 500 feet above sea level and five of them are above 750 feet. One might expect that most of these courses would have a moorland character, but this is not the case. The only course classed as moorland is that at Leadhills (B111), which is Scotland's highest golf course at 1,200 feet above sea level. The relatively high altitude of all the Lanarkshire courses means that they tend to receive above average rainfall and experience more snow and frost. The growing season is shorter and they are therefore in good condition for shorter periods than courses at lower altitudes or on the coast.

The courses at Leadhills (B111) and Douglas Water (B58) are both of nine holes. There are reasonable quality parkland courses at Strathaven (B152), Lesmahagow (B87),

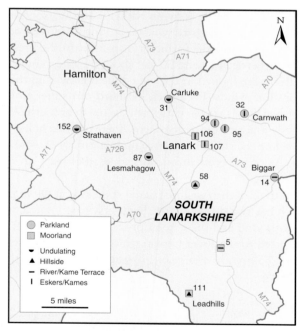

FIG. 6.10 *The landforms and vegetation of golf courses in South Lanark.*

Carluke (B31) and Biggar (B14). The course at Biggar is a municipal course laid out on the flat-floored valley of the Biggar Gap.

The courses at Carnwath (B32), Mouse Valley (Kames CC, B94) and Lanark are built on sand and gravel laid down by the meltwaters of the last ice sheet. The Lanark Club was founded in 1851, which makes it one of the oldest clubs in the West of Scotland. The history of the club has been written by A. D. Robertson *(The Story of Lanark Golf Club 1851–1951)* and it makes interesting reading. The first course used by the club consisted of six holes on Lanark Moor. The course was reduced to five holes in 1853, extended to ten holes in 1857, to 13 holes in 1869, to 14 holes in 1885 and to 18 holes in 1897. The final layout was arranged by Tom Morris who received £3.10s. for his services. Ben Sayers devised a new layout in 1909 and further modifications were made by James Braid in 1926–7. The 1st and 18th holes have remained unchanged since 1851. Such additions and modifications to golf courses are probably typical of all nineteenth century Scottish golf courses, but few are as well-documented as the development of Lanark.

Lanark golf course is built on an area of undulating fluvioglacial sand and gravel. The hollows and undulations (Fig. 6.11) are the product of the melting out of blocks of glacier ice buried beneath the sand and gravel spread. This type of landscape is the nearest inland equivalent to coastal links land. It is well-drained and tends to support good short grassland or moorland vegetation. In the early days the grass was kept short

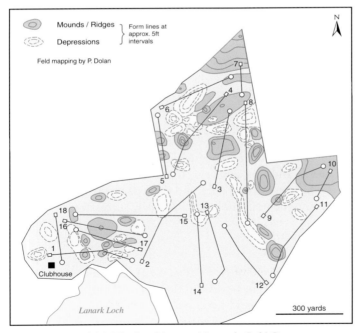

FIG. 6.11 *The landforms of Lanark Golf Course.*

by the burghers' cows under the charge of a hind or cowherd. The only implement used on the course until 1880 was a scythe. After that date, mowers were acquired and a roller was bought in 1882. The first horse-drawn mower was purchased in 1897. Since the altitude of the course is some 600 feet above sea level, frosts can occur at any time of the year. Play can be interrupted both by frost, snow lying (an average of 28 days per year) and by periods of heavy rain. The course consists of a series of low mounds which rise some ten to 20 feet above the intervening hollows. The northern part of the course (holes three to eight) crosses the most complicated topography. With the exception of the greens which are generally located on elevated plateau areas, both mounds and hollows have been used for fairway and rough areas. Much of the course itself is characterised by moorland vegetation—coarse grasses, heather and whin. However, the surrounding stands of coniferous and deciduous trees tend to give the general landscape a parkland appearance. This is a good quality inland golf course maintained to a high standard.

Just a few miles east of Lanark is the Carnwath Golf Club (B32). The course is built mainly over a series of mounds (kames) and hollows underlain by sand and gravel. The course designer, Henry McKenzie, used the mounds (which rise to 10 to 50 feet) for rough, and the hollows for fairways and greens, although some greens and tees are located on a large mound (9th, 12th and 15th tees and 8th green). The deciduous and coniferous trees on the course introduce a parkland landscape but there are also strong moorland characteristics. Although the course is only 5,955 yards long it is a most interesting course and well worth a visit.

One of the first commercial 'pay and play' golf facilities in Scotland was opened in 1994 at Mouse Valley, three miles north-east of Lanark. The Kames Golf and Country Club (B94, 95) was originally a basic 18-hole course with temporary clubhouse, but it has matured and been extended to 27 holes with a fine clubhouse. This facility has an attached members club but welcomes visitors.

A recent addition to the golf facilities of this area is the Armory Golf Club (B5), a 9-hole course at Abington which is an attempt by two brothers, Harry and Alfie Ward, to recreate nineteenth century golf. A 9-hole course was laid out by Willie Fernie on this site in 1892. The Ward brothers have established World Heritage Golf Links Ltd, and have built new greens and tees similar to those which existed last century. Players are encouraged to use hickory-shafted clubs and gutta-percha balls. It will be interesting to see if this journey into the past will be commercially successful.

ARRAN

The golf courses on the Island of Arran (Fig. 6.12) are notable for three reasons: their fine scenic setting, their low green fees and their accessibility to visitors. No great championship courses are to be found here, but the seven courses on the island provide excellent holiday golf.

There are three 18-hole courses: Brodick (B121), Lamlash (B105) and Whiting Bay

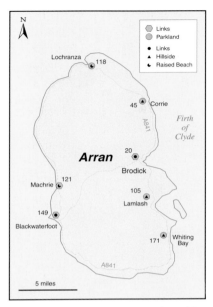

FIG. 6.12 *The landforms and vegetation of the golf courses on Arran.*

(B171). They are all short courses (less than 4,700 yards) but a round of golf cost (in 1999) less than £13. There is a 12-hole links course at Blackwaterfoot (Shiskine Golf and Tennis Club, B149) and 9-hole courses at Corrie (B45), Lochranza (B118) and Machrie (B121) on each of which a round of golf cost less than £10 (in 1999). All of Arran's golf courses occur at coastal sites, but only three of them are links courses—Brodick, Machrie Bay and Blackwaterfoot.

KINTYRE, MID-ARGYLL, OBAN

There are twelve golf courses between Oban and the southern tip of the Kintyre peninsula (Fig. 6.13). The three 9-hole courses at Lochgilphead (B116), Tarbert (B154) and Carradale (B33) are very unsophisticated. The course at Lochgilphead was designed by the head physiotherapist at the local hospital, Dr Ian MacCammond, and the course was built by the hospital's patients and staff. The Dunaverty Golf Club at Southend (B64) was begun by local farmers in 1889. It is a links course, with small greens protected from grazing animals by wire fences, and has some fine views. This is the home course of Belle Robertson, the Curtis Cup player and winner of many tournaments.

A very distinctive golf course is to be found in Oban (B77). Designed by James Braid, the course contains rock knolls and cliffs which provide some thrilling drives from the tees perched high on hillsides.

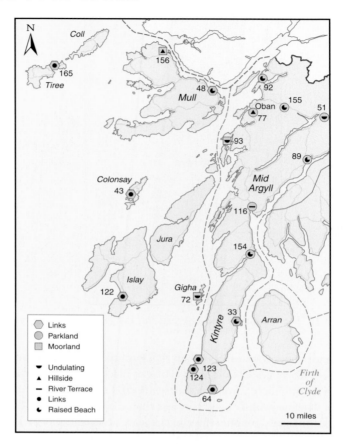

FIG. 6.13 *The landforms and vegetation of golf courses in Kintyre, Argyll and the Islands.*

Ten miles north of Oban a new 9-hole course at the Isle of Eriska Hotel (B92) was designed by Howard Swan and opened in 1998. It is built on the post-glacial raised beach. East of Oban at Taynuilt (B155) and Dalmally (Ph. 6.10, B51), and 30 miles south-east of Oban at Inveraray (B89) are three 9-hole courses all opened for play since 1986. All three courses are in the tradition of the late nineteenth-century Scottish golf boom in that they are laid out across the existing landscape with minimal earth moving, they have small greens and tees and they are cheap to maintain. They were created by local enthusiasts who have no objection to visitors helping to pay for their up-keep. A visitor's day ticket in 1999 cost £10 on each of these courses. The magnificent scenery surrounding each of these courses also generates high rainfall, and therefore the courses can be rather wet. Lack of roll on the ball is more than adequately compensated by the fine surrounding scenery. However, on humid summer evenings the Highland midge (small black flies) can deter even the most enthusiastic golfer.

Ph. 6.10 *Dalmally.*

Ph. 6.11 *Macrihanish, the first tee.*

One course in this sub-region is often discussed in a whisper, as if those who know it simply do not wish to pass on the good news. The town of Campbeltown has two rather distinctive attributes—its nearby coal mine (now closed) and one of the finest links courses in Scotland at Machrihanish (B123). On the west shore of the Kintyre peninsula the wide sweep of Machrihanish Bay (Ph. 6.11) is open to the full force of the Atlantic winds and waves. A magnificent dune system backed by undulating links land has been used for golf since 1876. It has been said that, had this links course of 6,228 yards not been in such an isolated place, it would have hosted many championships. Those golfers who have made the journey, either by road through the delightful scenery around Loch Fyne and down the Kintyre peninsula, or by plane from Glasgow to Campbeltown, always speak very highly of this course.

THE ISLANDS OF ISLAY, GIGHA, COLONSAY, TIREE AND MULL

A short flight from Campbeltown to Islay brings yet another golfing surprise. The Machrie course (Bl22), just outside Port Ellen, has 18 holes set amidst high dunes and rolling links land with every hole offering a challenge (Ph. 6.12). There is an adjoining hotel and daily flights from Glasgow. Not only is the golf of good quality, but Islay has many attractions including fine malt whisky, excellent fishing and a wide variety of bird life.

Ph. 6.12 *Machrie, Islay.*

Although there are golf courses on the islands of Gigha, Colonsay, Tiree and Mull, all but one fall into the category of 'holiday courses'. The exception is that at Tobermory, not because it is of championship standard, but because it has some very distinctive characteristics. The course is located on a hill high above the village, and it has magnificent views down the Sound of Mull and up Loch Sunart and to the surrounding mountains. It is a moorland course of nine holes with small greens and fairways which utilise the 'flats' of the step-like landscape of the basalt lavas on which the course is built. Some of the fairways are transverse to the line of the drive from tee to green and small cliffs can cause a well-hit ball to ricochet in all directions. Accuracy is more important than length on this course.

❧ Seven
East Central Scotland (Region C)

This region, which many regard as the heartland of Scottish golf, contains 125 golf courses (Fig. 7.1). This claim is based on both the antiquity of some of the clubs and courses (e.g. St Andrews 1754, Crail 1786, Tayport 1817, Leven 1820, Royal Perth 1824, Carnoustie 1842, Earls Ferry (Elie) 1858, Lundin Links 1869, Stirling 1869) and the wide variety and large number of courses found in this region. From St Andrews in the east to Aberfoyle in the west, and from Stirling in the south to Pitlochry in the north, the golfing landscapes are full of variety and surrounded by delightful scenery. To some, the famous courses at St Andrews, Gleneagles and Carnoustie are the main attraction, but to others the delights of Ladybank (C80), Lundin Links (C86), Elie (C55), Glenbervie (C64), Dunblane (C47), Pitlochry (C101), Alyth (C6) or Edzell (C54) are the basis for planning golfing holidays in this part of Scotland. Since 1980 there have been 27 new golf courses opened in the region, twenty of which were constructed and are operated by commercial companies.

FALKIRK, STIRLING AND CLACKMANNAN

This sub-region incorporates industrial areas adjacent to the Firth of Forth in the east, the shores of Loch Lomond in the west, the edge of the Highlands from Aberfoyle to Callander and the foothills of the Ochil Hills in the north-east (Fig. 7.2). There are 24 golf courses: 10 are of 9 holes, 14 of 18 holes. Only four are moorland courses: Dollar (C45), Muckhart (C93) and Balfron (C12). The other 20 courses are classed as parkland, there being no true links courses in this sub-region.

The industrialised area of Falkirk-Grangemouth, on the south bank of the Forth estuary, contains several interesting golf courses which owe their character to their location, either on carse clays (raised mud-flats) associated with former high sea levels, or sand and gravel deposited by the meltwaters of the last ice sheet (see Chapter 3). Some 6,000 years ago the Forth estuary was much wider than it is at present, and the area around Falkirk, Larbert and Glenbervie was below sea level. The raised mud-flats and coastal terraces of the former estuary are now the sites of three courses: Falkirk (C58), Falkirk Tryst (C59) and Glenbervie (C64). Both Falkirk and Glenbervie are built partly

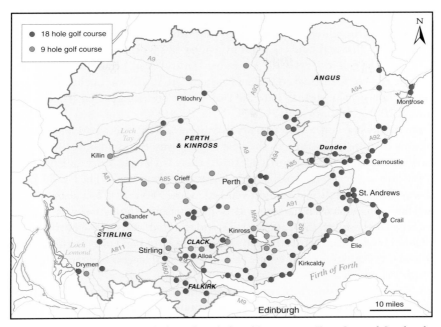

FIG. 7.1 *The location of 9-hole and 18-hole golf courses in East Central Scotland.*

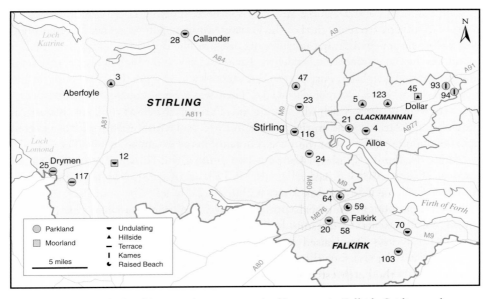

FIG. 7.2 *The landforms and vegetation of golf courses in Falkirk, Stirling and Clackmannan.*

145

on carse clays and partly on raised-beach gravels, while the clubhouse at Glenbervie stands on the old shoreline and looks across the fairly flat carseland which has now been developed into a fine parkland course. This course hosted the Scottish PGA championship in 1986. The Falkirk Tryst course is rather flat and bears some similarities to a links course. The 18-hole municipal course at Grangemouth (C70) was opened in 1973 and is an undulating upland course. There are two rather undistinguished 9-hole courses at Polmont (C103) and Bonnybridge (C20).

There is only one golf course actually in Stirling (C116). It is a parkland course built on volcanic lavas in Kings Park, to the west of the town. Stirling University has a short course on the campus and just north of Stirling there is a 9-hole course at Bridge of Allan (C23) and an excellent 18-hole parkland course at Dunblane (C47). The Dunblane course, which was opened in 1923, is built on a hillside some 250 to 400 feet above sea level. It is a well-maintained parkland course with some interesting holes and with magnificent views of the Forth Valley, the Campsie Hills and the Highlands to the northwest. Along the Highland 'edge', to the north-west, is a good-quality parkland course at Callander (C28), while the original 9-hole course at Aberfoyle (C3) has been extended to 18 holes and much improved.

On the south-east side of Stirling, at Bannockburn, a new 9-hole 'pay and play' course, an excellent driving range and a clubhouse containing a restaurant and pro-shop was opened in 1997. Brucefields (C24) is an excellent facility for those of all ages wishing to learn to play golf.

The two courses at Drymen, near the southern shore of Loch Lomond, and the course at Balfron, are really part of the Greater Glasgow golfing scene, Drymen being only half-an-hour's drive from the centre of Glasgow. The Buchanan Castle course (C25) is built on the flat terraces that border the River Endrick. It is a high-quality course set in fine parkland. The 9-hole course of the Strathendrick Golf Club (C117) is built on silts and clays deposited in a former glacial lake. There was a 9-hole course at Balfron (C12) at the turn of the century which was abandoned. Through the efforts of local enthusiasts, the club and a 9-hole course were reinstated in 1997, and with the assistance of a Lottery Sports Fund grant, the course is in the process of being extended to 18 holes.

Along the foot of the steep, southern face of the Ochil Hills is a series of four golf courses. Those at Alva (C5) and Tillicoultry (C123) are of nine holes; there is an 18-hole course at Dollar (C45) and Muckhart (C93) has 27 holes. The courses at Alva and Tillicoultry are built on hill-foot deposits of gravel and have a parkland character. The course at Dollar is built on the hillside between 250 and 500 feet above sea level and has a moorland character, while the courses at Muckhart are on an undulating upland some distance from the Ochil scarp, with nine holes built mainly on a hillside and 18 holes on undulating sand and gravel deposits.

The town of Alloa has two golf clubs. Alloa Braehead (C21) plays over a parkland course to the west of the town, built on a raised-beach to the north of the River Forth. The Alloa Shawpark (C4) course is to the north-east of the town and is set in undulating parkland.

FIFE

Between the Firth of Forth and the Firth of Tay there is a 15-mile-wide peninsula which contains 45 golf courses (Fig. 7.3). Several of these courses have long histories and many traditions. The game of golf, during the period from the fifteenth to mid-eighteenth centuries, was certainly played over the fine links land at St Andrews and Elie and possibly at other locations. The game became more organised from the mid-eighteenth century with the establishment of the following golf clubs in Fife: Society of St Andrews Golfers, 1754/1766; Crail Golfing Society, 1786; Scotscraig Golf Club, Tayport, 1817; Leven Golfing Society, 1820; Earlsferry and Elie Golf Club, 1858; Lundin Links Golf Club, 1869. All of these clubs used the links land associated with the sequence of raised beaches all along the coast from Leven to Tayport—a total of some 20 miles of links land which contains 16 golf courses. Apart from Ladybank (C80) founded in 1879 and Dunfermline (C48) founded in 1887, all the inland golf courses in Fife were founded after 1890.

Coastal Courses

The history of golf at St Andrews is discussed in Chapter One. The presence of a large area of links land between the old harbour, within the estuary of the River Eden, and the

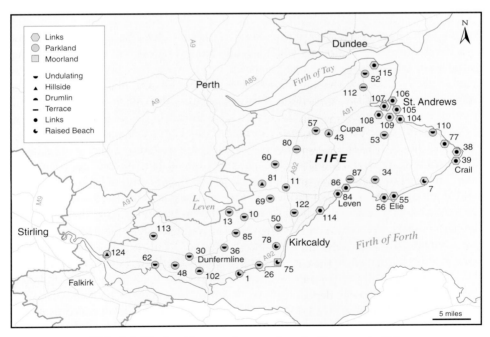

FIG. 7.3 *The landforms and vegetation of golf courses in Fife.*

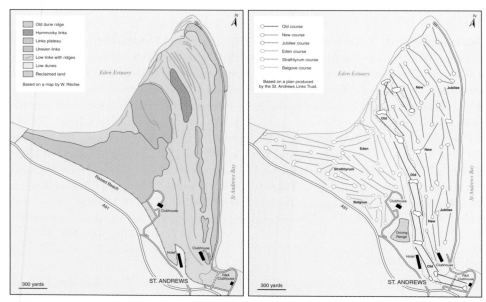

FIG. 7.4A *The landforms of the St Andrews golf courses.*

FIG. 7.4B *The 'Old', 'New', 'Jubilee', 'Eden' and 'Strathtyrum' courses at St Andrews.*

ecclesiastical centre and market of the old town, seems to have been significant in the early development of the game of golf. This links land was created as a result of the late-glacial and post-glacial sea level changes which are known to have occurred around the coast of Scotland during the past 13,000 years. Kincraig Point, one mile west of Elie, bears witness in the form of abandoned shore-platforms and cliffs to the former higher stand of the sea along this coast. The higher, abandoned shorelines (those over 30 feet above present sea level) were probably formed about 12–14,000 years ago. The lower raised beaches (10–30 feet above present sea levels) are related to a period of relatively higher sea level about 6,000 years ago. Since that time relative sea level has been dropping. The combination of a slowly falling sea level and the presence of large quantities of sand along the shoreline, either produced by the meltwaters of the last ice sheet or from the massive supply of sediment brought into the Tay and Eden estuaries, has permitted the development of extensive wind-blown sand spreads and dunes in several locations (see Chapter 3). The Pilmour Links at St Andrews are really a part of the large sand accumulation known as Tentsmuir. The area between the River Eden and St Andrews (Fig. 7.4) has emerged from beneath the sea during the past 6,000 years and is underlain by a raised beach associated with a shoreline which runs roughly parallel to and just south of the main road (A91) between St Andrews and Guard Bridge. As the sea retreated eastwards from the old shoreline (at about 25 feet), large expanses of sand would dry out in the intertidal area and could be picked up and blown inshore by strong winds.

Not only was the old raised beach buried by sand spreads, but lines of sand dunes developed, generally aligned in a north-south direction. Most of the Old Course and Eden Course were built on the gently undulating links land to the west of the main dune ridges (Ph. 7.1), while the New and Jubilee Courses include dune ridges which stand 15 to 25 feet above the surrounding links and are usually covered with rough vegetation. Much of the area between the highest dune ridge and the present beach is reclaimed land.

Although the first written record of golf in the Royal Burgh of St Andrews does not occur until 1552, the game has probably been played on these links since the twelfth century. Not until after the formation of the Society of St Andrews Golfers, on 14 May 1766, do we have much information about the course on the St Andrews links. The Society used the public links, and even after it became the Royal and Ancient Golf Club of St Andrews in 1834 it did not, and still does not, own its own course. However, the Royal and Ancient is much concerned with the running of the six courses controlled by the St Andrews Links Trust and run by the Links Management Committee through its representatives on both bodies.

The Old Course originally consisted of 22 holes—11 out and 11 home. By the time the first survey of the course was made in 1836, it had been reduced to nine holes out and nine home, and from 1832 homeward players holed out on the same green but in a different hole. There were no tees, the player simply teeing off within two clubs' length of

Ph. 7.1 *St Andrews.*

the previous hole. Since sand for teeing-up was obtained from the bottom of the hole, the holes became progressively deeper. Separate teeing grounds were introduced in 1846.

In 1895 the Royal and Ancient constructed the New Course (C105) on ground leased from St Andrews Town Council (Fig. 7.4). The Jubilee Course (C106) was built by the Town Council in 1897 at the time of Queen Victoria's Diamond Jubilee. Originally consisting of 12 holes, it was extended to 18 in 1912. In order to accommodate the ever-increasing number of golfers, the Town Council constructed the Eden Course (C107) in 1912. The 9-hole Balgove Course (C109) was built in 1971, primarily for the use of children and beginners, and the Strathtyrum Course (C108) was opened in 1993.

These six courses, the Royal and Ancient Clubhouse, some five local clubs, several golf equipment and clothing shops, numerous first class hotels and the Old Town and university buildings make St Andrews the major and most attractive golfing centre in Scotland. During the last decade, there have been some major additions to the golf facilities in St Andrews. Parts of the Jubilee course have been re-designed and a new 18-hole course, the Strathtyrum, of 5,094 yards, designed by Donald Steel, was opened for play in 1993. The Links Trust has invested large sums in constructing two new club-houses, open to all visitors, which contain high-quality locker rooms, restaurants, bars and a pro-shop, as well as a new maintenance facility and administration centre. New wells for sourcing irrigation water have been drilled and a new irrigation system in-stalled. Near to the R&A clubhouse an excellent Museum devoted to the history of golf has been built.

The owners of the Old Course Hotel have opened an 18-hole parkland course, de-signed by Peter Thompson, at Craigtoun, two miles to the south-west of the centre of St Andrews. The Duke's Course (C53), is 7,200 yards long off the championship tees, and is a challenging inland addition to the famous links courses of St Andrews. Another new golf complex, Kingask, consisting of two 18-hole golf courses and a hotel and conference centre, is under construction at St Andrews Bay (C110), three miles south-east of St Andrews on the A917.

A further five miles along the A917, at Kingsbarns, an American company has con-structed a magnificent 18-hole links course and clubhouse on the site originally occupied by the 9-hole course used by the Kingsbarns Golf Club founded in 1793. The original 9-hole course was closed in 1939. Four holes on the new course (6,7, 16 and 17) occupy the site of the original 9-hole course.

The writer walked this site with Mark Parsinen and Art Dunkley, the California-based developers, prior to any construction taking place. The morphology of the site was very simple (Fig. 7.5). The present shoreline was backed by a single dune ridge (6–9 feet), inland of which there was a sand plain (with minor depressions) one hundred to two hundred yards in width (the post-glacial raised beach circa 6,000 years old), which in turn was backed by an abandoned marine cliff some 30 feet high (Ph. 7.2, 7.3). Inland of this cliff line was an almost flat surface (the late glacial surface circa 13,000 years old), with occasional former and present water courses producing some undulations. A series

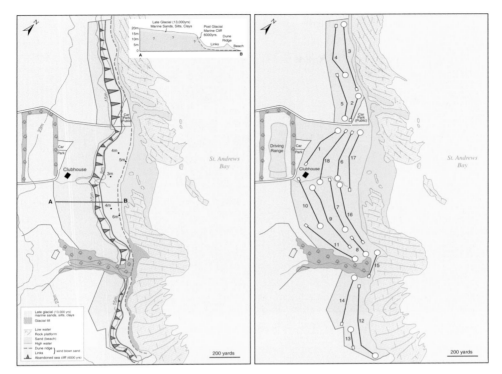

FIG. 7.5 *The landforms of Kingsbarns Golf Links.*

of inspection pits revealed that virtually the entire site had a covering of sand at least six feet thick. While it would have been possible to lay out an 18-hole course on the existing surfaces, the developers decided to use modern design and construction methods to create a series of classic links landforms and their associated vegetation. The course designer, Kyle Phillips, was given a brief to create a series of landforms of appropriate scale and form in order to replicate the features commonly encountered by golfers playing the several courses on the Pilmour Links in St Andrews. This writer made several site visits during the construction phase and made comments about the man-made landforms, and Walter Woods provided expert advice on vegetation. The turf created consists of the modern genetic equivalents of the fescues and bents found on the Old Course, St Andrews. The greens are 70% fescue (Slender Creeping Red, Chewings) and 30% Brown Top Bent. The fairways are 80% fescues, 10% Brown Top Bent and 10% Smooth Stalked Meadow Grass. The rough areas contain fescues, bents and meadow grass along with some heather and gorse.

This magnificent course was opened for play by the public in July 2000, and those who have already played it have been very complimentary. Because links courses are always close to the sea, it is often mistakenly believed that golfers enjoy many views of

Ph. 7.2 *Kingsbarns—the site prior to course construction.*

Ph. 7.3 *Kingsbarns Golf Links.*

the sea. Any classic links course, laid out amongst 10–30 foot high dune ridges and where tees, fairways and greens are usually in the inter-dune 'valleys', rarely provides the golfer with a view of the sea and only exposes players occasionally to the full force of onshore winds. At Kingsbarns, the course has been specifically designed to provide many sea views, and thus wind strength and direction will have a great part to play in determining the difficulty of the course.

Probably the best compliment to pay the designer and developers of Kingsbarns is that a visitor who had not visited the site before the creation of the golf course would be unlikely to conclude that the landforms and vegetation were anything other than 'natural'. The officers of the R&A obviously think highly of the course, as in return for an interest-free loan, they have secured preferred limited access to the course for R&A members and other specified local golfers. The facility will be operated primarily on a 'pay and play' basis with a green fee of £100.

Although early golf in Scotland is usually associated with St Andrews, other links in East Lothian, on the north-east coast of Scotland and in other parts of Fife, were undoubtedly used by golfers in the eighteenth century. The Crail Golfing Society (C38), which now plays over the Balcomie Links, was founded in 1786. This club claims to be the seventeenth oldest in the world and has a complete set of minutes of the club meetings since its inception. The minute relating to the club's foundation reads as follows:

> Several gentlemen in and about the town of Crail who were fond of the diversion of Golf, agreed to form themselves into a Society. The Society was accordingly instituted upon the 23rd day of February 1786.

The Society first used a course at Sauchope before moving to its present site. Crail has one of the earliest recorded uses of iron rings to maintain the holes (1874), before the development of metal cups. The present course is built on a rock-controlled raised-platform covered by wind-blown sand (Ph. 7.4), which has only minor undulations and no marked dune ridges. There are no trees and very little rough vegetation. The club built a second 18-hole course (Craighead C39), which was opened for play in 1998, with the assistance of a Lottery Sports Fund Grant.

Another early golf club was that at Tayport. The Scotscraig Golf Club (C115) was founded in 1817, making it the thirteenth oldest club in Scotland. The present layout was designed by James Braid. It is a gently undulating links course of 6,550 yards with much heather and gorse rough and surrounded by coniferous plantations. It has similarities with a moorland course.

Between Leven and Elie, around the shores of Largo Bay, there are six golf courses within an eight-mile stretch of coastline. Golf was played on the Earlsferry links in the sixteenth century and may well have been played on the Leven and Lundin links at the same time. The Leven Golfing Society (C84) was founded in 1820 and the Earlsferry and Elie Golf Club in 1858 (Elie Golf House Club 1875 and Earlsferry Thistle Club

Ph. 7.4 *Crail: Balcomie Links.*

1875). Formal golf was therefore well-established on the south coast of Fife by the mid-nineteenth century. The Earlsferry links (C55) are rather similar to those at Balcomie, in that they are gently undulating, with no marked dune ridges except along the seaward edge of the course. The first two holes and the third tee are built on higher ground above the main links surface. The drive from the first tee is up over a ridge and the starter makes use of an old submarine periscope to ensure the fairway is clear, before permitting golfers to drive off. An excellent history of golf at Elie has been written by A. M. Drysdale. Iron bands to protect the holes on the course were first used in 1874 and the Club purchased its first mower to cut the putting greens in 1877. The course is now kept in excellent condition.

Between Leven and Lundin Links there is a fine area of links land which has two quite distinct elements. Running parallel to the coast and extending some 400 yards inland is an area of wind-blown sand with a series of low (12–20 feet), parallel, old dune ridges. This true links land is backed by an old, abandoned cliff-line some 25 to 30 feet high, above which there is an almost flat raised-beach at an altitude of between 50 and 60 feet above present sea level. The Leven Golfing Society (C84) play on the Leven Links which are in the south-western part of this links system. The Leven Municipal course (The Scoonie Club, C114) is an 18-hole course, which apart from a few holes, is built mainly on the upper, flat raised beach. The Lundin Links course (C86) combines holes both on the low-level links (an extension of the Leven Links) and on the upper, flat raised-beach (Ph. 7.5). It is a first-class course and has been used for the qualifying rounds of the Open Championship when it has been held at St Andrews. The fourth course in this group is that played over by the Lundin Ladies Golf Club (C87), which is a 9-hole course located on the high raised beach. It is a gently undulating parkland with few trees.

There are three other courses along the south coast of Fife which, although they have coastal locations, are not typical links courses. The 9-hole course at Anstruther (C7) is built across two raised rock-platforms, both of which have a thin cover of sand. The 18-hole municipal course at Kinghorn (C75) is situated on a high coastal platform some 200 feet above sea level. It is a coastal moorland course and has fine views across the Firth of Forth. There is a delightful 18-hole course at Aberdour (C1) which is located on a series of raised marine-platforms. The first hole involves a drive across a valley to the green situated on a rocky promontory. Much of the course is parkland, developed on the sequence of raised beaches.

Although the Tulliallan course (C123) at Kincardine is primarily an inland course, with the majority of the holes on an upland some 150 to 200 feet above sea level, the first two and last two holes are in fact built across almost flat raised-beach deposits. The course is however, primarily in the parkland category.

Ph. 7.5 *Lundin Links.*

Inland Courses

While the coastal courses of Fife may be of prime interest to the visitor, a great deal of local golf in this region is played on the 29 inland courses (13 of which are 9-hole courses). It must be admitted, however, that of the 29 courses, only ten can be regarded as good-quality 18-hole courses—Dunfermline (C48), Burntisland (C26), the two courses in Kirkcaldy (C78, C50), Glenrothes (C69), Balbirnie Park (C11), Drumoig (C52), The Dukes (C53), Elmwood (C57) and Ladybank (C62). A large part of Fife, south-east of a line from Glenrothes to Kincardine, has had a long industrial history. The juxtaposition of delightful rural landscapes and attractive coastal villages with areas of both past and present industrial and mining activity is a major characteristic of this area. Perhaps the courses at Lochgelly (C85) and Auchterderran (C10) are the best examples of golf in the old industrial areas. The town of Dunfermline has three golf courses (C30, 48, 102) and a fourth is under construction at Forrester Park (C62) while Kirkcaldy has two (C78, 50), all of 18 holes and of parkland character. In a more rural setting there are interesting 9-hole courses at Saline (C113), Bishopshire (C15), Leslie (C81) and an 18-hole course at Thornton (C112).

The Dunfermline Golf Club (C48), founded in 1887, plays over some fine undulating parkland in the grounds of Pitfirrane House to the west of the town. The old house is the heart of the clubhouse to which has been added a new extension. This high-quality parkland course of 6,126 yards is well worth a visit. Burntisland golf course (C26) is situated high above the town on an undulating upland. The two courses at Kirkcaldy are in considerable contrast. Kirkcaldy Golf Club (C78), founded in 1904, plays over hilly parkland to the south-west of the town while the municipal course (C50), opened in 1963 in the grounds of Dunnikier Park, is on undulating upland with old Scots pines and more recently planted deciduous trees.

Another newcomer to the Fife golfing scene is the fine parkland course at Glenrothes (C69) which was developed in association with the creation of Glenrothes New Town. The 18-hole course of 6,444 yards was laid out in an estate of fine mature parkland and opened in 1958.

Inland from St Andrews there are four new golf facilities which exemplify the four types of new commercial golf development taking place in Scotland. The owner of Charleton House Estate near Colinsburgh on the B942 (ten miles south-west of St Andrews, three miles north of Elie) opened one of Scotland's first commercial 'pay and play' golf courses in 1994 (C34). The course was designed by John Salvesen, former Captain of the R&A, and the construction involved minimal earth movement. Set in a very pleasant undulating parkland and with a most attractive clubhouse, the course of 6,149 yards provides enjoyable golf at a reasonable price.

Another estate owner at Craigie, three miles north of Leuchars on the A914 (nine miles north of St Andrews), developed the 18-hole Drumoig (C53) golf course along with a large clubhouse and associated housing. The 7,000 yard course, located on an undulating upland, was opened in 1996. This facility was subsequently chosen as the new headquarters of the Scottish Golf Union and the Ladies Golf Association which share offices adjacent to the Drumoig clubhouse. The Scottish Golf Union, assisted by a large grant from the Lottery Sports Fund, has constructed a first-class golf academy on the site, the Scottish National Golf Centre, which provides excellent indoor and out-door practice facilities. The centre is open to the general public.

A golf course already existed at nearby Leuchars. Founded in 1903, the St Michaels Club (C112), played for many years over a 9-hole course built on undulating land underlain by sand and gravel. The course has been extended to 18 holes and welcomes visitors.

A golf club was established in Cupar (C43) in 1855. The present course is a simple, 9-hole layout on the side of a hill. A level stance is hard to find on this course and it is probably the only course in Scotland where the path to the clubhouse passes through a cemetery. A little further inland is the excellent Ladybank course (C80). Tom Morris designed the original six holes and the present 18 holes constitute one of Scotland's finest inland courses. The course measures 6,641 yards over fairly flat terrain. The turf has a heathland quality but there is much heather and gorse and extensive pine woods. This course has been used as a qualifying course for the Open Championship.

Within the Kingdom of Fife (i.e. within a 30-mile radius of St Andrews) there are 45 golf courses ranging from the most basic of 9-hole layouts to courses designed by internationally renowned golf course architects which cost many millions of pounds to construct. There are also courses of great historical significance. Most of the courses in Fife are owned and operated by members clubs but they all welcome visitors. The most famous golf club in the world, the all-male Royal and Ancient Golf Club of St Andrews, does not own its own course but plays its competitions mainly over the Old and New courses in St Andrews. When the two new courses under construction at St. Andrews Bay are opened, the St Andrews Links Trust, which is Scotland's largest golf business even though it is a non-profit making organisation, will be in competition with three commercial golf facilities (four courses) operated by two American and one Japanese company.

PERTH AND KINROSS, DUNDEE AND ANGUS

This beautiful area of Scotland extends from Loch Tay in the west to Montrose in the east. It not only contains the famous golfing centres of Carnoustie and Gleneagles but also courses of great antiquity in places such as Montrose, Monifieth and Perth. Both along the Highland edge (Crieff, Blairgowrie, Alyth, Kirriemuir, Edzell) and within the Highland glens there are numerous golf courses of a wide range of quality and difficulty, surrounded by fine scenery. Within this sub-region there are 56 golf courses. The nine coastal courses are all of 18 holes. Forty-two of the 47 inland courses are classed as parkland, there being only five moorland courses (C37, C49, C44, C125, C63). Thirty-three of the inland courses are of 18 holes (Fig. 7.6).

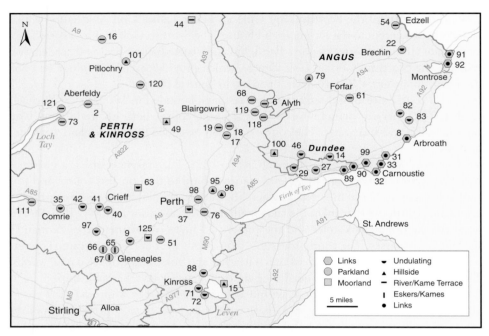

FIG. 7.6 *The landforms and vegetation of golf courses in Perth and Kinross, Dundee and Angus.*

Golf is known to have been played on the links at Carnoustie and Montrose, and on the gravel terraces of the Tay at Perth in the sixteenth century. It is believed by locals that golf was played in Forfar in 1651. However, the majority of the present golf courses of Tayside had their formal beginnings in the last half of the nineteenth century.

Of more recent vintage is the golf complex at Gleneagles developed during the 1920s. Over the past twenty years this sub-region has seen the addition of 14 courses so that Perth and Kinross now has one of the highest levels of golf facility provision in Scotland. There is one 18-hole unit per 4,600 resident population, and therefore many of the golf courses in this sub-region welcome visitors. The quality of the facilities range from the magnificent Gleneagles Hotel and its three courses, the championship course at Carnoustie and the adjacent new hotel, the hotels and associated golf courses at Murrayshall (Perth) and Letham Grange (Arbroath), to basic 9-hole layouts where a day's golf can be obtained for £15.

Coastal Courses

Between Monifieth, some six miles east of Dundee, and Montrose (a distance of 25 miles), there are nine links courses. Six of these are located on a triangular area of raised beach covered by blown-sand known as Barry Links. Much of this area lies a mere 10 to

20 feet above sea level, with a few old dune-ridges rising to 30 feet. The former coastline of some 6,000 years ago is located north of the A930 road between Monifieth and Carnoustie. Just to the south of this road is a strip of land about half a mile wide and four miles long, where golf has been played since 1527 and where formal golf clubs at Monifieth, Barry and Carnoustie have existed since the middle of last century. There are two 18-hole courses at Monifieth—the Medal (C89) and the Ashludie (C90). They are built over undulating links with some old dune-ridges, often covered by gorse, between the fairways. The Monifieth Links were first formally used for golf in 1845 when Allan Robertson and Alexander Pirie of St Andrews designed a 9-hole course which was subsequently extended to 18 in 1880. Almost contiguous with the eastern end of Monifieth's Medal course is another links course played over by the Panmure Golf Club (founded 1845) of Barry (C99). The members of this club originally played over the Monifieth Links but opened their own course in 1899. This course at 6,317 yards is of good quality with many low dune-ridges and numerous plateau greens. The Panmure clubhouse is of great character.

There are now three golf courses at Carnoustie—the Championship Course (C32), the Burnside Course (C33) and the newest, only opened in 1981, the Buddon Links Course (C31). The first record of golf being played at Carnoustie is dated 1650. The

Ph. 7.6 *Carnoustie* (© *Angus McNicol*).

original ten holes of the present Championship Course were created by Allan Robertson in the mid-nineteenth century and later extended to 18 holes by Tom Morris. Further modifications were made by James Braid in 1926 in the form of several new greens, tees and bunkers, but since that time the course has remained basically unchanged. Each hole is different from the next and never do more than two holes follow the same direction. This fine links course has hosted five Open Championships—the last in 1999, which was won by Paul Lawrie of Scotland (Ph. 7.6).

Two miles south-west of Arbroath, at the village of Elliot, is the clubhouse of the Arbroath Golf Club, founded in 1877. It stands on a flat terrace (probably a raised beach) with the steep slope of the abandoned shoreline leading down to an undulating links course. The course is bounded on the south-east side by the Dundee to Aberdeen railway line and beyond that is a dune-ridge some 12 to 15 feet high.

At Montrose there are two 18-hole links courses—the Medal Course (C91) and the Broomfield (C92). There is evidence to suggest that golf was played on these links in 1567, with a formal layout existing after 1810. The original course was of 17 holes, but it was extended to 18 holes in 1863 and the Medal course has been changed little since that time. The undulating links upon which both courses are built are bounded to the east by a 30-foot high marram-covered dune-ridge. Five different golf clubs (The Royal Albert, The Caledonia, The Mercantile, The Victoria, The North Links Ladies) play over these courses. However, visitors are still made welcome and the courses provide good-quality golf.

The links courses of Angus bear many similarities to those of Fife. In both regions there is a long history of golf being played on the links and in several towns a number of clubs play over one course. Apart from the two championship courses (St Andrews Old Course and Carnoustie), all the links courses are generally accessible to visitors.

Inland Courses

The two major urban centres in Tayside, Dundee and Perth (a combined population of some 200,000) can only muster ten golf courses between them. However, this may reflect the proximity of the two towns to a large number of golf courses throughout Perth and Kinross, Angus and Fife. The five courses in Dundee are all on the north side of the city and all, in Scottish terms, are relatively recent developments. The Downfield Course (C46) is an undulating parkland course which, although it was originally opened in 1933, was developed into its present layout in 1964. This course has hosted many amateur and professional tournaments, including the 1972 Scottish Open Championship. Peter Thomson, the five-times Open Champion, once described Downfield as '...one of the finest inland courses I've played anywhere in the world'. The other two courses in Dundee—Caird Park (C27) and Camperdown (C29)—are both municipal courses. The Camperdown course is set in fine mature parkland and is a stiff test of golfing skill.

Two new commercial golf facilities have been opened recently on the outskirts of

Dundee. Six miles north-west of the city, on the A923, an 18-hole course of 6,500 yards with clubhouse, driving range and a property development is located at Piper Dam (C100). On the north-east periphery of Dundee, at Balumbie (C14) an 18-hole course, clubhouse and driving range were opened in 2000.

Perth was once the capital of Scotland, and in 1503 King James IV is known to have bought expensive golf clubs from a bow-maker in Perth. The sand and gravel river-terraces on the banks of the River Tay, now known as the North Inch and South Inch, were probably used as golf links in the sixteenth and seventeenth centuries. The Royal Perth Golfing Society was founded in 1824 and until recently held competitions over the municipal course on the North Inch (C98). This course is fairly flat and is set in a fine mature parkland along the west bank of the Tay. The Royal Perth claims to be the oldest of the Royal clubs. When the Scottish Parliament met in Perth the Kings of Scotland would attend. The King James VI Golf Club, founded in 1858, is named in honour of the golfing King. The course now played on by the King James VI club is located on an island between two channels of the River Tay. Its mid-river location makes it unique amongst Scottish golf courses, but it is also distinctive in that it can only be reached by a narrow walkway attached to the railway bridge over the River Tay. The clubhouse therefore has no adjacent car park.

Perth has a third course which is totally different from the two courses on the banks of the Tay. The Craigie Hill Course (C37) is located on volcanic rocks and is very hilly and rugged and has a moorland classification. There are some fine views from the higher parts of the course. Three miles north-east of Perth near New Scone, there is a fine modern golf development. In 1981 an undulating parkland course designed by J. Hamilton Stutt was opened. It was laid out in the mature parklands of Murrayshall House, the house itself being converted to a hotel. A second 18-hole course has recently been constructed. Perth, therefore, has both the traditional North Inch municipal course with its long history, and also a modern golfing development. In many ways Perth makes an ideal centre for a golfing holiday, in that within a 50-mile radius there are some 70 golf courses catering for golfers of all levels of skill and in surroundings which are of high scenic quality.

To the south-west of Perth is the district known as Strathearn. The valleys of the Earn and its tributaries provide some beautiful golfing country, the centrepiece of which is the Gleneagles complex (Ph. 7.7, 7.8). It was Donald Matheson, general manager of the Caledonian Railway Company, who conceived the idea of a Grand Hotel to be built close to his company's railway line between Stirling and Perth. He was aware that the Glasgow and South-West Railway Company had already built the Turnberry Hotel and he was not to be outdone. The construction of the Gleneagles Hotel began in 1914, but was interrupted by the First World War, when part of the building was used as a hospital and rehabilitation centre for coal miners. Work was resumed in 1922 and James Braid was invited to design the King's (C65) and Queen's (C66) courses which were opened in 1924. The Prince's course (C67) was originally of nine holes, but was extended to 18 holes in 1974. A fourth 18-hole course, the Glendevon, was opened in 1980. The Prince's and Glendevon courses were replaced in 1993 by a new championship course of 7,081 yards, designed by Jack Nicklaus.

There can be few pieces of land anywhere in Scotland better suited to the construction of golf courses. Like the older links courses, the Gleneagles courses are also built on sand and gravel, but instead of being the product of wave and wind action, the sand and gravel deposits of the Gleneagles area were laid down by the meltwaters of the last ice sheet. They are ice-contact, fluvioglacial (meltwater) deposits (see Chapter 3). Immense quantities of sand and gravel were brought to this site by large meltwater rivers some 15,000 years ago. They were deposited in tunnels in the ice and on top of and against large blocks of glacier ice. When all the ice melted, long sinuous ridges of sand and gravel (eskers), flat-topped mounds (kames) and enclosed hollows (kettles) were left on the south facing slope of Muir of Ochil (Fig. 7.7) between 400 and 500 feet above sea level. The three golf courses have been built across this series of sub-parallel, 20 to 50

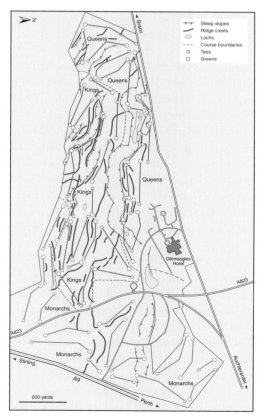

FIG. 7.7 *The landforms of the Gleneagles golf courses.*

Ph. 7.7 *Gleneagles: 14th green on the King's Course.*

Ph. 7.8 *Gleneagles: PGA Centennial Course.*

feet high, ridges and mounds which are aligned in a west-north-west to east-south-east direction. This complex land system covers an area about two miles from west to east and one mile from north to south. There are many similarities between the parallel ridges and hollows found on this inland site and the parallel, old dune-ridges and intervening hollows found on many coastal links courses. James Braid and subsequent designers made full use of these convolutions in the Gleneagles landscape. This is particularly true of the King's Course, where the golfer has the luxury of the feeling of playing his own private course because so many of the fairways and greens are isolated from neighbouring holes by the high gravel ridges. The highest part of the courses is in the west, with a gentle slope down towards the south-east.

The Jack Nicklaus-designed course has only six holes which thread their way through gravel ridges and mounds. The twelve holes east of the road (A823) are largely the product of mechanised shaping and are more akin to a typical American resort course, thus they are in stark contrast to the natural forms utilised by James Braid in the design of the King's and Queen's courses. The Monarchs (C67), recently renamed the PGA Centenary Course, was the first course in Scotland to have a purpose-built concrete cart-path constructed to allow the use of powered golf carts. While such a feature is regarded by some as an unnecessary scar on the landscape, the fact that the routing plan of this course is such that the length of the 18 holes plus the distance between greens and tees amount to some 8,000 yards explains, in part, the necessity for the use, at least by some players, of a golf cart. During and after the construction of the Monarchs, the Gleneagles maintenance staff, under the leadership of Jimmy Kidd and with advice from numerous experts, have embarked on a major environmental conservation programme for the entire Gleneagles estate.

Some writers have referred to the Gleneagles courses as having a moorland or heathland character. This is understandable in that they are located on an upland plateau with firm turf and with rough of heather and gorse. However, all three courses have fine coniferous (often Scots pine) and deciduous trees and the general aspect is that of parkland.

Although the courses were designed for 'resort golf' in association with the first-class hotel, they have been the venue for various championships. The King's Course has been used for the Ladies Championship and a Curtis Cup match. Both the King's and the Queen's have become internationally famous as the venues of the BBC Television Pro-Celebrity series. The King's Course has recently been lengthened for championship play and hosted the Scottish Open Championship in 1987 and 1988 and several LPGA events. The PGA Centenary Course will host the Ryder Cup in 2014.

Golf at Gleneagles is expensive by Scottish standards, but there is no other golfing complex to match it in terms of facilities, accommodation, scenery and overall quality. Even for the dedicated coastal-links golfer, Gleneagles has something special in the way that natural features have been incorporated into these inland courses.

Just a mile east of Gleneagles Hotel is the village of Auchterarder, which has had its own golf club (C9) and course since 1892. The facilities and character of this course are much more in keeping with traditional Scottish golf than those of its illustrious neighbour. It is a course of 5,757 yards built over undulating parkland. There is also a 9-hole course at nearby Dunning (C51) and an 18-hole 'pay and play' course at Whitemoss (C125).

The view to the south from Gleneagles is dominated by a steep-sided valley which cuts through the Ochil Hills. On the north side of these hills this deep cut is known as Glen Eagles, while on the south side it is known as Glen Devon. A drive south through this beautiful country of some 16 miles (the A823 and A91), to Milnathort, will permit visits to three rather flat, parkland courses on the banks of Loch Leven. The one at Milnathort (C 88) is of nine holes, and at Kinross, The Green Hotel (C71, C72) has two challenging 18-hole courses. To the north of Gleneagles (A823) there is a 9-hole course at Muthill (C97) and an 18-hole and a 9-hole course at Crieff. The original course at Crieff was opened in 1891 but major changes have been made resulting in the present 18-hole course which opened in 1980. This new Ferntower course (C40) comprises 11 new holes and some of the original 18 holes, nine of which now make up the shorter Dornoch Course (C41). They combine to form a good quality golfing facility with magnificent views over Strathearn.

Crieff is located at the edge of the Highlands and two miles further west (on the A85) the River Earn flows through a steep-sided valley. There is an interesting 9-hole course on the north side of the Earn Valley at Comrie. Outside the small clubhouse there is a list of fauna and flora to be observed during a round of golf. Another couple of miles up the Glen there is another 9-hole course at St Fillans (C89) built on the gravel terraces and protruding rock knolls of the valley floor. The Comrie and St Fillans courses are a far cry from the sophisticated facilities of Gleneagles, but anyone who wishes to experience traditional Scottish golf should include such courses in their itinerary.

The so-called 'Highland edge' is very marked between Blairgowrie and Edzell (Fig. 7.6). This is one of the very distinctive natural boundaries in Scotland which is closely associated with a geological fault (the Highland Boundary Fault). To the north and west lie the ancient metamorphic rocks of the Grampians, while to the south-east, the broad valley of Strathmore is underlain by the younger Old Red Sandstone rocks. A series of rivers (Rivers Shee, Isla, South Esk, North Esk) flow south-eastwards through deep, glacial valleys within the Grampians and suddenly emerge on to the broad plain of Strathmore. During the last glaciation (see Chapter 3) these valleys contained large glaciers and when they melted the meltwaters carried large quantities of sand and gravel which were dumped along the Highland Boundary. These gravels were either deposited as large outwash-fans, as river-terraces, or as ice-contact accumulations (eskers, kames), and it is these sand and gravel areas that provide excellent sites for golf courses at Blairgowrie, Alyth, Kirriemuir, Forfar and Edzell.

There are two fine 18-hole courses and one 9-hole course at Blairgowrie (C17, 18, 19, Ph. 7.9) built over a large, gently sloping outwash fan (sandur) of sand and gravel. The

Ph. 7.9 *Blairgowrie.*

Ph. 7.10 *Strathmore.*

old meltwater routeways across the surface can still be seen and there are several lake-filled depressions (kettle holes). This well-drained surface has been extensively planted with pine and birch and the fairways have been developed as routeways for the golfer through the forest. The three courses are kept in fine condition, and are stern tests of golfing skill. The Rosemount course has hosted the British Boys' Championship and the Martini International, which was won in 1977 by Greg Norman.

Five miles east of Blairgowrie the pleasant village of Alyth now boasts four golf courses, all located on well-drained undulating sand and gravel deposits. The Alyth Golf Club Course (C6) was designed by James Braid and opened in 1894. Its original heathland character has been modified by extensive pine plantations. Two new, commercial golf facilities have been developed near Alyth since 1995. Strathmore Golf Centre (C118, 119) has an 18-hole and a 9-hole course, driving range and clubhouse (Ph. 7.10). The courses were designed by John Salvesen and constructed using minimal earth move-ment with generous fairways and large but challenging greens, and are set in a most pleasant landscape with some fine views. This complex has a core membership and attracts many visitors. A similar facility, the Glenisla 18-hole course (C68, Ph. 7.11), is to be found immediately north of Alyth Golf Club. The Alyth Golf Desk provides a tee reservation and accommodation booking service, not only for the three Alyth courses, but for other courses and accommodation throughout the region.

Ph. 7.11 *Glenisla.*

167

The courses at Kirriemuir (C79) and Brechin (C22) were also designed by Braid but are a little different in that they are both built on rolling uplands above the floor of Strathmore. There is much less woodland on the Brechin course and therefore some excellent views across to the Highlands.

There is a delightful 18-hole course at Forfar (C61) where the locals claim golf has been played since 1651. Tom Morris was responsible for the original layout in 1871, which was added to and modified by James Braid in 1926. Today, the beautiful tree-lined fairways, many of which are crossed by old cultivation ridges, constitute an interesting 6,052 yard course. Again, this is a course built on ridges, mounds and spreads of sand and gravel. James Braid also designed the course at Edzell (C54) in the North Esk Valley which is built on gravel terraces. This is a good-quality parkland course with some fine surrounding woodland.

There are seven golf courses north-west of the Highland edge in Perthshire. The main road north (the A9) follows the deep valley of the Tay at Dunkeld. High up on a coll to the north of Dunkeld is an interesting 9-hole moorland course (C49) which has recently been extended to 18 holes. The course makes use of rugged terrain with some tees placed so that the golfer is required to drive across deep ravines to small greens. This is a very different type of golf when compared to traditional links courses, but the combination of new golfing experiences and spectacular surrounding scenery makes such a course well worth a visit.

The course at Pitlochry (C101), although also built across a steep rocky hillside, is more of a traditional parkland course. No two holes are alike and again there are some delightful views. There are three courses in the Tay Valley to the west of Pitlochry. There is a 9-hole course at Strathtay (C124) and an 18-hole course at Aberfeldy (C2), the latter being built on flat river terraces. Where Loch Tay empties into the River Tay at Kenmore there is another fine parkland course (C121) built on flat river terraces. The Taymouth Castle Golf Course (C121) is one of the most beautiful in the Scottish Highlands. It was designed by James Braid in 1923 and he made full use of the mature parkland surrounding the castle. There is also an attractive 9-hole 'pay and play' course at Kenmore (C73). Two other 9-hole courses, to the north and north-east of Pitlochry respectively, are sited on river terraces. That at Blair Atholl (C44) is rather flat and of an open parkland character, while that at the head of Glen Shee (C44) at the Dalmunzie Hotel is a moorland course.

With over 56 courses ranging in type from those used for great championships to unsophisticated and yet challenging 9-hole layouts set in beautiful scenery, this sub-region has a great deal to offer the golfing enthusiast. Visitors to the region should not restrict themselves to the famous golfing centres of St Andrews, Carnoustie and Gleneagles, but explore the many other delightful courses described in this chapter.

✿ Eight
The North of Scotland
(Region D)

In the first edition of this book I was able to state (p. 181) that in this region: 'There are numerous courses where (in 1987) a round of golf costs £5 or less and a few at which a one pound coin deposited in an honesty box entitles you to play the course.' The development of the oil-related industry in Aberdeen and around the shores of the Moray Firth and of tourism in the Highlands and Islands means that, at least in some parts of the region, very cheap golf is no longer available. Nevertheless, a weekday visitor's green fee for a round of golf on 75% of the 122 courses, one-third of nine holes (Fig. 8.1), still costs less than £20. However, there is an increasing tendency for rural basic 9-hole courses to offer only day tickets for £10 to £15. There are only six courses where a weekday round costs more than £40.

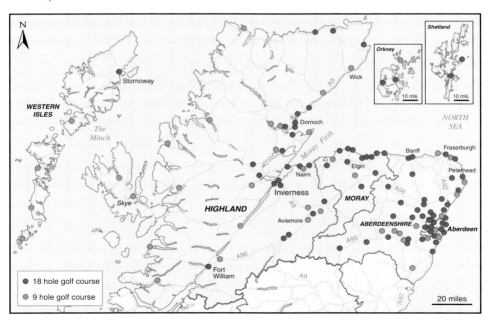

FIG. 8.1 *The location of the 9-hole and 18-hole courses in the North of Scotland.*

169

TABLE 8.1
Membership and Weekday Visitors Green Fees at Six Aberdeenshire Clubs
1973-1998

GOLF CLUB	1973		1984		1994		1998	
	A	B	A	B	A	B	A	B
Oldmeldrum	100	25p	220	£1.50	700	£10	800	£12
Newburgh	125	20p	180	£5.00	50	£10	520	£13
Kemnay	100	25p	300	£1.50	500	£10	820	£14
Kintore	25	18p	260	£2.50	460	£9	700	£11
Inverurie	100	25p	460	£4.00	475	£12	585	£14
Ellon	250	30p	650	£3.50	650	£14	650	£15
Total/average	700	24p	2070	£3.00	3035	£11	4075	£13

A: Total Membership
B: Weekday visitors green fee

At many courses in the north of Scotland the game is played on natural features very little modified by the golf course designer. The combination of unsophisticated courses and clubhouses and the fine surrounding scenery makes the north of Scotland a golfing region of great character. With the expansion of tourism and oil-related industry during the past two decades, many members clubs have expanded their membership and improved their facilities. Major changes have taken place in the provision, quality and management of golf facilities in the area within 20 miles of the centre of Aberdeen. There are six members clubs to the north of Aberdeen (Table 8.1) which clearly demonstrate the impact of the period of oil-related economic and population growth on the golf market in this area. The total membership of the six clubs increased three-fold between 1973 and 1984 and doubled again in the next fourteen years. While the cost of club membership in 1973 is not known (it was probably about £30 per year), an indication of the increase in the cost of playing golf in this area between 1973 and 1998 is provided by the data on visitor weekday green fees at these six clubs. In 1973 the average weekday green fee was 24p per round. It had risen to £3 by 1984 and to £13 in 1997. The average male annual membership fee in 1998 at these clubs was £225 and most of the clubs had long waiting lists. These figures were well below the Scottish average and were cheap compared with members clubs in other parts of the UK. There were two reasons for these low fees. Firstly, all six clubs were originally very basic golf facilities developed by the local population for local use at low cost. With a rapid increase in income from new members and from visitors' green fees, significant VAT refunds (in 1994) and the availability of Sports Lottery Fund grants (post 1995), these clubs were able to improve the quality of their courses and clubhouses. Oldmeldrum, Kemnay, Kintore and Newburgh have extended their courses to 18 holes and built new clubhouses. Secondly, these clubs generated

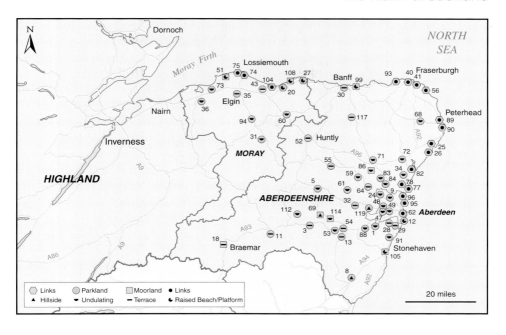

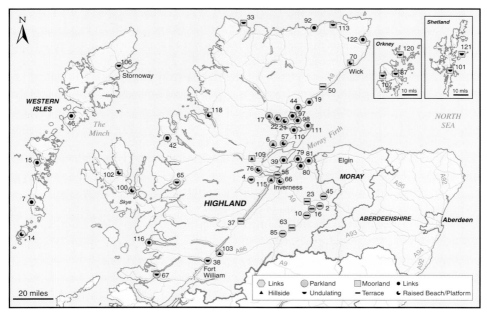

FIGS. 8.2A and 8.2B The landforms and vegetation of the golf courses in the North of Scotland.

a high proportion (30-40%) of their income from non-members (green fees, bar profits, gaming machine profits) and used this income to keep annual membership fees low.

As recently as 1998 the Aberdeen golf market was characterised by demand exceeding supply. In the last two years, seven new golf courses have been constructed, Aberdeen Petroleum Club (9 holes), Newmachar (second 18-hole course), Inchmarlo (9 and 18), Meldrum House (18), East Aberdeenshire (18) and Craibstone (18). Two additional 18-hole courses are in the planning stage. The level of golf facility provision within 20 miles of Aberdeen has increased by 25%, and a situation in which supply is exceeding demand has probably been attained. This is reflected in the reduction or elimination of membership waiting lists at some of the long-established members clubs. Five of the new golf facilities and the two being planned are commercial, primarily 'pay and play'.

The area dealt with in this chapter (Fig. 8.1 and 8.2A and B) consists of the Scottish mainland north of a line from Stonehaven in the east to Fort William in the west, plus the western islands of Skye, North and South Uist, Lewis and Harris and the northern islands of Orkney and Shetland.

There are records of golf having been played on the Aberdeen links in 1538 and on the Dornoch links in 1616. There is a reference in the records of the Banff magistrates for 1773 to the first hole of the 'links'. The history of the game in the north of Scotland goes back to the sixteenth century. The oldest formal golf club in the area is the Royal Aberdeen (1815), which was preceded by the Society of Golfers at Aberdeen (1780). Other early clubs were Cruden Bay (Port Errol 1791), Peterhead (1841), Wick (1870), Aberdeen Bon Accord (1872), Muir of Ord (1875) and Dornoch (1877). However, it was the last quarter of the nineteenth century which saw a major expansion in the number of golf clubs, some 38 clubs being established during the 25-year period. This expansion probably largely reflects the completion of the rail network between Perth, Aberdeen, Fraserburgh, Banff, Elgin, Nairn, Inverness, Wick and Thurso (Fig. 2.3) by 1880. A further 12 clubs were founded between 1901 and 1910 and another 10 clubs between 1920 and 1933. A further 36 courses have been opened since 1954. Most of these recent courses have been opened in response to either tourist development in the Spey Valley or population increases associated with industrial developments (Fort William, Thurso, Invergordon, Nigg Bay, Aberdeen).

The courses of this area fall into two distinct groups—those along the coastline and the inland courses. Most, but not all, of the coastal courses are on links land, while the inland courses are either in the undulating landscape of Aberdeenshire or in the valleys of the Don, Dee, Spey and Great Glen.

COASTAL COURSES

Most of the coastal courses are located in the east between Stonehaven and Wick (40 courses). There are only three courses on the north coast, seven on the west coast, four in the western islands and four in the islands of Orkney and Shetland.

There are 165 miles of coastline between Stonehaven and Inverness, of which some 50% is links land. It is almost surprising that there are only 19 golf courses built on this classic golfing landscape. Between Inverness and Brora there are a further 130 miles of coastline of which some 30 per cent is links land. North of Brora, the only extensive links are to be found at Wick. The coastal courses of the north-east of Scotland either occur on platforms some 100 to 150 feet above sea level and are bounded by steep cliffs, or they occur on low-lying platforms or sand accumulations, often within 20 to 50 feet of present sea level. (For explanations of the origins of these coastal features see chapter 4).

Stonehaven to Fraserburgh (Fig. 8.2A)

Although not a long course (5,128 yards), Stonehaven (D105) produces some unusual challenges to the golfer. It is perched on a dissected platform between rocky cliffs and the railway line to Aberdeen, just north of the town. It is rather atypical of most of the coastal courses described in this section. It is perhaps best described as coastal moorland with some spectacular cliff scenery, and is very exposed to winds off the North Sea.

In historical terms the King's Links at Aberdeen (D62), which form the coastline between the mouths of the Rivers Dee and Don, are one of the ancient foundations of Scottish golf. The formation of the Society of Golfers of Aberdeen in 1780, which used the King's Links, establishes that golf has been played on this site for over 200 years. The appearance of this area has been much changed by human activity over that period. Originally, both river mouths were choked by shifting sandbanks, and between the rivers there was a broad, low sand-plain with several small lochs, especially in the north of the area. The links merged landwards into a raised beach surface of marine sands and gravels underlain by glacial till. Between the links and the beach there used to be an extensive dune ridge, but only remnants of the northern part of this system still remain. These remnants occur to the west of the main road, attaining altitudes of about 25 to 30 feet, and parts of the lower back slopes of the dunes are incorporated into the design of the golf course. Much of the King's Links golf course is of a low undulating nature about 10 to 15 feet above sea level, with a few sand hills and ridges up to 20 feet. The King's Links course is now a municipal course managed by Aberdeen's Department of Leisure and Recreation. The same department also manages two 18-hole and one 9-hole course at Hazlehead (D47, 48, 49), and the 18-hole courses at Balnagask (D12) and Auchmill (D9). The Balnagask golf course lies on a promontory between Nigg Bay and Aberdeen Harbour. It is an area of undulating glacial and fluvioglacial deposits with occasional rock outcrops. There are no trees on the course and the occasional patches of heather and broom give the course a moorland appearance.

The Royal Aberdeen Golf Club (D95, 96) was founded in 1815, and originally the club played over seven holes on the King's Links. In 1866 the club moved to Balgownie to the north of the River Don and has developed two 18-hole courses on classic links

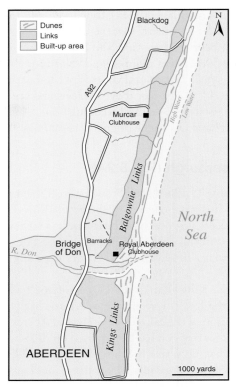

FIG. 8.3 *The landforms of the golf courses north of Aberdeen.*

Ph. 8.1 *Royal Aberdeen (© Angus McNicol).*

land (Fig. 8.3, Ph. 8.1). These links continue for some 10 miles to the north-east, as far as the famous Sands of Forvie at the mouth of the River Ythan. Right next to the Royal Aberdeen Club's main course is the course of the Murcar Golf Club. Both courses are characterised by a large, single coastal dune-ridge some 25 to 40 feet high, which merges inland with hillocks and ridges of sand which in turn merge into undulating links generally 20 to 50 feet above sea level. Most of these blown-sand deposits are underlain by raised-beach sands and gravels. The sand hills on Murcar are somewhat larger than on Royal Aberdeen. Robert Simpson designed Royal Aberdeen and his namesake Andrew, who was the greenkeeper at the new course, designed Murcar which was opened in 1902. Both courses can be regarded as excellent examples of the golf course designer's use of links land.

The links on which the Royal Aberdeen and Murcar courses have been constructed continue northward for a further eight miles to the mouth of the River Ythan, where another golf course is encountered. At Newburgh (D82) a 9-hole course was created on an area of low-lying links with a series of low sandhills and dunes. Most of this area is only 10 to 20 feet above sea level, and the rough consists of gorse and heather. The course sits on a neck of land between the Foveran Burn and the River Ythan, and there are some excellent views of the large sand hills at Forvie on the north-east side of the beautiful Ythan estuary. In 1998 the course was extended inland to add nine holes on undulating upland.

At Cruden Bay (D25), some seven miles south of Peterhead, there are two courses—one of 18 holes which has been described as being of championship standard, and a

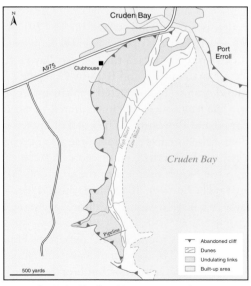

FIG. 8.4 *The landforms of Cruden Bay.*

Ph. 8.2 *Cruden Bay* (© *Angus McNicol*).

9-hole course. The Cruden Bay Golf Club started life in 1791 playing over a course at Port Errol, but in 1899 a new course was opened over the large sand hills and links at the foot of the abandoned cliff on top of which the Cruden Bay Hotel had been built (Fig. 8.4, Ph. 8.2) by the Great North of Scotland Railway Company. The magnificent hotel was built of pink Peterhead granite and attracted wealthy golfers to travel north on the railway from Aberdeen. The new course was inaugurated by a tournament attended by Harry Vardon, James Braid and Ben Sayers. The hotel did not re-open after the Second World War and was demolished in 1947. The course was purchased by a syndicate of local people from the British Transport Commission. Even the arrival of the pipeline, from the Forties Field in the North Sea, just to the south of the course, has had little impact. Many of the fairways lie between 30 feet high dune ridges at the north end of the course, and these give way to a single asymmetric dune ridge some 15 feet high backed by undulating links land.

The shoulder of Buchan sweeps round from Peterhead to Fraserburgh in a series of cuspate bays, each of which is backed by some impressive sand dunes and links land. Some of these dunes are 30 to 40 feet high. On the north side of the town of Peterhead a golf club (D89) was established in 1841. The original clubhouse was abandoned because of the threat of erosion and the course is now served by a large modern clubhouse. Along with the courses at Inverallochy (D56) and Fraserburgh (D40), the Peterhead course has been built on a sand-covered raised beach backed by an abandoned cliff cut in glacial till. The fishermen golfers of Inverallochy are believed to be the last players in the world to have given up the gutty ball.

Fraserburgh to Nairn

Whereas much of the coastline between Fraserburgh and Aberdeen is dominated by dunes and links, that between Fraserburgh and Lossiemouth is dominated by steep rock cliffs leading up to a coastal platform some 100 to 150 feet above sea level (Fig. 8.5). Only in Cullen Bay, Spey Bay and just west of Lossiemouth is there any links land. However, from Burghead to Fort George at the entrance to the Inner Moray Firth there are great expanses of sand and shingle but only the three golf courses at Nairn (D79, 80, 81).

Between Macduff (D99) in the east and Lossiemouth (D74) in the west, a distance of some 30 miles, there are 11 coastal courses which provide a variety of golfing land-scapes. Although in close proximity to the coast (the clubhouse is a mere 200 yards from the beach), the Duff House Royal course (D30) at Banff is in parkland and will be considered in the section devoted to the inland courses of Aberdeenshire.

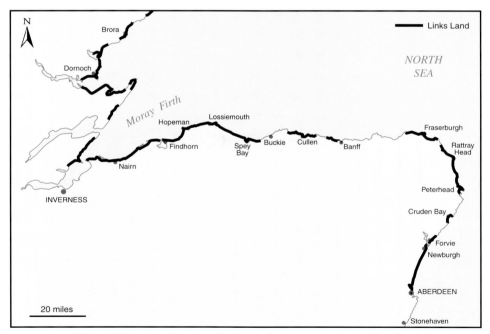

FIG. 8.5 *The distribution of links land in the north-east of Scotland.*

177

This north-facing coast, although a relatively dry part of Scotland (annual precipitation of 22 to 30 inches) is an exposed coastline with frequent sea fogs in summer. The 11 golf courses are built on five types of coastal landforms: coastal dunes at Nairn (D79, 81) and Lossiemouth (D74, 75); raised shingle ridges at Spey Bay (D104); marine platforms and raised beach at Cullen (D27); high raised marine platforms at Hopeman (D51), Buckpool (D20), Strathlene (D108) and Royal Tarlair (D99); and river terraces at Garmouth and Kingston (D43). This variety of landforms provides a remarkable range of golfing landscapes within a relatively small coastal area. All the courses, except Hopeman, are of 18 holes.

Classic links courses are to be found only at Nairn and Lossiemouth and even these are in considerable contrast. The two 18-hole courses at Nairn were both designed by A. Simpson. The Nairn Golf Club course (D79) to the west of the town was built on a raised shingle-beach covered by blown sand (Ph. 8.3). Simpson's original design (1887) was improved both by Tom Morris and James Braid, and although there are no dramatic sandhills or spectacular views, it is a challenging seaside course which has been ranked in the top 40 courses in the British Isles by *Golf World*. The Ladies British Amateur Championship was held here in 1979 and the Walker Cup in 1999. The Nairn Dunbar

Ph. 8.3 *Nairn* (© *Angus McNicol*).

course (D81), to the east of the town, lies on an elevated surface 15–30 feet above sea level, and while providing an exacting test of golf skills, it has the appearance of a rather uninteresting area of links land. Both the Nairn clubs have constructed new clubhouses. In great contrast are the two links courses at Lossiemouth (D74, 75) which are built on sandhills up to 25 feet high along with undulating links land. The links land consists of blown sand covering raised shingle-ridges. The Moray Golf Club was established in 1889 and the Old Course was designed by Tom Morris. A second 18-hole course (the New) was designed by Henry Cotton and opened in 1979. While both courses are very attractive, being built close to the beach and having extensive colourful areas of gorse rough, their proximity to the Lossiemouth military airfield does lead to some noisy distractions.

A different type of links course is to be found at Spey Bay (D104). An 18-hole course has been laid out on a series of raised, storm-beach ridges which accumulated during periods of higher relative sea level some 6,000 years ago. The ridges consist of boulders and pebbles and largely coincide with the rough of gorse and heather, while the fairways are to be found in the shallow 'valleys' between the ridges. Wind direction and strength obviously play an important part in determining the difficulty of this course. Just half a mile to the west of the Spey Bay golf course, but on the other side of the River Spey and therefore a six-mile drive via the bridge at Fochabers, is the Garmouth and Kingston course (D43). While parts of this course have the characteristic of true links (mainly built on river gravels and raised-beach gravels) other parts have fairways lined by birch and alder and have a parkland character. Both the Spey Bay and Garmouth courses provide excellent, cheap golf at under £15 per round (in 1999).

Cullen (D27) is one of the most interesting golf courses in this district. It contains two distinct golfing landscapes and provides the golfer not only with a variety of challenges but also with some fine views. It is a short course of 4,610 yards, but it can be a difficult test particularly in windy conditions. The course starts out along the post-glacial raised beach and then the golfer is required to play a shot from the second tee up the face of the abandoned cliff to a green which sits up on the upper marine-platform (Fig. 8.6). This platform at about 100 feet above sea level is the 'moorland' section of the course and contains holes 3,

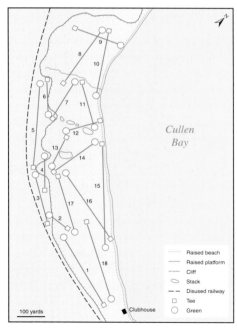

FIG. 8.6 *The landforms of Cullen Golf Course.*

Ph. 8.4 *Cullen.*

4, 5 and 6. The seventh tee is perched on the cliff edge (Ph. 8.4) with the green of this 231 yard, par three hole some 80 feet below on the links part of the course. I thoroughly enjoyed watching the result of a drive hang in the air for several seconds before pitching on the green, on the first occasion I played the course. During two subsequent rounds in the same week, it was impossible to see the green from the seventh tee because of sea fog (or 'haar') which can be another local hazard along this coastline in summer. The remainder of this course (i.e. holes 8 to 18) is close to sea level and is built on the post-glacial raised beach which is fronted by a low dune-ridge and partly covered by blown sand. However, this is not typical links land because on several holes the golfer has to negotiate abandoned sea-cliffs and stacks (Ph. 8.4). These upstanding rock ridges cause the player to make blind shots on the 12th, 13th and 14th holes, and if the golf ball hits any of the almost vertical rock faces, it can fly in almost any direction. The last few holes are played across links land back towards the town.

There are four cliff-top courses along this coast which are located on an old raised marine-platform some 70 to 150 feet above present sea level—Hopeman (D51), Buckpool (D20), Strathlene (D108) and Royal Tarlair at Macduff (D99). They are best described as coastal moorland courses, often with fine views and the occasional tricky hole which makes use of the cliff scenery. The course at Hopeman has one dramatic hole with a drop from tee to green of 100 feet and the short 13th (152 yards) at Royal Tarlair crosses a deep ravine.

The Beauly Firth to Reay (Thurso)

This part of the Scottish coastline (Fig. 8.2B) falls into two distinct sections. Between Inverness and Dornoch the sea penetrates far inland in the firths of Beauly (Moray), Cromarty and Dornoch. There are 12 golf courses which are either on the shores of or overlook these firths. To the north of Dornoch the character of the coastline changes, with high coastal plateaus bounded by a steeply-cliffed coastline and occasional pockets of links land. In this north-east corner of Scotland there are seven golf courses.

Excellent examples of raised beaches are found around the Beauly Firth: the 18-hole course at Muir of Ord (D76) is built on one of them. It is in pleasant parkland and utilises the terrace form of the raised beaches. One of the last courses to be designed by James Braid is at Fortrose (D38): it is built on a raised beach and a raised spit which extends out into the Moray Firth, and can best be described as a gentle links course.

For convenience, the very interesting inland course at Strathpeffer (D109) will be discussed in this section, even though it cannot be described as a coastal course. However, from the higher parts of the course there are fine views of the Cromarty Firth. It is a very hilly, moorland course located in a col some 500 feet above sea level and surrounded by coniferous plantations. The course was opened in 1888 in association with the development of the spa town of Strathpeffer. There are some very interesting holes on this golf course but it is its beautiful scenic setting which makes it well worth a visit.

On the north shore of the Cromarty Firth are two 18-hole courses—one at Alness (D6) and the other at Invergordon (D57). The former is a moorland course while the latter is a parkland course built on raised-beach deposits with views of the Cromarty Firth and its oil-related activities.

Around the shores of the Dornoch Firth are some fine links golf courses which owe their origins to the dramatic environmental changes which have taken place in the area over the past 15,000 years (Price 1983). At the maximum of the last ice sheet, great glaciers descended the Oykel and Shin valleys, moving southeast down the Kyle of Sutherland and Strath Fleet. As the glaciers retreated, the land was still depressed by the former weight of the ice and sea-levels were at least 100 feet higher than at present. Vast quantities of sand and gravel were deposited in Loch Fleet, the inner Dornoch Firth, the Brora Valley and along the coastline from Tarbat Ness to Brora. Sea level fell to about six feet below its present level about 9,000 years ago, before rising rapidly again to reach some 20 feet above present levels about 6,000 years ago. It began to decline again about 4,000 years ago. The combination of the provision of large quantities of sediment (sand and gravel) by the retreating glaciers and the re-working of these sediments by fluctuating sea levels has created the very distinctive 'soft' coastal landscapes around the shores of the Dornoch Firth (Fig. 8.7). Underlying most of the area below the 50 foot contour are gravel and shingle deposits put in place by wave action associated with the high postglacial sea level of 6,000 years ago. Since that time areas such as Morrich Moor, east of Tain (12 square miles), Cuthill Links, Dornoch Links, Coul Links, Ferry Links (Golspie)

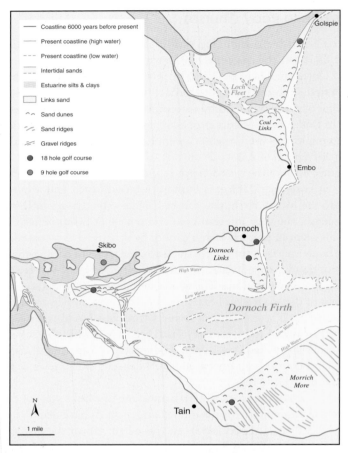

Legend:
- Coastline 6000 years before present
- Present coastline (high water)
- Present coastline (low water)
- Intertidal sands
- Estuarine silts & clays
- Links sand
- Sand dunes
- Sand ridges
- Gravel ridges
- 18 hole golf course
- 9 hole golf course

FIG. 8.7 *The present and former coastline (6,000 years ago) of the Dornoch Firth.*

and Brora Links have been modified by a thin cover of wind-blown sands (sand plains) or by the development of sand-dune ridges. This links land was ideally suited to the game of golf and golf clubs were established at Dornoch in 1877, Golspie in 1899, Tain in 1890 and Brora in 1891, although the game was probably played at these places long before the creation of formal clubs.

On the southern shore of the Dornoch Firth are two links courses—one at Tain (D110) and a 9-hole course at Portmahomack (D111). The course at Tain was designed by Tom Morris and is an interesting mixture of links and inland parkland golf. At Bonar Bridge at the head of the Firth there is a 9-hole moorland course (D17).

Royal Dornoch (D97, 98) is undoubtedly the most famous golf course in the north-east of Scotland (Ph. 8.5). *Golf World* has ranked it in the top ten in Britain and the British Amateur Championship was played here in 1986. Tom Watson has described the course '...as one of the great courses of the five continents. I have played none finer, a natural masterpiece'. There is little doubt that the Open Championship would have been played here if the course were not located in the north-east corner of Scotland. Although golf was probably played on the Dornoch links in the seventeenth century, the Dornoch Club was founded in 1877 and in 1886 the Club invited the veteran champion golfer, Old Tom Morris, to make a survey of the links and lay out a planned course. The club received its royal status in 1906. John Sutherland was Secretary of the club for 53 years until 1935 and had a great influence on the development of the course. By 1939 there were two 18-hole courses, but the RAF requisitioned several holes for a wartime airstrip. After the war George Duncan built six new holes. The course is built on an area of blown sand resting on top of a raised beach. The combination of sand ridges, mounds and hollows, and gorse and heather rough, provides some classic links golf. This is one course where the so-called 'Scottish shot' of a pitch and run up to the hole is rarely possible, as many of the greens sit on top of mounds with steep banks surrounding the putting surface. A famous son of Dornoch, Donald Ross, emigrated to America in 1898 where he designed the Seminole, Oakland Hills and Pinehurst courses among many others, and the characteristic 'perched' green, so familiar in Dornoch, is seen on some of his American courses—particularly at Pinehurst No 2. Not only Donald Ross but many

Ph. 8.5 *Royal Dornoch (© Angus McNicol).*

other Scottish golfers who learned the game on the now famous links at St Andrews, Royal Dornoch, Musselburgh, Troon or Prestwick and who then emigrated to America and embarked on a career of golf course design, took with them the memory of many of the natural features of Scottish links land and incorporated them in their new man-made golfing landscapes.

When Andrew Carnegie bought Skibo Castle in 1898 he soon established contact with John Sutherland, the famous secretary of Royal Dornoch Golf Club. He asked Mr Sutherland to design a 9-hole course on the Skibo estate so that he could learn the game of golf and he subsequently became a member of the Dornoch club. He also presented to the club the Carnegie Shield, which remains the club's foremost trophy. When Peter de Savery bought the Skibo Estate in 1990 for the establishment of the Carnegie Club, he commissioned Donald Steel to design an 18-hole championship course on the narrow spit of land which juts out into the Dornoch Firth and is bounded to the north by Loch Evelix. This spit was produced during the high stand of sea level some 6,000 years ago and consists of marine gravels overlain by a thin cover of blown sand. This is a land-scape typical of the margins of the Dornoch Firth and Donald Steel has created a magnificent traditional links course of 6,650 yards from which there are some dramatic views. An interesting 9-hole parkland course, also designed by Donald Steel, can either be played from one set of tees as a par 3 course of 1,545 yards, or from another set of tees as a par 3.5 course of 2,825 yards.

The Carnegie Club is a luxurious, international members club which has some very famous members. A limited number of tee-times are available to non-members (on week-days between 11am and 12 noon) at a green fee of £130.

After turning inland from Dornoch to pass around Loch Fleet, the main road north (A9) returns to the coast at Golspie. There is another raised beach/blown sand combina-tion here which is the location of Golspie golf course (D44) designed by James Braid who also designed the course at Brora, some five miles further north. The Brora course was set in a series of 20 to 40 foot high sand hills with several elevated tees and greens.

At Helmsdale (D50) and Lybster (D70) there are 9-hole courses, both of moorland character although close to the coast. North of Lybster the almost flat, wind-blown land-scape of eastern Caithness is sometimes rather bleak. Three miles to the north of the town of Wick is the exposed links of the Wick Golf Club (D122), founded in 1870. Much of the course is built on gently undulating links land which is given some protec-tion from the easterly winds by the presence of a larger outer dune ridge. Thurso Golf Course (D84), opened in 1964, sits on the almost flat moorland surface south of the town. Golf has been played at Reay (D92), 12 miles west of Thurso, since 1893 on a delightful links course—the only links course on the entire north coast of Scotland. A sixty-mile journey, west from Reay along a narrow twisting road with some spectacular views, leads to the village of Durness where a group of enthusiastic golfers have laid out a 9-hole course of 2,762 yards. The course (D33) was opened in 1988 and is located on a limestone bench partly covered by wide-blown sand. This is definitely not a modern,

Ph. 8.6 *Durness.*

expensive piece of golf course design, but a delightful natural course where golfers share the moorland turf with grazing sheep (Ph. 8.6). The par 3 ninth hole involves a carry of 150 yards across an embayment occupied by the Atlantic Ocean. The small clubhouse, which sells refreshments during the season, is not always staffed and visitors are requested to place a £12 fee, for a day ticket, in the honesty box. The views from the clubhouse and from the course, of coastal cliffs and mountains, can only be described as spectacular. Durness golf course is the most northerly course on mainland Scotland (58° 34′) and it is only marginally further north than the courses at Reay and Thurso. One of the delights of these northern courses is to play golf late into the evening of the long summer days—it is not at all uncommon to be able to conclude an evening round at 11pm.

The West Coast, Western Isles, Orkney and Shetland

There are only four golf courses on the west coast of the Scottish mainland north of Fort William—Loch Sunart (D67), Mallaig (D116), Loch Carron (D65) and Gairloch (D42). The courses at Mallaig (Ph. 8.7) and Gairloch are on links land, the latter being built across some high sand dunes. There is a 9-hole course on the east coast of Skye at Sconser (D100) and another at Skeabost (D102). In the Outer Hebrides there are five courses. Information about these courses has been provided by Mike Williamson (MW

Ph. 8.7 *Traigh, Mallaig.*

Associates) as it is some thirty years since I last visited the Outer Hebrides. Four of the courses are of nine holes, Barra (D14), Askernish South Uist (D7), Benbecula (D15) and Harris (D46), while the 18-hole parkland course at Stornoway (D106) is the only professionally maintained course. All four of the 9-hole courses are on machair land (links land) and are best described as 'natural' courses maintained by enthusiastic members. All of the courses welcome visitors and apart from Stornoway (weekday green fee, £15) a round of golf can be enjoyed by placing £6 in an honesty box.

Stornoway Golf Club was established in 1890 but its original course at Melbost was requisitioned for the construction of an airport and the present course was constructed in 1947. The club has a website and welcomes visitors.

The four 9-hole courses are all short (2,200–2,500 yards) and provide basic golf facilities in fine natural settings. The Harris Golf Club has sold 400 life-memberships to non-residents of the island for £100 each. The Benbecula course has two sets of tees for each hole, thus giving variety to a round of 18 holes. The course is very flat and set amongst various military buildings.

The 9-hole course at Askernish was part of an 18-hole course laid out by Old Tom Morris in 1891. Again, there are two sets of tees on each hole. The ground is common grazing, but with animals kept off from May to September.

The course on Barra was established in 1992 and is laid out on an area of hummocky topography, with a significant number of rock outcrops, blind shots and holes whose length and shape is determined by the lie of the land rather than by golf design. The greens are fenced to minimise damage by cattle, sheep and rabbits. This course is the most westerly in Britain.

Apart from the course at Stornoway, golf in the Outer Hebrides is much the same today as it was in 1900. Enthusiastic local golfers maintain their courses and pay annual membership fees of between £40 and £60 per year. The members of these clubs welcome visitors to their courses for nominal green fees, and while you will not find manicured greens, tees and fairways or luxurious clubhouses, you will enjoy cheap golf in the form of the early traditions of Scottish golf.

The Orkney Islands contain two 18-hole courses (D87, 107) and one 9-hole course (D120) and there are two 18-hole courses (D101, 121) in Shetland.

INLAND COURSES

There are four distinct areas of inland golf courses in the North of Scotland (Fig. 8.1)—Aberdeenshire, Moray, the Upper Spey Valley and the Great Glen (Fort William to Inverness).

Aberdeen City and Aberdeenshire (Fig. 8.8)

The city of Aberdeen has ten golf courses, six of which are municipal. The Kings Links course (D62) has a long history which pre-dates its operation as a municipal facility. At Hazlehead (D47, 48, 49) there is a municipal complex of two 18-hole and one 9-hole course, and there are 18-hole municipal courses at Auchmill (D9) and Balnagask (D12).

Royal Deeside is justly famous for its beautiful scenery and for salmon fishing. Since the glaciers disappeared from the area some 10,000 years ago, the River Dee has been depositing, and subsequently eroding, large quantities of gravel along the valley bottom. Throughout much of the valley there are sequences of gravel terraces which have provided excellent sites for inland golf courses. Seven courses were built between 1891 and 1908 and a further four courses, Peterculter (D88), Aberdeen Petroleum Club (D1) and Inchmarlo's 27 holes (D53, 54) have been built in the last decade as the Dee Valley below Banchory has become a commuter suburb of Aberdeen.

On the outskirts of Aberdeen is the fine parkland course of Deeside (D28) while further up the Dee Valley the course at Banchory (D13) has recently been renovated and lengthened and makes full use of the stepped-landscape of the river terraces. A new commercial golf facility at Inchmarlo (D53), to the west of Banchory, was opened in 1997 as a 9-hole course on a gravel terrace plus a driving range and clubhouse/restaurant. This facility, in June 2000, opened a new 18-hole course (D54) designed by Graeme Webster. Along with the courses at Aboyne (D3) and Ballater (D11), these parkland courses provide some delightful golfing landscapes. The course at Braemar (D18) is also largely laid out on river gravels but it has a moorland character. A second 9-hole course at Aboyne (D112), played over by the Tarland Golf Club, is located in the grounds of a

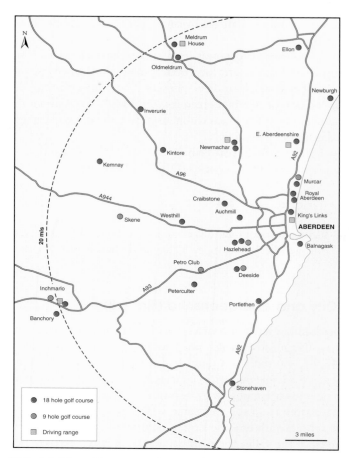

FIG. 8.8 The golf courses within 20 miles of Aberdeen city centre.

large mansion which was used as a wartime hospital. A 9-hole moorland course at Torphins (D114), some seven miles north-west of Banchory, is not actually in the Dee Valley, but it stands on an upland area some 500 feet above sea level, and from the course there are excellent views of the mountains to the south of the Dee Valley.

The impact of the economic activity associated with the North Sea oil industry led to the development of 11 new golf courses in this sub-region. The first was built at Westhill, a new suburb of Aberdeen, in 1977, and the second, at Portlethen (D119), was built in 1983. Neither of these parkland courses are particularly attractive. In 1989, at Newmachar (12 miles north of Aberdeen on the A947), Dave Thomas designed a challenging 18-hole course (D83) for a new members club (Ph. 8.8). A fine clubhouse, a driving range and a second 18-hole course (D84) opened in 1998, have made this a significant addition to the golf facilities of the sub-region. Within the last two years a new commercial 18-hole

Ph. 8.8 *Newmachar.*

course (East Aberdeenshire Golf Club, D34) has been opened at Balmedie on the A90, and the Scottish Agricultural College has constructed an 18-hole 'pay and play' course (D24) on its estate at Craibstone to the north-west of Aberdeen on the A96. The long-established members clubs at Ellon (D72), Inverurie (D89), Kintore (D64), Kemnay (D61), Insch (D55) and Oldmeldrum (D86) have all upgraded their courses and clubhouses in recent years.

Twenty miles north of Aberdeen on the A94, in the village of Oldmeldrum, a high-quality 18-hole golf course, clubhouse and practice facility have been built in the grounds of Meldrum House (D71). This course was designed by Graeme Webster and built by Glen Andrews Ltd of Dyce, in a fine parkland estate adjacent to the Meldrum House Hotel. This facility is currently operated as an exclusive members club and is not available to non-members unless they are resident at the hotel or are guests of members.

The series of coastal courses between Peterhead and Nairn is strongly supported by an interesting group of seven inland courses. Although within a few hundred yards of the coastline, Duff House Royal Golf Club (D30) plays over a very fine parkland course built on the gravel terraces of the River Deveron. The history of golf in the town of Banff has a macabre beginning. In 1637 a boy was convicted and hanged for stealing golf balls. There is also a reference in the records of the Banff magistrates for 1733 to the 'first hole of the links'. It is doubtful whether these early references refer to activities on the present course, which was designed by Dr A. McKenzie who later designed both the Augusta National and Cypress Point courses in the United States. The club was given its Royal

189

status in 1923 and is the only club in the world to use the term as a suffix. The modern clubhouse and high quality of this parkland course make it one of the most attractive courses in this area.

Further up the valley of the River Deveron, two more courses are built on gravel terraces, one at Turriff (D117) and another at Huntly (D52). Both are pleasant parkland courses and along with the more recently developed course at Keith (D60) offer an interesting change of scene for the golfer who may have decided to visit this corner of Scotland mainly to play the coastal courses. In a similar way the two courses at Elgin (D35) and Forres (D36) offer parkland golf of a high quality to the visitors staying at Nairn and Lossiemouth.

The Spey Valley

Although the villages of Newtonmore, Kingussie, Boat of Garten, Carrbridge and Granton on Spey are most famous for their winter sports, the Spey Valley is also a major tourist attraction during the summer months and each of these villages has a golf course. Like the Dee Valley, most of the courses are built on the gravel terraces which are conspicuous features along the valley floor. The three 18-hole courses at Newtonmore (D85), Boat of Garten (D16) and Grantown on Spey (D45), as well as the two 9-hole courses at Carrbridge (D23) and Abernethy (D12), make use of these well-drained gravels. The course at Newtonmore is partly built on a kame terrace with kettle holes—that is, the gravels were

Ph. 8.9 *Boat of Garten.*

deposited up against the retreating margin of a glacier and lumps of glacier ice were buried in the gravels only to melt subsequently and produce the kettle holes (depressions) in the terrace surface. There are magnificent views of the Cairngorm Mountains from this course. Many visitors have extolled the virtues of the courses at Grantown on Spey and Boat of Garten (Ph. 8.9). Both are characterised by rolling parkland with fine stands of conifers and birches plus heather rough. Robert Green, writing in *Golf World's* 'The World of Scottish Golf' in 1985, stated that Boat of Garten '... is probably the finest "short" golf course I have ever played'. The one course which is markedly different from the others in the Spey Valley is that at Kingussie (D63). It is a combination of holes on terraced parkland and heather moorland with rocky outcrops.

The Great Glen

One of Scotland's most dramatic topographic features is the Great Glen. It is a long, straight and steep-sided trough resulting from many tens of millions of years of erosion by water and glacier ice along the line of a major fault (fracture) in the earth's crust. It is aligned in a south-west to north-east direction with the town of Fort William in the south-west and the town of Inverness at the north-east end.

There are six golf courses in the Great Glen. Apart from the Inverness Club (D58) which was founded in 1883, golf arrived late in the Great Glen. The interesting 9-hole course built on gravel terraces (with kettle holes) at Fort Augustus was opened in 1930. Another 9-hole course at Spean Bridge (D103) was opened in 1954. There is a municipal course in Inverness at Torvean (D48) built on river gravels in attractive parkland (opened 1962). North of Fort William (D39) a course was built in 1975 over hummocky ground created by the last glaciers to occupy this area some 10,000 years ago. It is a mixture of moorland and parkland.

A new commercial golf facility consisting of an 18-hole course, driving range and clubhouse, the Loch Ness Club (D66), was opened in 1996 on the south side of Inverness.

The marked concentration of golf courses on the eastern side of the Scottish Highlands is probably a reflection of two sets of circumstances. Firstly, golf had its early development in the east, and the coastal and inland landscapes of Aberdeenshire, Easter Ross and Caithness were conducive both to the expansion of the game and to the development of tourism. The climatic differences between west and east are also such that the building and upkeep of courses is easier in the east. The golfers of Fort William 'enjoy' an annual rainfall of 78 inches while those in Nairn, with an annual average rainfall of 20 inches, have problems in maintaining their greens through periods of drought.

𝒲 Bibliography

*Titles marked * are particularly informative on the history of golf in Scotland.*

Alliss, P. (ed) 1987. *Golf, a Way of Life.* Stanley Paul.

*Baird, A. 1985. *Golf on Gullane Hill.* Edinburgh.

*Behrend, J. and Lewis, P.N. 1998. *Challenges and Champions—The Royal and Ancient Golf Club: 1754-1883.* The Royal and Ancient Golf Club of St. Andrews.

Campbell, M. 1999. *The Scottish Golf Book.* Lomond Books, Edinburgh.

Colville, J. 1907. *The Glasgow Golf Club.* Glasgow.

Cornish, S. and Whitten, R.E. 1983. *The Golf Course.* Windward, Leicester.

Crampsey, R.A. 1988. *St. Mungos Gowfers—The History of Glasgow Golf Club 1987-1987.* Glasgow.

*Darwin, B. *et al* 1952. *The History of Golf in Britain.* Cassell, London.

Davis, P. 1993. *The Historical Dictionary of Golfing Terms.* Robson Books Ltd, London.

Dickson, J. H. 1991. *Wild Plants of Glasgow.* Aberdeen University Press.

Drysdale, A. M. 1975. *The Golf House Club, Elie.* Elie, Fife.

European Golf Association Ecology Unit 1996. *An Environmental Management Programme for Golf Courses.*

European Golf Association Ecology Unit 1997. *The Committed to Green Handbook for Golf Courses.*

Forgan, R. 1880. *Golfers Handbook.* (Now published annually by Macmillan).

Furnie, H.B. 1857. *Golfer's Manual.* Whitehead & Orr, Cupar, Fife.

Hamilton, D. 1985. *Early Golf in Aberdeen.* The Partick Press.

Hamilton, D. 1985. *Early Golf in Glasgow: 1589-1787.* The Partick Press.

*Hamilton, D. 1998. *Golf—Scotland's Game.* The Partick Press.

Hawtree, F.W. 1983. *The Golf Course—Planning, Design, Construction.* Spon Ltd. London.

*Henderson, I. & Stirk, D. 1979. *Golf in the Making.* Henderson & Stirk Ltd, Winchester.

Highland Golf Development Group 1999. *Highland Golf Development Strategy.*

Laidlaw, R. (ed) 1999. *The Royal and Ancient Golfers Handbook.* Macmillan—published annually.

Menzies, G. (ed) 1982. *The World of Golf.* BBC Publications, London.

Price, R. J. 1983. *Scotland's Environment During the Last 30,000 Years.* Scottish Academic Press, Edinburgh.

Price, R. J. 1988. The Landforms of Scotland's Golf Courses. *Sport Place International,* Vol. 2, No 1, 2-13.

Price, R. J. 1992. Environmental Aspects of 250 Years of Golf Development in Scotland. *Proceedings of the World Golf Forum, Tokyo, Japan.* 192-202.

Price, R. J. 1993. Can Scottish Golf Get Out of the Bunker? *Scottish Banker* (Chartered Institute of Bankers).

Price, R. J. 1997. The Scottish Golf Industry—Performing Below Par. *Scottish Banker* (Chartered Institute of Bankers).

Price, R. J. 1998. Golf Course Provision, Usage and Revenues in Scotland. *Proceedings Third World Scientific Congress of Golf,* 594-599. Human Kinetics.

Price, R. J. 1998. *The Golf Industry in Scotland—Current Status and Future Prospects.* Research Report.

Price, R. J. 2000. *The Management and Marketing of Scotland's Golf Facilities.* Research Report.

Ransomes, Sims & Jefferies. *Ransomes—A Great Tradition 1832–1982.* Ipswich.

Robertson, A.D. 1951. *The Story of Lanark Golf Club 1851–1951.* Lanark.

Robertson, J. K. 1984. *St Andrews Home of Golf.* Macdonald, Edinburgh.

Royal and Ancient Golf Club, St Andrews 1989. *The Demand for Golf.*

Scottish Sports Council 1991. *Study of Golf in Scotland.*

Smith, J. A. 1998. The Role of Golf Clubs in the Conservation of Scotland's Natural And Cultural Heritage. *Proceedings of the Third World Scientific Congress of Golf.* 729-734. Human Kinetics.

Smith, R. H. 1866. *Golfers Yearbook.* Smith and Grant, Ayr.

Stubbs, D. 1998. The Importance of Environmental Management for Golf. *Proceedings of the Third Scientific Congress of Golf,* 710-720. Human Kinetics.

The Henley Centre 1997. *EMAP Futures—Future Trends in the British Golf Market.*

T.M.S. 1998. *Golf Tourism Review—Issues and Recommendations.* (produced for Scottish Enterprise).

*van Hengel, S.J.H. 1985. *Early Golf.* F.P. van Eck, Vaduz, Liechtenstein.

Ward Thomas, P. et al., 1976, *The World Atlas of Golf.* Mitchell Beazley, London.

Ward Thomas, P. 1980. *The Royal and Ancient.* Scottish Academic Press, Edinburgh.

Williamson, M. G. 1998. Golf Tourism: Measurement and Marketing. *Proceedings of the Third World Scientific Congress of Golf.* 600-608. Human Kinetics.

Young, Arthur. 1987. *Study of Golf Facilities in Scotland.* (for the Scottish Tourist Board).

🌿 Appendix
Regional listing of 538 Golf Courses

KEY

Ref. No.: Reference number used in text with prefix for each region (A,B,C,D)

Name: Name of facility or golf club

Address, Postcode: Name of location with postcode

Date: Based either on the date of foundation of the oldest club to use the course, or on the known date of opening of the course

H: Number of holes

Yds: Length of course in yards. Length of 9-hole courses is stated as 18-hole equivalent.

Man: Type of management

    MC—Members Club
    Mu—Municipal or Links Management Committee
    Co—Commercial Company

GF: Weekday Green Fee

    A—Less than £10
    B—£10–£19
    C—£20–£29
    D—£30–£39
    E—£40–£49
    F—over £50

L: Landforms

U	Undulating
H	Hillside
D	Drumlin
E	Esker
K	Kame
KT	Kame Terrace
RT	River Terrace
S	Sandur (outwash fan)
RB	Raised Beach
RM	Raised Marine Platform
L	Links

V: Vegetation

P	Parkland
PW	Woodland
M	Moorland
L	Links

Region A: South and South-east Scotland

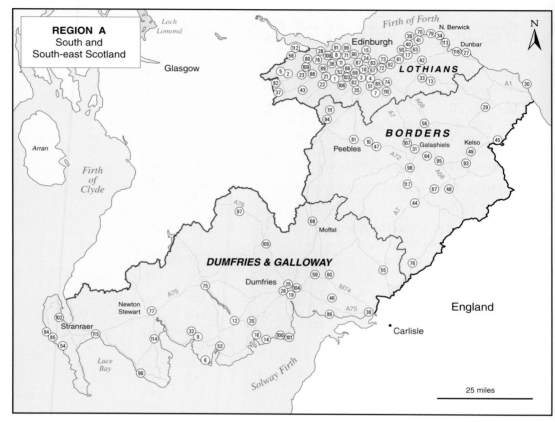

	NAME	ADDRESS	POSTCODE	DATE	H	YDS	MAN	GF	L	V
1	**Baberton**	Edinburgh	EH14 5DU	1893	18	6123	MC	C	U	P
2	**Bathgate**	Bathgate	EH48 1BA	1892	18	6326	MC	B	U	M
3	**Braid Hills 1**	Edinburgh	EH10 6JY	1893	18	5731	Mu	B	H	M
4	**Braid Hills 2**	Edinburgh	EH10 6JY	1894	18	4832	Mu	B	H	M
5	**Bridge Castle**	Armadale	EH48 3NX	1999	10	6042	Co	B	U	P
6	**Brighouse Bay**	Kirkcudbright	DG6 4TS	1996	18	6030	Co	B	U	L/M
7	**Broomieknowe**	Bonnyrigg	EH19 2HZ	1906	18	6200	MC	B	U	P
8	**Bruntsfield Links**	Edinburgh	EH4 6JH	1761	18	6407	MC	D	RB	P
9	**Cally Palace**	Gatehouse of Fleet	DG7 2DL	1995	18	5802	Co	D	RT	P
10	**Cardrona**	Peebles	EH44 6PH	2001	18		Co		RT	P

	NAME	ADDRESS	POSTCODE	DATE	H	YDS	MAN	GF	L	V
11	Carrick Knowe	Edinburgh	EH12 5VZ	1930	18	6299	Mu	A	U	P
12	Castle Douglas	Castle Douglas	DG7 1BA	1905	9	5408	MC	B	K	P
13	Castle Park	Gifford	EH41 4PL	1995	9	5592	Co	B	U	P
14	Colvend	Dalbeattie	DG5 4PY	1908	18	4700	MC	B	H	M
15	Craigentinny	Edinburgh	EH7 6RG	1891	18	5418	Mu	A	RB	P
16	Craigieknowes	Kippford	DG5 4QS	1996	9	2782	Co	A	H	P
17	Craigielaw	Aberlady	EH32 0PY	2001	18	6601	Co	D	L	L
18	Craigmillar Park	Edinburgh	EH9 3HG	1895	18	5859	MC	C	H	P
19	Crichton	Dumfries	DG1 4TH	1884	9	3084	MC	B	U	P
20	Dalbeattie	Dalbeattie	DG5 4JR	1897	9	4200	MC	B	H	M
21	Dalmahoy 1, east	Kirknewton	EH27 8EB	1926	18	6677	Co	F	U	P
22	Dalmahoy 2, west	Kirknewton	EH27 8EB		18	5185	Co	D	U	P
23	Deer Park	Livingston	EH54 9PG	1978	18	6636	Co	B	U	P
24	Duddingston	Edinburgh	EH15 3QB	1895	18	6438	MC	C	U	P
25	Dumfries & County	Dumfries	DG1 1JX	1912	18	5928	MC	C	KT	P
26	Dumfries & Galloway	Dumfries	DG2 7NY	1880	18	6325	MC	C	K	P
27	Dunbar	Dunbar	EH42 1LT	1856	18	6426	MC	C	RB	L
28	Dundas Park	South Queensferry	EH30 9SS	1957	9	6025	MC	B	U	P
29	Duns	Duns	TD11 3NR	1894	18	6209	MC	B	U	P
30	Eyemouth	Eyemouth	TD14 5DX	1880	18	6472	MC	B	RM	M
31	Galashiels	Galashiels	TD1 2NJ	1884	18	5309	MC	B	H	M
32	Gatehouse of Fleet	Gatehouse	DG7 2PW	1921	9	5042	MC	B	H	M
33	Gifford	Gifford	EH41 4JN	1904	9	6256	MC	C	U	P
34	Glen	North Berwick	EH39 4LE	1906	18	6079	MC	B	RM	L
35	Glencorse	Penicuik	EH26 0RD	1890	18	5217	MC	B	U	P
36	Gogarburn	Newbridge	EH28 8NN	1975	12	3021	MC	B	U	P
37	Greenburn	Fauldhouse	EH47 9HG	1953	18	6210	MC	B	RT	P
38	Gretna	Gretna	DG16 5HD	1991	9	6430	Co	A	RB	P
39	Gullane 1	Gullane	EH31 2BB	1882	18	6466	MC	F	L	L
40	Gullane 2	Gullane	EH31 2BB	1898	18	6244	MC	C	L	L
41	Gullane 3	Gullane	EH31 2BB	1909	18	5252	MC	B	L	L
42	Haddington	Haddington	EH41 4PT	1865	18	6317	MC	B	RT	P
43	Harburn	West Calder	EH55 8RS	1921	18	5921	MC	B	U	P
44	Hawick	Hawick	TD9 0NY	1877	18	6066	MC	C	H	M
45	Hirsel	Coldstream	TD12 4NJ	1948	18	6092	MC	C	RT	P
46	Hoddom Castle	Lockerbie	DG11 1AS	1993	9	4548	Co	A	RT	P
47	Innerleithen	Innerleithen	EH44 6NL	1886	9	6066	MC	B	RT	P
48	Jedburgh	Jedburgh	TD8 6LA	1892	9	5492	MC	B	U	M

	NAME	ADDRESS	POSTCODE	DATE	H	YDS	MAN	GF	L	V
49	Kelso	Kelso	TD5 7SL	1887	18	6066	MC	B	RT	P
50	Kilspindie	Aberlady	EH32 0QD	1867	18	5452	MC	C	L	L
51	Kings Acre	Lasswade	EH18 1AU	1997	18	5935	Co	B	RT/U	P
52	Kingsknowe	Edinburgh	EH14 2JD	1908	18	5966	MC	B	U	P
53	Kirkcudbright	Kirkcudbright	DG6 4EZ	1893	18	5739	MC	B	H	P
54	Lagganmore	Portpatrick	DG9 9AB	1992	18	5807	Co	B	U	M
55	Langholm	Langholm	DG13 0JR	1892	9	5246	MC	B	H	P
56	Lauder	Lauder	TD2 6QD	1896	9	6002	Mu	B	U	M
57	Liberton	Edinburgh	EH16 5UJ	1920	18	5299	MC	C	U	P
58	Linlithgow	Linlithgow	EH49 6QF	1913	18	5729	MC	C	U	P
59	Lochmaben	Lochmaben	DG11 1NT	1926	18	5357	MC	B	KT	P
60	Lockerbie	Lockerbie	DG11 2ND	1889	18	5418	MC	B	U	P
61	Longniddry	Longniddry	EH32 0NL	1921	18	6219	MC	D	RB	L/P
62	Lothianburn	Edinburgh	EH10 7DU	1893	18	5568	MC	B	H	M
63	Luffness New	Aberlady	EH32 0QA	1894	18	6122	MC	D	L	L
64	Melrose	Melrose	TD6 9HS	1880	9	5579	MC	B	H	M
65	Melville	Lasswade	EH18 1AN	1996	9	3834	Co	B	U	P
66	Merchants	Edinburgh	EH10 5PY	1907	18	4889	MC	B	H	P
67	Minto	Hawick	TD9 8SH	1928	18	5460	MC	B	U	P
68	Moffat	Moffat	DG10 9SB	1884	18	5263	MC	B	H	M
69	Mortonhall	Edinburgh	EH10 6PB	1892	18	6557	MC	D	H	M
70	Muirfield	Gullane	EH31 2EG	1744	18	6963	MC	F	L	L
71	Murrayfield	Edinburgh	EH12 6EU	1896	18	5752	MC	D	H	P
72	Musselburgh	Musselburgh	EH21 6SA	1938	18	6623	MC	C	RT	P
73	Musselburgh Old	Musselburgh	EH21 7SD	1774	9	5380	Mu	A	L	L
74	Newbattle	Dalkeith	EH22 3AD	1896	18	6012	MC	B	RT	P
75	New Galloway	New Galloway	DG7 3RN	1902	9	5006	MC	B	U	M
76	Newcastleton	Newcastleton	TD9 0QD	1994	9	5748	Co	A	H	P
77	Newton Stewart	Newton Stewart	DG8 6PF	1981	18	5903	MC	B	KT	P
78	Niddry Castle	Winchburgh	EH52 4RQ	1983	9	5476	MC	B	U	P
79	North Berwick	North Berwick	EH39 4BB	1832	18	6420	MC	D	L	L
80	Oatridge	Broxburn	EH52 6NH	2000	9	5842	Co	B	U	P
81	Peebles	Peebles	EH45 8EU	1892	18	6160	MC	C	U	P
82	Polkemmet	Whitburn	EH47 0AD	1981	9	6496	Mu	A	U	P
83	Portobello	Edinburgh	EH15 1JJ	1853	9	4838	Mu	A	RB	P
84	Portpatrick 1	Portpatrick	DG9 8TB	1903	18	5908	MC	C	RM	M
85	Portpatrick 2	Portpatrick	DG9 8TB		9	3008	MC	A	RM	M
86	Powfoot	Annan	DG12 5QE	1903	18	6266	MC	D	L	L
87	Prestonfield	Edinburgh	EH16 5HS	1920	18	6212	MC	C	RT	P
88	Pumpherston	Pumpherston	EH53 0LF	1895	18	5154	MC	B	U	P
89	Ratho Park	Ratho	EH28 8NX	1928	18	5900	MC	C	U	P

	NAME	ADDRESS	POSTCODE	DATE	H	YDS	MAN	GF	L	V
90	Ravelston	Edinburgh	EH4 5NZ	1912	9	5332	MC	B	U	P
91	Royal Burgess	Edinburgh	EH4 6BY	1735	18	6494	MC	D	U	P
92	Royal Mussel-burgh	Prestonpans	EH32 9RP	1774	18	6237	MC	C	RB	P
93	Roxburghe	Kelso	TD5 8JZ	1997	18	7111	Co	E	U	P
94	Rutherford Castle	West Linton	EH46 7AS	1998	18	6525	Co	B	U	P
95	St Boswells	St Boswells	TD6 0DE	1899	9	5250	MC	B	RT	P
96	St Medan	Newton Stewart	DG8 8NJ	1905	9	4554	MC	B	RM	M
97	Sanquhar	Sanquhar	DG4 6JZ	1894	9	5630	MC	B	RT	P
98	Selkirk	Selkirk	TD7 4NW	1883	9	5560	MC	B	H	M
99	Silverknowes	Edinburgh	EH4 5ET	1947	18	6202	Mu	A	RB	P
100	Solway Links	Southerness	DG12 8AD	1996	11	3062	Co	A	L	L
101	Southerness	Southerness	DG12 8AZ	1947	18	5466	MC	D	L	L
102	Stranraer	Stranraer	DG9 0LF	1906	18	6308	MC	C	RB	P
103	Swanston	Edinburgh	EH10 7DS	1927	18	5004	MC	B	H	M
104	The Pines	Dumfries	DG1 3PF	1998	18	5850	Co	B	U	P
105	Thornhill	Thornhill	DG3 5DW	1893	18	6011	MC	B	RT	P
106	Torphinhill	Edinburgh	EH13 0PG	1895	18	5025	MC	B	H	M
107	Torwoodlee	Galashiels	TD1 2NE	1895	18	6200	MC	B	RT	P
108	Turnhouse	Edinburgh	EH12 0AD	1897	18	6171	MC	C	U	P
109	Uphall	Uphall	EH52 6JT	1895	18	5588	MC	B	U	P
110	Vogrie	Gorebridge	EH23 4NU	1989	9	4626	Mu	A	U	P
111	West Linton	West Linton	EH46 7HN	1890	18	6132	MC	C	KT	M
112	West Lothian	Linlithgow	EH49 7RH	1892	18	6406	MC	B	H	M
113	Whitekirk	North Berwick	EH39 5PR	1995	18	6526	Co	B	H	M
114	Wigtown & Bladnock	Wigtown	DG8 9EF	1960	9	5424	MC	B	D	P
115	Wigtownshire Co	Newton Stewart	DG8 0NN	1894	18	5847	MC	B	L	L
116	Winterfield	Dunbar	EH42 1AU	1935	18	5035	Mu	B	L	L
117	Woll	Askirk	TD9 4NY	1993	9	6406	MC	A	U	P

Region B: West Central Scotland

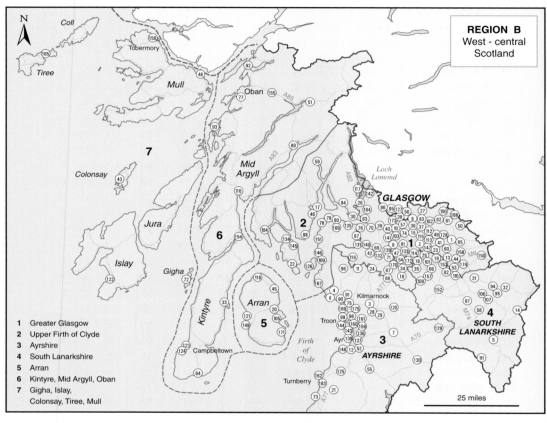

	NAME	ADDRESS	POSTCODE	DATE	H	YDS	MAN	GF	L	V
1	**Airdrie**	Airdrie	ML6 0PQ	1877	18	6004	MC	B	U	P
2	**Alexandra Park**	Glasgow	G31 8SE	1880	9	4562	Mu	A	D	P
3	**Annanhill**	Kilmarnock	KA3 2RT	1957	18	6270	Mu	A	D	P
4	**Ardeer**	Stevenston	KA20 4JX	1880	18	6409	MC	B	D	P
5	**Arbory**	Abington	ML12 6RW	1999	9	3224	Co	B	KT	M
6	**Auchenharvie**	Saltcoats	KA20 3HU	1981	9	5050	Mu	A	U	P
7	**Ballochmyle**	Mauchline	KA5 6LE	1937	18	5982	MC	B	U	P
8	**Balmore**	Torrance	G64 4AW	1906	18	5735	MC	C	D	P*
9	**Barshaw**	Paisley	PA1 3TJ	1920	18	5703	Mu	A	D	P
10	**Bearsden**	Glasgow	G61 4BP	1891	9	6014	MC	B	D	P
11	**Beith**	Beith	KA15 2JR	1896	18	5616	MC	B	H	M

200

	NAME	ADDRESS	POSTCODE	DATE	H	YDS	MAN	GF	L	V
12	Belleisle	Ayr	KA7 4DU	1927	18	6477	Mu	C	RB	P
13	Bellshill	Bellshill	ML4 2RZ	1908	18	5900	MC	B	U	P
14	Biggar	Biggar	ML12 6AH	1895	18	5416	Mu	B	RT	P
15	Bishopbriggs	Bishopbriggs	G64 2DX	1906	18	6041	MC	B	RT	P
16	Blairbeth	Rutherglen	G73 4SF	1910	18	5518	MC	B	H	P
17	Blairmore & Stone	Dunoon	PA23 8JJ	1896	9	4244	MC	A	H	M
18	Bonnyton	Eaglesham	G76 0QA	1957	18	6252	MC	D	U	P
19	Bothwell Castle	Bothwell	G71 8PS	1912	18	6243	MC	C	U	P
20	Brodick	Isle of Arran	KA27 8DL	1897	18	4736	MC	B	L	L/P
21	Brunston Castle	Dailly	KA26 9GD	1992	18	6792	Co	C	RT	P
22	Bute	Isle of Bute	PA20 0BG	1888	9	4994	MC	A	RB	L
23	Calderbraes	Uddingston	G71 7TS	1891	9	5046	MC	B	H	P
24	Caldwell	Uplawmoor	G78 4AU	1903	18	6195	MC	B	H	P
25	Cambuslang	Cambuslang	G72 7NA	1892	9	6072	MC	–	RT	P
26	Cameron House	Loch Lomond	G83 8QZ	1992	9	4523	Co	B	RT	P
27	Campsie	Lennoxtown	G66 7HX	1897	19	5517	MC	B	H	P
28	Caprington 1	Kilmarnock	KA1 4UW	1907	18	5748	Mu	A	D	P
29	Caprington 2	Kilmarnock	KA1 4UW		9	3538	Mu	A	D	P
30	Cardross	Cardross	G82 5LB	1895	18	6469	MC	C	D	P
31	Carluke	Carluke	ML8 5HG	1894	18	5805	MC	C	U	P
32	Carnwath	Carnwath	ML11 8JX	1907	18	5955	MC	C	K	P
33	Carradale	Campbeltown	PA28 6SA	1906	9	4784	MC	B	RB	L
34	Cathcart Castle	Clarkston	G76 7YL	1895	18	5832	MC	B	D	P
35	Cathkin Braes	Rutherglen	G73 4SE	1888	18	6208	MC	C	U	M
36	Cawder 1 (Cawder)	Bishopbriggs	G64 3QD	1933	18	6295	MC	D	RT	P
37	Cawder 2 (Keir)	Bishopbriggs	G64 3QD	1937	18	5877	MC	C	RT	P
38	Clober	Milngavie	G62 7HP	1951	18	4963	MC	B	D	P
39	Clydebank	Clydebank	G81 3RE	1927	18	5349	Mu	B	D	P
40	Clydebank & District	Clydebank	G81 5QY	1904	18	5823	MC	B	D	P
41	Coatbridge	Coatbridge	ML52 2HX	1971	18	6020	MC	B	U	P
42	Cochrane Castle	Johnstone	PA5 0HF	1895	18	6226	MC	B	H	P
43	Colonsay	Isle of Colonsay	PA61 7YP	1880	18	4775	MC	A	L	L
44	Colville Park	Motherwell	ML1 4UG	1923	18	6265	MC	C	U	P
45	Corrie	Isle of Arran	KA27 8JD	1892	9	3896	MC	A	H	P
46	Cowal	Dunoon	PA23 8LT	1891	18	6063	MC	B	H	P
47	Cowglen	Glasgow	G43 1EU	1906	18	6006	MC	C	D	P
48	Craignure	Isle of Mull	PA64 5AP	1895	9	5072	MC	B	RB	L
49	Crow Wood	Muirhead	G69 9JF	1925	18	6261	MC	C	D	P
50	Cumbernauld	Cumbernauld	G67 3HU	1975	18	6444	Mu	A	U	P

	NAME	ADDRESS	POSTCODE	DATE	H	YDS	MAN	GF	L	V
51	Dalmally	Dalmally	PA33 1AS	1986	9	4554	MC	B	RT	P
52	Dalmilling	Ayr	KA8 0QY	1961	18	5724	Mu	B	RB	P
53	Dalziel	Motherwell	ML1 5RZ	1997	18	5508	Co	B	U	P
54	Deaconsbank	Eastwood	G46 7UZ	1922	18	4800	Co	B	D	P
55	Doon Valley	Patna	KA6 7JT	1927	9	5856	MC	A	H	M
56	Dougalston	Milngavie	G62 8HJ	1977	18	6415	Co	C	D	PW
57	Douglas Park	Bearsden	G61 2TJ	1897	18	5982	MC	C	D	P
58	Douglas Water	Lanark	ML11 9NB	1922	9	5832	MC	A	H	P
59	Drimsynie	Lochgoil	PA24 8AD	1990	9	6400	Co	B	U	P
60	Drumpellier	Coatbridge	ML5 1RX	1894	18	6227	MC	C	U	P
61	Dullatur 1	Dullatur	G68 0AR	1896	18	6253	MC	C	U	P
62	Dullatur 2	Dullatur	G68 0AR	1998	18	5940	MC	C	U	P
63	Dumbarton	Dumbarton	G82 2BQ	1888	18	5968	MC	C	RT	P
64	Dunaverty	Campbeltown	PA28 6RF	1889	18	4799	MC	B	L	L
65	Easter Moffat	Airdrie	ML6 8NP	1922	18	6221	MC	B	U	P
66	East Kilbride	East Kilbride	G74 4PF	1900	18	6419	MC	C	U	P
67	East Renfrewshire	Newton Mearns	G77 6RT	1922	18	6097	MC	D	U	M
68	Eastwood	Newton Mearns	G77 6RX	1893	18	5864	MC	C	U	M
69	Elderslie	Elderslie	PA5 9AZ	1909	18	6165	MC	C	D	P
70	Erskine	Bishopton	PA7 5PH	1904	18	6287	MC	C	RT	P
71	Fereneze	Barrhead	G78 1HJ	1904	18	5962	MC	C	H	M
72	Gigha	Isle of Gigha	PH41 7AA	1992	9	5042	MC	B	U	M
73	Girvan	Girvan	KA26 9HW	1900	18	5095	Mu	B	RB	L
74	Glasgow Killermont	Bearsden	G61 2TW	1787	18	5982	MC	·	D	P
75	Glasgow Gailes	Irvine	KA11 5AE	1892	18	6515	MC	F	L	L
76	Gleddoch	Langbank	PA14 6YE	1974	18	6375	Co	D	H	P
77	Glencruitten	Oban	PA34 4PU	1905	18	4452	MC	B	H	P
78	Gourock	Gourock	PA19 1HD	1896	18	6512	MC	B	H	M
79	Greenock 1	Greenock	PA16 8RE	1890	18	5888	MC	C	H	M
80	Greenock 2	Greenock	PA16 8RE		9	4298	MC	B	H	M
81	Haggs Castle	Glasgow	G41 4SN	1910	18	6464	MC	D	RB	P
82	Hamilton	Hamilton	ML3 7UE	1892	18	6255	MC	C	U	P
83	Hayston	Kirkintilloch	G66 1RN	1926	18	6042	MC	C	D	P
84	Helensburgh	Helensburgh	G84 9HZ	1893	18	6058	MC	C	H	P
85	Hilton Park 1	Milngavie	G62 7HB	1927	18	6054	MC	C	D	M
86	Hilton Park 2	Milngavie	G62 7HB		18	5487	MC	C	D	M
87	Holland Bush	Lesmahagow	ML11 0JS	1954	18	6233	Mu	A	U	P
88	Innellan	Inellan	PA23 7SG	1891	9	4878	MC	B	H	M
89	Inveraray	Inveraray	PA32 8YH	1893	9	5600	MC	B	RB	P
90	Irvine	Irvine	KA12 8SN	1887	18	6408	MC	D	RB	L

	NAME	ADDRESS	POSTCODE	DATE	H	YDS	MAN	GF	L	V
91	Irvine Ravenspark	Irvine	KA12 8SR	1907	18	6429	Mu	B	RB	P
92	Isle of Eriska	Benderloch	PA37 1SD	1997	9	5000	Co	A	RB	L
93	Isle of Seil	Oban	PA34 4TP	1998	9	4670	MC	A	U	M
94	Kames 1	Cleghorn	ML11 8NR	1994	18	6006	Co	B	K	P
95	Kames 2	Cleghorn	ML11 8NR	1999	9	4796	Co	B	K	P
96	Kilbirnie Place	Kirbirnie	KA25 7AT	1922	18	5521	MC	B	KT	P
97	Kilmacolm	Kilmacolm	PA13 4PD	1891	18	5960	MC	C	U	M
98	Kilmarnock Barassie 1	Troon	KA10 6SY	1887	18	6484	MC	E	L	L
99	Kilmarnock Barassie 2	Troon	KA10 6SY	1997	9	5776	MC	—	L	L
100	Kilsyth Lennox	Kilsyth	G65 0RS	1900	18	5930	MC	B	H	M
101	Kirkhill	Cambuslang	G72 8YN	1910	18	6030	MC	B	U	M
102	Kirkintilloch	Kirkintilloch	G66 1RN	1895	18	5269	MC	B	D	P
103	Knightswood	Glasgow	G71 5QZ	1929	9	5584	Mu	A	U	P
104	Kyles of Bute	Tighnabruich	PA21 2EE	1907	9	4778	MC	A	U	M
105	Lamlash	Isle of Arran	KA27 8JU	1889	18	4640	MC	B	H	P
106	Lanark 1	Lanark	ML11 7RX	1851	18	6426	MC	C	K	M
107	Lanark 2	Lanark	ML11 7RX		9	4796	MC	A	K	M
108	Langlands	East Kilbride	G75 0QQ	1985	18	6201	Mu	A	U	P
109	Largs	Largs	KA30 8EU	1891	18	5707	MC	C	RB	P
110	Larkhall	Larkhall	ML9 3AB	1904	9	6754	Mu	A	U	P
111	Leadhills	Leadhills	ML12 6XR	1935	9	4062	MC	A	H	M
112	Lenzie	Lenzie	G66 5DA	1889	18	5984	MC	B	D	P
113	Lethamhill	Glasgow	G33 1AH	1933	18	5946	Mu	A	D	P
114	Linn Park	Glasgow	G44 5TA	1924	18	4592	Mu	A	D	P
115	Littlehill	Glasgow	G64 1UT	1926	18	6228	Mu	A	D	P
116	Lochgilphead	Lochgilphead	PA31 8LD	1963	9	4484	MC	B	RT	P
117	Loch Lomond	Luss	G83 8NT	1994	18	7060	Co	F	RB	P
118	Lochranza	Isle of Arran	KA27 8HL	1991	9	5600	Co	B	RB	P
119	Lochwinnoch	Lochwinnoch	PA12 4AH	1897	18	6243	MC	C	H	P
120	Loudon Gouf	Galston	KA4 8PA	1909	18	6016	MC	C	RT	P
121	Machrie Bay	Isle of Arran	KA27 8DZ	1900	12	4400	MC	A	RB	L
122	Machrie Hotel	Isle of Islay	PA42 7AT	1891	18	6226	Co	C	L	L
123	Machrihanish 1	Campbeltown	PA28 6PT	1876	18	6228	MC	C	L	L
124	Machrihanish 2	Campbeltown	PA28 6PT		9	—	MC	B	L	L
125	Maybole	Maybole	KA19 7DX	1970	9	5270	Mu	A	U	P
126	Millport	Isle of Cumbrae	KA28 0HB	1888	18	5828	MC	C	U	P
127	Milngavie	Milngavie	G62 8EP	1895	18	5818	MC	B	D	M
128	Mount Ellen	Gartcosh	G69 9EY	1905	18	5525	MC	B	D	P
129	Muirkirk	Muirkirk	KA18 3QR	1991	9	5366	Co	A	U	M

	NAME	ADDRESS	POSTCODE	DATE	H	YDS	MAN	GF	L	V
130	New Cumnock	New Cumnock	KA18 4BQ	1901	9	5176	MC	A	U	P
131	Old Ranfurly	Bridge of Weir	PA11 3DE	1905	18	6089	MC	C	U	M
132	Paisley	Paisley	PA2 8TZ	1895	18	6466	MC	C	U	M
133	Pollok	Glasgow	G43 1BG	1893	18	6295	MC	D	RB	P
134	Port Bannatyne	Isle of Bute	PA20 0PH	1912	13	5085	MC	B	H	P
135	Port Glasgow	Port Glasgow	PA14 5XE	1895	18	5712	MC	B	U	M
136	Prestwick	Prestwick	KA9 1QG	1851	18	6668	MC	F	L	L
137	Prestwick St Cuthbert	Prestwick	KA9 2SX	1899	18	6470	MC	C	L	L
138	Prestwick St Nicholas	Prestwick	KA9 1SN	1851	18	5952	MC	D	L	L
139	Ralston	Paisley	PA1 3DT	1904	18	6100	MC	C	D	P
140	Ranfurly Castle	Bridge of Weir	PA11 3MN	1889	18	6284	MC	D	U	M
141	Renfrew	Renfrew	PA4 9EG	1894	18	6818	MC		RT	P
142	Ross Priory	Gartocharn	G83 8NL	1989	9	5800	MC		U	P
143	Royal Troon Old	Troon	KA10 6EP	1878	18	7097	MC	F	L	L
144	Royal Troon Portland	Troon	KA10 6EP		18	6289	MC	F	L	L
145	Rothesay	Rothesay	PA20 9HN	1892	18	5395	MC	B	H	M
146	Routenburn	Largs	KA30 9AH	1914	18	5650	MC	B	H	M
147	Sandyhills	Glasgow	G32 9NA	1905	18	6253	MC	B	U	P
148	Seafield	Ayr	KA7 4DU	1930	18	5498	Mu	B	RB	P
149	Shiskine	Isle of Arran	KA27 8HA	1896	12	3055	MC	B	L	L
150	Shotts	Shotts	ML7 5BJ	1895	18	6205	MC	B	U	P
151	Skelmorlie	Skelmorlie	PA17 5ES	1891	18	5056	MC	B	U	M
152	Strathaven	Strathaven	ML10 6NL	1908	18	6226	MC	C	U	P
153	Strathclyde Park	Hamilton	ML3 6BY	1920	9	6350	Mu	A	RT	P
154	Tarbert	Tarbert	PA29 6XX	1910	9	4460	MC	A	RB	P
155	Taynuilt	Taynuilt	PA35 1JE	1989	9	4510	MC	B	RB	P
156	Tobermory	Isle of Mull	PA75 6PS	1896	9	4984	MC	B	H	M
157	Torrance House	East Kilbride	G75 0QZ	1969	18	6415	Mu	B	U	P
158	Torrance Park	Motherwell		UC	18		Co		U	P
159	Troon Lochgreen	Troon	KA10 6NE	1907	18	6822	Mu	C	L	L
160	Troon Darley	Troon	KA10 6NE		18	6501	Mu	B	L	L
161	Troon Fullarton	Troon	KA10 6NE		18	4869	Mu	B	L	L
162	Turnberry 1 Ailsa	Turnberry	KA26 9LT	1906	18	6976	Co	F	L	L
163	Turnberry 2 Kintyre	Turnberry	KA26 9LT	UC	18		Co	F	L	L
164	Vale of Leven	Alexandria	G83 9ET	1907	18	5156	MC	B	H	P
165	Vaul	Isle of Tiree	PA77 6TP	1920	9	5674	MC	A	L	L
166	Westerwood	Cumbernauld	G68 0EW	1989	18	6616	Co	C	U	P

	NAME	ADDRESS	POSTCODE	DATE	H	YDS	MAN	GF	L	V
167	West Kilbride	West Kilbride	KA23 9HT	1893	18	6452	MC	C	L	L
168	Western Gailes	Irvine	KA11 5AE	1897	18	6639	MC	F	L	L
169	Whinhill	Greenock	PA16 9LN	1911	18	5504	MC	B	H	M
170	Whitecraigs	Giffnock	G46 6SW	1905	18	6013	MC	D	U	P
171	Whiting Bay	Isle of Arran	KA27 8PR	1895	18	4405	MC	B	H	P
172	Williamwood	Netherlee	G44 3YR	1906	18	5878	MC	C	U	P
173	Windyhill	Bearsden	G61 4QQ	1908	18	6254	MC	C	D	M
174	Wishaw	Wishaw	ML2 7PH	1897	18	5999	MC	B	U	P

Region C: East Central Scotland

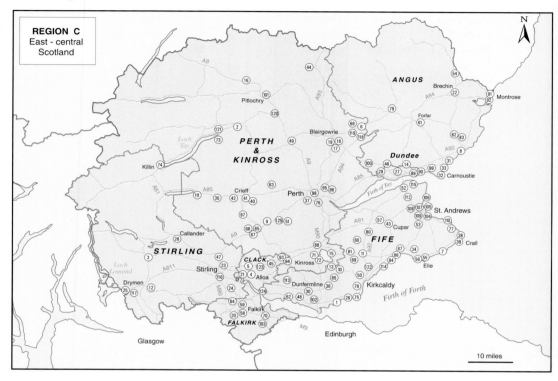

	NAME	ADDRESS	POSTCODE	DATE	H	YDS	MAN	GF	L	V
1	**Aberdour**	Aberdour	KY3 0TX	1896	18	5460	MC	B	RB	P
2	**Aberfeldy**	Aberfeldy	PH15 2BH	1895	18	5600	MC	B	RT	P
3	**Aberfoyle**	Aberfoyle	FK8 3UY	1890	18	5218	MC	B	H	P
4	**Alloa**	Alloa	FK10 3AX	1891	18	6240	MC	C	U	P
5	**Alva**	Alva	FK12 4HL	1901	9	4846	MC	B	H	P
6	**Alyth**	Alyth	PH11 8HF	1894	18	6205	MC	C	K	P
7	**Anstruther**	Anstruther	KY10 3DZ	1890	9	4504	MC	B	RB	L
8	**Arbroath**	Arbroath	DD11 2PE	1903	18	6185	Mu	C	L	L
9	**Auchterarder**	Auchterarder	PH3 1LS	1892	18	5757	MC	B	U	P
10	**Auchterderran**	Cardenden	KY5 0NH	1904	9	5400	Mu	A	U	P
11	**Balbirnie Park**	Glenrothes	KY7 6NR	1983	18	6214	MC	C	U	P
12	**Balfron**	Balfron	G63 0RN	1997	18	5372	MC	B	U	M
13	**Ballingry**	Lochgelly	KY5 8BA	1908	9	6482	Mu	A	U	P

	NAME	ADDRESS	POSTCODE	DATE	H	YDS	MAN	GF	L	V
14	Balumbie Castle	Dundee	DD4 0PD	2000	18	6127	Co	B	U	P
15	Bishopshire	Kinross	KY13	1903	10	4830	MC	A	H	M
16	Blair Atholl	Blair Atholl	PH18 5TG	1896	9	5710	MC	B	RT	P
17	Blairgowrie Rosemount	Blairgowrie	PH10 6LG	1889	18	6588	MC	D	S	PW
18	Blairgowrie Landsdowne	Blairgowrie	PH10 6LG		18	6895	MC	D	S	PW
19	Blairgowrie Wee	Blairgowrie	PH10 6PG		9	4614	MC	B	S	PW
20	Bonnybridge	Bonnybridge	FK4 1NY	1924	9	6058	MC	B	U	P
21	Braehead	Alloa	FK10 2NT	1891	18	6013	MC	B	RB	P
22	Brechin	Brechin	DD9 7PD	1893	18	6200	MC	B	U	P
23	Bridge of Allan	Bridge of Allan	FK9 4LY	1895	18	4932	MC	B	U	P
24	Brucefields	Bannockburn	FK7 8EH	1997	9	4896	Co	B	U	P
25	Buchanan Castle	Drymen	G63 0HY	1936	18	6015	MC	C	RT	P
26	Burntisland	Burntisland	KY3 9EY	1898	18	5965	MC	B	U	P
27	Caird Park	Dundee	DD4 9BX	1926	18	6303	Mu	B	U	P
28	Callender	Callender	FK17 8EN	1890	18	5125	MC	B	U	P
29	Camperdown	Dundee	DD4 9BX	1960	18	6561	Mu	B	U	P
30	Canmore	Dunfermline	KY12 0PF	1897	18	5437	MC	B	U	P
31	Carnoustie Champion	Carnoustie	DD7 7JE	16C	18	6941	Mu	F	L	L
32	Carnoustie Burnside	Carnoustie	DD7 7JE	1914	18	6020	Mu	C	L	L
33	Carnoustie Buddon Links	Carnoustie	DD7 7JE	1981	18	5420	Mu	C	L	L
34	Charleton	Colinsburgh	KY9 5HG	1994	18	6149	Co	B	U	P
35	Comrie	Comrie	PH6 2LR	1891	9	5966	MC	A	H	P
36	Cowdenbeath	Cowdenbeath	KY4 8AD	1988	18	6522	Mu	B	U	P
37	Craigie Hill	Perth	PH2 0NE	1909	18	5386	MC	B	H	M
38	Crail Balcomie	Crail	KY10 3XN	1786	18	5922	MC	C	L	L
39	Crail Craighead	Crail	KY10 3XN	1998	18	6152	MC	B	L	L
40	Crieff Ferntower	Crieff	PH7 3LR	1891	18	6402	MC	C	U	P
41	Crieff Dornock	Crieff	PH7 3LR	1980	9	4772	MC	B	U	P
42	Crieff Hydro	Crieff	PH7 4JN	2001	18	4520	Co	B	U	P
43	Cupar	Cupar	KY15 4JT	1855	9	5074	MC	B	H	P
44	Dalmunzie	Glenshee	PH10 7QG	1948	9	4070	Co	B	RT	M
45	Dollar	Dollar	FK14 7EA	1890	18	5144	MC	B	H	M
46	Downfield	Dundee	DD2 3QP	1932	18	6822	MC	D	U	P
47	Dunblane New	Dunblane	FK15 0LJ	1923	18	5957	MC	C	U	P
48	Dunfermline	Dunfermline	KY12 8QW	1887	18	6126	MC	C	U	P
49	Dunkeld & Birnam	Dunkeld	PH8 0HU	1892	18	5240	MC	B	H	M

	NAME	ADDRESS	POSTCODE	DATE	H	YDS	MAN	GF	L	V
50	Dunnikier Park	Kirkcaldy	KY1 3LP	1963	18	6601	Mu	B	U	P
51	Dunning	Dunning	PH2 0QX	1953	9	4777	MC	B	RT	P
52	Drumoig	Leuchars	KY16 0BE	1996	18	7017	Co	C	U	P
53	Dukes	St Andrews	KY16 8NS	1995	18	7271	Co	F	U	P
54	Edzell	Edzell	DD9 7TF	1895	18	6348	MC	C	S	P
55	Elie 1	Elie	KY9 1AS	1875	18	6261	MC	D	L	L
56	Elie 2	Elie	KY9 1AS		9	4554	MC	A	L	L
57	Elmwood	Cupar	KY15 5RS	1997	18	5951	Co	B	U	P
58	Falkirk	Falkirk	FK2 7YP	1922	18	6282	MC	B	RB	P
59	Falkirk Tryst	Larbert	FK5 4BD	1885	18	6053	MC	B	RB	P
60	Falkland	Falkland	KY7 7AA	1976	9	4814	Mu	A	U	P
61	Forfar	Forfar	DD8 2RL	1871	18	6052	MC	B	KT	P
62	Forrester Park	Cairneyhill	KY12 8RF	2001	18		Co		U	P
63	Glen Almond	Glen Almond	PH1 3RZ	1923	9	5812	MC		U	M
64	Glenbervie	Larbert	FK5 4SJ	1932	18	6423	MC	D	RB	P
65	Gleneagles Kings	Auchterarder	PH3 1NF	1924	18	6471	Co	F	E	P
66	Gleneagles Queens	Auchterarder	PH3 1NF	1924	18	5965	Co	F	E	P
67	Gleneagles PGA Centenary	Auchterarder	PH3 1NF	1993	18	7081	Co	F	E	P
68	Glenisla	Alyth	PH11 8JJ	1998	18	6402	Co	C	KT	P
69	Glenrothes	Glenrothes	KY6 2LA	1958	18	6444	Mu	B	U	P
70	Grangemouth	Polmont	FK2 0YA	1973	18	6527	MC	B	U	P
71	Green Hotel Red	Kinross	KY13 8AS	1900	18	6257	Co	C	U	P
72	Green Hotel Blue	Kinross	KY13 8AS	1990	18	6456	Co	C	U	P
73	Kenmore	Kenmore	PH15 2HN	1992	9	6052	Co	B	RT	P
74	Killin	Killin	FK21 8TX	1913	9	5016	MC	B	H	P
75	Kinghorn	Kinghorn	KY3 9RE	1887	18	5629	Mu	B	RB	M
76	King James VI	Perth	PH2 8NR	1858	18	5664	MC	B	RT	P
77	Kingsbarns	Kingsbarns	KY16 8QD	2000	18	7100	Co	F	L	L
78	Kirkcaldy	Kirkcaldy	KY2 5LT	1904	18	6040	MC	B	H	P
79	Kirriemuir	Kirriemuir	DD8 4PN	1908	18	5510	MC	C	U	P
80	Ladybank	Ladybank	KY15 7RA	1879	18	6641	MC	D	S	P
81	Leslie	Glenrothes	KY6 3EZ	1898	9	4940	MC	A	H	P
82	Letham Grange Old	Arbroath	DD11 4RL	1987	18	6968	Co	D	U	P
83	Letham Grange New	Arbroath	DD11 4RL	1988	18	5528	Co	B	U	P
84	Leven Links	Leven	KY8 4HS	1846	18	6434	MC	C	L	L
85	Lochgelly	Lochgelly	KY5 9PB	1895	18	5454	MC	B	U	P
86	Lundin Links	Leven	KY8 6BA	1868	18	6394	MC	C	L	L
87	Lundin Ladies	Leven	KY8 6AR	1891	9	4730	MC	B	U	P

	NAME	ADDRESS	POSTCODE	DATE	H	YDS	MAN	GF	L	V
88	Milnathort	Milnathort	KY13 9XA	1910	9	5985	MC	B	U	P
89	Monifieth Medal	Monifieth	DD5 4AW	1858	18	6650	Mu	C	L	L
90	Monifieth Ashludie	Monifieth	DD5 4AW		18	5123	Mu	B	L	L
91	Montrose Medal	Montrose	DD10 8SW	1562	18	6495	Mu	C	L	L
92	Montrose Bloomfield	Montrose	DD10 8SW	1858	18	4815	Mu	C	L	L
93	Muckhart 1	Dollar	FK14 7JH	1908	18	6034	MC	B	K/H	P/M
94	Muckhart 2	Dollar	FK14 7JH	1998	9	6400	MC	B	K	P
95	Murrayshall 1	New Scone	PH2 7PH	1981	18	6416	Co	C	H	P
96	Murrayshall 2	New Scone	PH2 7PH	2000	18	5174	Co	B	H	P
97	Muthill	Muthill	PH5 2DA	1935	9	4742	MC	B	U	P
98	North Insch	Perth	PH1 4JS	1842	18	5165	Mu	B	RT	P
99	Panmure	Carnoustie	DD7 7RT	1845	18	6317	MC	C	L	L
100	Piper Dam	Muirhead	DD2 5LP	1998	18	6526	Co	B	H	M
101	Pitlochry	Pitlochry	PH16 5NE	1909	18	5811	MC	C	H	P
102	Pitreavie	Dunfermline	KY11 5PR	1922	18	6031	MC	B	D	P
103	Polmont	Falkirk	FK2 0LS	1901	9	6088	MC	B	U	P
104	St Andrews Old	St Andrews	KY16 9SF	15C	18	6566	Mu	F	L	L
105	St Andrews New	St Andrews	KY16 9SF	1895	18	6604	Mu	E	L	L
106	St Andrews Jubilee	St Andrews	KY16 9SF	1897	18	6805	Mu	D	L	L
107	St Andrews Eden	St Andrews	KY16 9SF	1914	18	6112	Mu	C	L	L
108	St Andrews Strathtyrum	St Andrews	KY16 9SF	1993	18	5094	Mu	B	L	L
109	St Andrews Balgove	St Andrews	KY16 9SF	1993	9	3040	Mu	A	L	L
110	St Andrews Bay	Kingask	KY16 8PN	2001	36	7020	Co		U	P
111	St Fillans	St Fillans	PH26 2NJ	1903	9	5796	Mc	B	RT	P
112	St Michaels	Leuchars	KY16 0DX	1903	18	5802	MC	B	RB	P
113	Saline	Saline	KY12 9LT	1912	9	5302	MC	B	U	P
114	Scoonie	Leven	KY8 4SP	1951	18	5028	Mu	B	L	L
115	Scotscraig	Tayport	DD6 9DZ	1817	18	6550	MC	C	L	L
116	Stirling	Stirling	FK8 3AA	1869	18	6409	MC	C	U	P
117	Strathendrick	Drymen	G63 0AA	1901	9	5116	MC	B	KT	P
118	Strathmore Rannaleroch	Alyth	PH11 8NZ	1996	18	6454	Co	C	KT	P
119	Strathmore Leitfie	Alyth	PH11 8NZ	1995	9	3332	Co	A	KT	P
120	Strathtay	Dunkeld	PH9 0PG	1909	9	4082	MC	B	RT	P
121	Taymouth Castle	Kenmore	PH15 2NT	1923	18	6066	MC	B	RT	P
122	Thornton	Thornton	KY14 4DW	1921	18	6175	MC	B	U	P

	NAME	ADDRESS	POSTCODE	DATE	H	YDS	MAN	GF	L	V
123	**Tillicoultry**	Tillicoultry	FK13 6BL	1899	9	5056	MC	B	H	P
124	**Tulliallan**	Kincardine	FK10 4BB	1902	18	5982	MC	B	H	P
125	**Whitemoss**	Auchterarder	PH2 0QX	1994	18	6200	Co	B	U	M

Region D: The North of Scotland

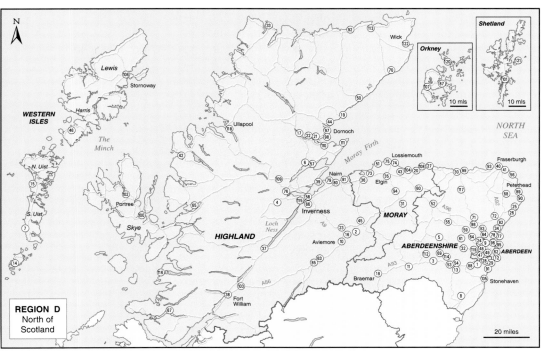

	NAME	ADDRESS	POSTCODE	DATE	H	YDS	MAN	GF	L	V
1	**Aberdeen Petrol Club**	Milltimber	AB13 0AB	1997	9	3000	MC	–	U	P
2	**Abernethy**	Nethybridge	PH25 3EB	1893	9	5040	MC	B	KT	P
3	**Aboyne**	Aboyne	AB34 5HP	1883	18	5910	MC	B	RT	P
4	**Aigas**	Beauly	IV4 7AD	1996	9	4878	Co	B	U	P
5	**Alford**	Alford	AB33 8AE		18	5483	MC	B	U	P
6	**Alness**	Alness	IV17 0QR	1904	18	4886	MC	B	H	P
7	**Askernish**	South Uist	HS81 5SY	1891	9	5114	MC	B	L	L
8	**Auchenblae**	Laurencekirk	AB30 1BU	1894	9	4416	Mu	A	H	M
9	**Auchmill**	Aberdeen	AB2 7FQ	1975	18	5883	Mu	A	U	P
10	**Aviemore**	Aviemore	PH22	1982	9	4908	Co	B	K	P
11	**Ballater**	Ballater	AB35 5QX	1892	18	6094	MC	B	KT	P
12	**Balnagask**	Balnagask	AB13 3QT	1949	18	6055	Mu	A	RB	P
13	**Banchory**	Banchory	AB31 5TA	1905	18	5775	MC	B	RT	P
14	**Barra**	Isle of Barra	HS9 5XX	1992	9	4792	MC	A	L	L

211

	NAME	ADDRESS	POSTCODE	DATE	H	YDS	MAN	GF	L	V
15	Benbecula Station	Isle of Benbecula	HS7 5LA	1980	9	4311	MC	A	L	L
16	Boat of Garten	Boat of Garten	PH24 3BQ	1898	18	5866	MC	C	KT	P
17	Bonar Bridge	Ardgay	IV24 3EJ	1901	9	5284	MC	B	H	P
18	Braemar	Braemar	AB35 5XX	1902	18	4916	MC	B	RT	M
19	Brora	Brora	KW9 6QS	1891	18	6110	MC	C	L	L
20	Buckpool	Buckie	AB56 1DU	1933	18	6257	MC	B	RM	L
21	Carnegie Club 1	Dornoch	IV25 3RQ	1995	18	6671	Co	F	RB	L
22	Carnegie Club 2	Dornoch	IV25 3RQ	1998	9	2825	Co	E	RB	L
23	Carrbridge	Carrbridge	PH23 3AU	1980	9	5402	MC	B	RT	M
24	Craibstone	Craibstone	AB21 9YA	1999	18	5779	Co	B	U	P
25	Cruden Bay 1	Peterhead	AB42 0NN	1899	18	6395	MC	E	L	L
26	Cruden Bay 2	Peterhead	AB42 0NN		9	5106	MC	B	L	L
27	Cullen	Cullen	AB56 4WB	1879	18	4610	MC	B	RB/ RM	L/M
28	Deeside 1	Bieldside	AB15 9DL	1903	18	5972	MC	D	RT	P
29	Deeside 2	Bieldside	AB15 9DL		9	3316	MC	B	RT	P
30	Duff House Royal	Banff	AB45 3SX	1909	18	6161	MC	C	RT	P
31	Dufftown	Dufftown	AB55 4BX	1896	18	5308	MC	B	U	P
32	Dunecht House	Skene	AB3 7AX	1925	9	6270	MC	B	RT	P
33	Durness	Durness	IV27 4PN	1988	9	5555	MC	B	RM	M
34	East Aberdeen-shire	Balmeddie	AB23 8YY	1998	18	6187	Co	B	U	P
35	Elgin	Elgin	IV30 8SX	1906	18	6411	MC	C	U	P
36	Forres	Forres	IV36 0RD	1889	18	6141	MC	B	U	P
37	Fort Augustus	Fort Augustus	PH32 4AU	1930	9	5454	MC	B	KT	P
38	Fortrose & Rosemarkie	Fortrose	IV10 8SE	1888	18	5973	MC	C	RB	L
39	Fort William	Fort William	PH33 6SN	1975	18	6217	MC	B	U	M
40	Fraserburgh 1	Fraserburgh	AB43 8TL	1881	18	6278	MC	B	L	L
41	Fraserburgh 2	Fraserburgh	AB43 8TL	1998	9	4800	MC	B	L	L
42	Gairloch	Gairloch	IV21 2BE	1898	9	4562	MC	B	L	L
43	Garmouth & Kingston	Fochabers	IV32 7NJ	1932	18	5847	MC	B	RT	P
44	Golspie	Golspie	KW10 6ST	1889	18	5890	MC	C	L	L
45	Grantown on Spey	Grantown on Spey	PH26 3HY	1890	18	5710	MC	C	KT	P
46	Harris	Isle of Harris	HS55 3UE	1986	9	4884	MC	B	L	L
47	Hazlehead 1	Aberdeen	AB15 8BD	1927	18	6240	Mu	A	U	P
48	Hazlehead 2	Aberdeen	AB15 8BD		18	5833	Mu	A	U	P
49	Hazlehead 3	Aberdeen	AB15 8BD		9	5568	Mu	A	U	P
50	Helmsdale	Helmsdale	KW8 6JA	1895	9	3720	MC	A	RT	M
51	Hopeman	Hopeman	IV30 2YA	1923	18	5564	MC	B	RM	M

	NAME	ADDRESS	POSTCODE	DATE	H	YDS	MAN	GF	L	V
52	Huntly	Huntly	AB54 4SH	1892	18	5399	MC	B	RT	P
53	Inchmarlo 1	Banchory	AB31 4BQ	1997	9	4300	Co	B	U	P
54	Inchmarlo 2	Banchory	AB31 4BQ	2001	18	6494	Co	C	RT	P
55	Insch	Insch	AB52 6JY	1982	18	5287	MC	B	U	P
56	Inverallochy	Fraserburgh	AB43 8XY	1890	18	5244	Mu	B	L	L
57	Invergordon	Invergordon	IV18 0BD	1893	18	6040	MC	B	RB	P
58	Inverness	Inverness	IV2 3XQ	1883	18	6226	MC	D	RB	P
59	Inverurie	Inverurie	AB51 5JB	1923	18	5711	MC	B	U	P
60	Keith	Keith	AB55 5DF	1963	18	5802	MC	B	U	P
61	Kemnay	Kemnay	AB51 5RA	1908	18	5903	MC	B	U	P
62	King's Links	Aberdeen	AB24 5QB	1925	18	5838	Mu	B	L	L
63	Kingussie	Kingussie	PH21 1LR	1891	18	5615	MC	B	RT	M
64	Kintore	Kintore	AB51 0UR	1911	18	6019	MC	B	KT	P
65	Lochcarron	Lochcarron	IV54 8YU	1991	9	3578	MC	B	U	P
66	Loch Ness	Inverness	IV2 6AA	1996	18	6700	Co	C	H	P
67	Loch Sunart	Resipole	PH36 4HX	1997	9	3642	MC	B	U	P
68	Longside	Peterhead	AB42 4XJ	1996	18	5215	MC	B	U	P
69	Lumphanan	Lumphanan	AB31 4PX	–	9	3176	MC	B	H	M
70	Lybster	Lybster	KW1 6BL	1926	9	3792	MC	A	RM	M
71	Meldrum House	Oldmeldrum	AB51 0AE	1998	18	6350	Co	–	U	P
72	McDonald	Ellon	AB41 9AW	1927	18	5986	MC	B	U	P
73	Miltonhill	Kinloss	IV36 0UA	1997	9	5070	Co	A	U	P
74	Moray 1	Lossiemouth	IV31 6QS	1889	18	6643	MC	C	L	L
75	Moray 2	Lossiemouth	IV31 6QS	1979	18	6005	MC	C	L	L
76	Muir of Ord	Muir of Ord	IV6 7SX	1875	18	5557	MC	B	RB	P
77	Murcar 1	Bridge of Don	AB23 8BD	1909	18	6287	MC	D	L	L
78	Murcar 2	Bridge of Don	AB23 8BD		9	5360	MC	B	L	L
79	Nairn 1	Nairn	IV12 4HB	1887	18	6722	MC	F	L	L
80	Nairn 2	Nairn	IV12 4HB		9	3542	MC	–	L	L
81	Nairn Dunbar	Nairn	IV12 5AE	1899	18	6720	MC	D	L	L
82	Newburgh on Ythan	Newburgh	AB41 6BE	1888	18	6162	MC	B	L/U	L/M
83	Newmachar 1	Newmachar	AB21 7UU	1989	18	6623	MC	D	U	P
84	Newmachar 2	Newmachar	AB21 7UU	1998	18	6388	MC	B	U	P
85	Newtonmore	Newtonmore	PH20 1AT	1893	18	6029	MC	B	KT	P
86	Oldmeldrum	Oldmeldrum	AB51 0DJ	1885	18	5988	MC	B	U	M
87	Orkney	Kirkwall	KW15 1RD	1889	18	5411	MC	B	U	M
88	Peterculter	Peterculter	AB14 0LN	1989	18	5924	MC	B	U	P
89	Peterhead 1	Peterhead	AB42 6TL	1841	18	6173	MC	C	L	L
90	Peterhead 2	Peterhead	AB42 1TL		9	4474	MC	B	L	L
91	Portlethen	Portlethen	AB12 4YA	1983	18	6735	MC	B	U	P

213

	NAME		ADDRESS	POSTCODE	DATE	H	YDS	MAN	GF	L	V
92	Reay		Thurso	KW14 7RE	1893	18	5856	MC	B	L	L
93	Roseharty		Fraserburgh	AB43 7JJ		9	6736	MC	A	L	L
94	Rothes		Rothes	AB38 7AN	1990	9	4956	MC	B	U	P
95	Royal Aberdeen	1	Balgownie	AB23 8AT	1780	18	6372	MC	F	L	L
96	Royal Aberdeen	2	Balgownie	AB23 8AT		18	4066	MC	C	L	L
97	Royal Dornoch	1	Dornoch	IV25 3LW	1877	18	6514	MC	F	L	L
98	Royal Dornoch	2	Dornoch	IV25 3LW	1900	18	5438	MC	B	L	L
99	Royal Tarlair		MacDuff	AB44 1TA	1926	18	5866	MC	C	RM	M
100	Sconser		Isle of Skye	IV48 8TD	1964	9	4789	MC	B	RB	L
101	Shetland		Lerwick	ZE2 9SB	1891	18	5776	MC	B	U	M
102	Skeabost		Isle of Skye	IV5 9NP	1982	9	3224	Co	A	RB	M
103	Speanbridge		Speanbridge	PH33	1954	9	4406	MC	B	U	P
104	Spey Bay		Spey Bay	IV32 7PJ	1907	18	6092	Co	B	L	L
105	Stonehaven		Stonehaven	AB39 3RH	1888	18	5128	MC	B	RM	M
106	Stornoway		Stornoway	HS2 0XP	1947	18	5252	MC	B	U	P
107	Stromness		Stromness	KW16 3DU	1890	18	4762	MC	B	U	M
108	Strathlene		Buckie	AB56 2DJ	1877	18	5977	MC	B	RM	M
109	Strathpeffer		Strathpeffer	IV14 9AS	1888	18	4792	MC	B	H	M
110	Tain		Tain	IV19 1JE	1890	18	6404	MC	D	L	L
111	Tarbat		Tain	IV20 1YA	1909	9	5136	MC	B	L	L
112	Tarland		Tarland	AB34 4TB	1908	9	5812	MC	B	U	P
113	Thurso		Thurso	KW14 7XF	1893	18	5853	MC	B	U	M
114	Torphins		Torphins	AB31 4JU	1896	9	4738	MC	B	U	M
115	Torvean		Inverness	IV3 8JN	1962	18	5784	Mu	B	RT	P
116	Traigh		Arisaig	PH39 4NT	1900	9	4912	MC	B	L	L
117	Turriff		Turriff	AB53 4HD	1896	18	6145	MC	B	RT	P
118	Ullapool		Ullapool	IV26 2TH	1998	9	5338	MC	B	RB	M
119	Westhill		Westhill	AB32 6RY	1977	18	5849	MC	B	H	P
120	Westray		Orkney	KW17 2DH	1890	9	4810	MC	A	U	M
121	Whalsay		Shetland	ZE2 9AL	1976	18	6009	MC	B	U	M
122	Wick		Wick	KW1 5LJ	1870	18	6200	MC	B	L	L

💥 Index